Moodle 2.0 E-Learning Course Development

A complete guide to successful learning using Moodle

William Rice

PUBLISHING

open source
community experience distilled

BIRMINGHAM - MUMBAI

Moodle 2.0 E-Learning Course Development

First published: August 2011

Production Reference: 1180811

Published by Packt Publishing Ltd.
Livery Place
35 Livery Street
Birmingham B3 2PB, UK.

ISBN 978-1-849515-26-9

www.packtpub.com

Cover Image by Filippo (filosarti@tiscali.it)

Credits

Author
William Rice

Reviewers
Mary Cooch
Ângelo Marcos Rigo

Acquisition Editor
Sarah Cullington

Development Editor
Neha Mallik

Technical Editors
Kavita Iyer
Pallavi Kachare

Project Coordinator
Srimoyee Ghoshal

Proofreader
Dirk Manuel

Indexer
Hemangini Bari

Production Coordinator
Shantanu Zagade

Cover Work
Shantanu Zagade

About the Author

William Rice is a training manager who lives, works, and plays in New York City. He has written several books for Packt on Moodle. He has a special interest in rapid e-learning development.

William's indoor hobbies include writing books, spending way too much time reading sites like slashdot and mashable, and chasing after his sons. His outdoor hobbies include practicing archery within sight of JFK airport, foraging for edible wild plants in New York City parks, and chasing after his sons.

William is fascinated by the relationship between technology and society: how we create our tools, and how our tools in turn shape us. He is married to an incredible woman who encourages his writing pursuits, and has two amazing sons.

William can be reached through his blog at `williamriceinc.blogspot.com`, and his LinkedIn profile at `linkedin.com/in/williamrice4`.

About the Reviewers

Mary Cooch (known online as @moodlefairy) is a teacher and VLE trainer based in the United Kingdom. She is the author of *Moodle 1.9 for Teaching 7-14 Year Olds* and *Moodle 2.0 First Look*, both also published by Packt. She blogs at www.moodleblog.net and can be contacted for consultation on mco@olchs.lancs.sch.uk. Mary will go anywhere to help you with Moodle!

Ângelo Marcos Rigo is a 35 years-old senior web developer who has enjoyed creating systems, performing customizations, and fixing many web systems since the launch of the Internet in Brasil in 1995. Some of the Ângelo's work can be found at www.u4w.com.br and he can be contacted for consultation on angelo.rigo@gmail.com.

He has worked in the past for companies in the field of telecoms, and for Primary Education and State Departments, and currently works in the PUCRS faculty for the CEAD Department of Distance Learning

I would like to thank my wife Janaína and my daughter Lorena for their support, and for understanding how reviewing a book is fascinating.

www.PacktPub.com

Support files, eBooks, discount offers and more

You might want to visit www.PacktPub.com for support files and downloads related to your book.

Did you know that Packt offers eBook versions of every book published, with PDF and ePub files available? You can upgrade to the eBook version at www.PacktPub.com and as a print book customer, you are entitled to a discount on the eBook copy. Get in touch with us at service@packtpub.com for more details.

At www.PacktPub.com, you can also read a collection of free technical articles, sign up for a range of free newsletters and receive exclusive discounts and offers on Packt books and eBooks.

http://PacktLib.PacktPub.com

Do you need instant solutions to your IT questions? PacktLib is Packt's online digital book library. Here, you can access, read and search across Packt's entire library of books.

Why Subscribe?
- Fully searchable across every book published by Packt
- Copy and paste, print and bookmark content
- On demand and accessible via web browser

Free Access for Packt account holders

If you have an account with Packt at www.PacktPub.com, you can use this to access PacktLib today and view nine entirely free books. Simply use your login credentials for immediate access.

For Gavin Bradford. You bring curiosity, joy,
and boundless energy into our home!

Table of Contents

Preface

Moodle is the leading open source learning management system. Using Moodle, teachers can easily construct richly-textured web-based courses. A course can consist of a number of lessons, with each lesson including reading materials; activities such as quizzes, tests, surveys, and projects; and social elements that encourage interaction and group work between students.

Moodle 2.0 E-Learning Course Development shows you how to use Moodle as a tool to enhance your teaching. It will help you to analyze your students' requirements, and come to an understanding of what Moodle can do for them. After that, you'll see how to use every feature of Moodle to meet your course goals. Moodle is relatively easy to install and use, but the real challenge lies in developing a learning process that leverages its power and maps effectively onto the established learning situation. This book guides you through meeting that challenge.

Whether you are the site creator or a course creator, you can use this book as you would a project plan. As you work your way through each chapter, the book provides guidance on making decisions that meet your goals for your learning site. This helps you to create the kind of learning experience that you want for your teachers (if you're the site creator) or students (if you're the teacher). You can also use this book as a traditional reference manual, but its main advantages are its step-by-step, project-oriented approach, and the guidance it gives you on creating an interactive learning experience.

Moodle is designed to be intuitive to use, and its online help is well written. It does a good job of telling you how to use each of its features. What Moodle's help files don't tell you is, when and why to use each feature, and what effect the feature will have on the students' experience. That is what this book provides.

This book shows you how to add static learning material, interactive activities, and social features to your courses, so that students can reach their full learning potential. This book is a complete guide to successful teaching using Moodle, focused on course development and delivery, and using the best educational practices.

What this book covers

Chapter 1, A Guided Tour of Moodle: In this chapter, you will learn what Moodle can do and what kind of user experiences you can create for your students and teachers. You will also learn how the Moodle philosophy shapes the user experience. This helps you to decide how to make the best use of Moodle, and to plan your learning site.

Chapter 2, Installing Moodle: This chapter guides you through the installation of Moodle on your Web server.

Chapter 3, Configuring Your Site: This chapter helps you to configure your site so that it behaves in the way that you envision, and helps to create the user experience that you want. If someone manages your Moodle site for you, you can use this chapter to learn about configuration options that will make the creation and teaching of courses easier for you and your teachers.

Chapter 4, Creating Categories and Courses: This chapter shows you how to create course categories and new courses. It covers course settings that affect the behavior of the course. It also shows you how to enroll teachers and students in a course.

Chapter 5, Adding Static Course Material: Static course materials are resources that students view or listen to, but don't interact with. This chapter shows you how to add web pages, graphics, Adobe Acrobat documents, and media to a course.

Chapter 6, Adding Interaction with Lessons and Assignments: Lessons and Assignments are Moodle activities that allow the student to interact with Moodle, and with the teacher. This chapter shows you how to create and use those activities.

Chapter 7, Evaluating Students with Quizzes, Choices, and Feedback: This chapter shows you how to evaluate your students' knowledge and attitudes to your course.

Chapter 8, Adding Social Activities to Your Course: Moodle excels at peer interaction. This chapter shows you several tools for making student-to-student interaction an integral part of your course.

Chapter 9, Blocks: Every block adds functionality to your site or your course. This chapter describes many of Moodle's blocks, helps you decide which ones will meet your goals, and tells you how to implement them.

Chapter 10, Features for Teachers: This chapter shows you how to use Moodle's gradebook and logs to track student activity.

What you need for this book

This book is designed for people who are creating and delivering courses in Moodle. To make the best use of this book, you will need to have the role of Teacher on a Moodle site. That is, you will need the ability to edit a course on a Moodle site.

This book also contains some information for the Administrator of a Moodle site. Even if you're not the Site Administrator, you can use this information to work with your Administrator to configure the site and use logs and reports.

Who this book is for

This book is for anyone who wants to make the most of Moodle's features to produce an interactive online learning experience. If you're an educator, corporate trainer, or just someone with something to teach, this book can guide you through the installation, configuration, creation, and management of a Moodle site. It is suitable for people who perform the task of creating and setting up the learning site, and for those who create and deliver courses on the site. That is, this book is for Site Administrators, Course Creators, and Teachers.

Conventions

In this book, you will find a number of styles of text that distinguish between different kinds of information. Here are some examples of these styles, and an explanation of their meaning.

Code words in text are shown as follows: "The PHP installed on your server uses a file called `php.ini` to store its settings."

A block of code is set as follows:

```
$CFG->dbtype      = 'mysql';
$CFG->dbhost      = 'localhost';
$CFG->dbname      = 'info-overload';
$CFG->dbuser      = 'info-overload';
$CFG->dbpass      = 'badpassword';
$CFG->dbpersist   = false;
$CFG->prefix      = 'mdl20_';
```

When we wish to draw your attention to a particular part of a code block, the relevant lines or items are set in bold:

```
<meta name="description" content="
Welcome to the Wilderness Skills site
title>Wilderness Skills</title>
<meta name="keywords" content="moodle, Wilderness Skills " />
```

New terms and **important words** are shown in bold. Words that you see on the screen, in menus or dialog boxes for example, appear in the text like this: "Go to the **Download Moodle** page and select the version and format that you need".

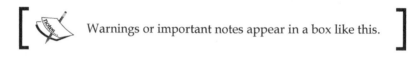

Warnings or important notes appear in a box like this.

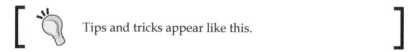

Tips and tricks appear like this.

Reader feedback

Feedback from our readers is always welcome. Let us know what you think about this book—what you liked or may have disliked. Reader feedback is important for us to develop titles that you really get the most out of.

To send us general feedback, simply send an e-mail to feedback@packtpub.com, and mention the book title via the subject of your message.

If there is a book that you need and would like to see us publish, please send us a note in the **SUGGEST A TITLE** form on www.packtpub.com or e-mail suggest@packtpub.com.

If there is a topic that you have expertise in and you are interested in either writing or contributing to a book, see our author guide on www.packtpub.com/authors.

Customer support

Now that you are the proud owner of a Packt book, we have a number of things to help you to get the most from your purchase.

Downloading the example code

You can download the example code files for all Packt books you have purchased from your account at http://www.PacktPub.com. If you purchased this book elsewhere, you can visit http://www.PacktPub.com/support and register to have the files e-mailed directly to you.

Errata

Although we have taken every care to ensure the accuracy of our content, mistakes do happen. If you find a mistake in one of our books—maybe a mistake in the text or the code—we would be grateful if you would report this to us. By doing so, you can save other readers from frustration and help us improve subsequent versions of this book. If you find any errata, please report them by visiting http://www.packtpub.com/support, selecting your book, clicking on the **errata submission form** link, and entering the details of your errata. Once your errata are verified, your submission will be accepted and the errata will be uploaded on our website, or added to any list of existing errata, under the Errata section of that title. Any existing errata can be viewed by selecting your title from http://www.packtpub.com/support.

Piracy

Piracy of copyright material on the Internet is an ongoing problem across all media. At Packt, we take the protection of our copyright and licenses very seriously. If you come across any illegal copies of our works, in any form, on the Internet, please provide us with the location address or website name immediately so that we can pursue a remedy.

Please contact us at copyright@packtpub.com with a link to the suspected pirated material.

We appreciate your help in protecting our authors, and our ability to bring you valuable content.

Questions

You can contact us at questions@packtpub.com if you are having a problem with any aspect of the book, and we will do our best to address it.

1
A Guided Tour of Moodle

Moodle is a free learning management system that allows you to create powerful, flexible, and engaging online learning experiences. I use the phrase "online learning experiences" instead of "online courses" deliberately. The phrase "online course" often connotes a sequential series of web pages, some images, maybe a few animations, and a quiz, provided online. There might also be some email or bulletin board communication among the teacher and students. However, online learning can be much more engaging than that.

Moodle's name gives you insight into its approach to e-learning. From the official Moodle documentation:

> *The word Moodle was originally an acronym for* **Modular Object-Oriented Dynamic Learning Environment***, which is mostly useful to programmers and education theorists. It's also a verb that describes the process of lazily meandering through something, doing things as it occurs to you to do them, an enjoyable tinkering that often leads to insight and creativity. As such it applies both to the way Moodle was developed, and to the way a student or teacher might approach studying or teaching an online course. Anyone who uses Moodle is a* **Moodler***.*

The phrase "online learning experience" connotes a more active, engaging role for the students and teachers. It connotes web pages that can be explored in any order, courses with live chats among students and teachers, forums where users can rate messages on their relevance or insight, online workshops that enable students to evaluate each other's work, impromptu polls that let the teacher evaluate what students think of a course's progress, and directories set aside for teachers to upload and share their files. All of these features create an active learning environment, full of different kinds of student-to-student and student-to-teacher interaction. This is the kind of user experience that Moodle excels at, and the kind that this book will help you to create.

Step-by-step: Using each chapter

When you create a Moodle learning site, you usually follow a defined series of steps. This book is arranged to support that process. Each chapter shows you how to get the most from each step. Each step is listed below, with a brief description of the chapter that supports that step.

As you work your way through each chapter, your learning site will grow in scope and sophistication. By the time you finish this book, you should have a complete, interactive learning site. As you learn more about what Moodle can do, and see your courses taking shape, you may want to change some of the things that you did in previous chapters. Moodle offers you this flexibility. And, this book helps you to determine how those changes will cascade throughout your site.

Step 1: Learn About the Moodle experience (Chapter 1)

Every Learning Management System (LMS) has a paradigm, or approach, that shapes the user experience and encourages a certain kind of usage. An LMS might encourage very sequential learning by offering features that enforce a given order for each course. It might discourage student-to-student interaction by offering few features that support it, while encouraging solo learning by offering many opportunities for the student to interact with the course material. In this chapter, you will learn what Moodle can do and what kind of user experience your students and teachers will have when they use Moodle. You will also learn about the Moodle philosophy, and how it shapes the user experience. With this information, you'll be ready to decide how to make the best use of Moodle's many features, and to plan your online learning site.

Step 2: Install Moodle (Chapter 2)

This chapter guides you through installing Moodle on your web server. It will help you to estimate the amount of disk space, bandwidth, and memory that you will need for Moodle. This can help you to decide upon the right hosting service for your needs.

Step 3: Configure your site (Chapter 3)

Most of the decisions that you make when installing and configuring Moodle will affect the user experience. Not just students and teachers, but also course creators and site administrators are affected by these decisions. Although Moodle's online help does a good job of telling you how to install and configure the software, it doesn't tell you how the settings you choose affect the user experience. *Chapter 3* covers the implications of these decisions, and helps you to configure the site so that it behaves in the way that you envision.

Step 4: Create the framework for your learning site (Chapter 4)

In Moodle, every course belongs to a category. *Chapter 4* takes you through the creation of course categories, and the creation of courses. Just as you chose sitewide settings during installation and configuration, you choose course-wide settings when creating each course. This chapter tells you the implications of the various course settings, so that you can create the experience that you want for each course. It also shows you how to add teachers and students to courses.

Step 5: Add basic course material (Chapter 5)

In most online courses, the core material consists of web pages that the students view. These pages can contain text, graphics, movies, sound files, games, and exercises: anything that can appear on the World Wide Web can appear on a Moodle web page. *Chapter 5* covers how to add web pages to Moodle courses, and also how to add other kinds of static course material: links to other websites, media files, labels, and directories of files. This chapter also helps you to decide when to use each of these types of material.

Step 6: Make your courses interactive (Chapter 6)

In this context, "interactive" means interaction between the student and teacher, or the student and an active web page. Student-to-student interaction is covered in the next step. This chapter covers activities that involve interaction between the student and an active web page, or between the student and the teacher. Interactive course material includes lessons that guide students through a defined path based upon their answers to review questions, and assignments that are uploaded by the student and then graded by the teacher. *Chapter 6* tells you how to create these interactions, and how each of them affects the student and teacher experience.

Step 7: Create tools to evaluate your students (Chapter 7)

In *Chapter 7, Evaluating Students with Quizzes, Choices, and Feedback*, you'll learn how to evaluate students' knowledge with a Quiz. You will also learn how to to evaluate their attitude towards the class by using the Feedback activity. Finally, you'll learn how to evaluate students' opinions by using the Choice activity.

Step 8: Make your course social (Chapter 8)

Social course material enables student-to-student interaction. Moodle allows you to add chats, forums, and **Wikis** to your courses. These types of interactions will be familiar to many students. You can also create glossaries that are site-wide and ones that are specific to a single course. Students can also add to the glossaries. Finally, Moodle offers a powerful workshop tool, which enables students to view and evaluate each others, work. Each of these interactions makes the course more interesting, but also makes it more complicated for the teacher to manage. *Chapter 8* helps you to make the best use of Moodle's social features. The result is a course that encourages students to contribute, share, and engage.

Step 9: Add functionality by using blocks (Chapter 9)

Every block adds functionality to your site or your course. You can use blocks to display calendars, enable commenting, enable tagging, show navigation features, and much more. This chapter describes many of Moodle's blocks, helps you decide which ones will meet your goals, and tells you how to implement them.

Step 10: Take the pulse of your course (Chapter 10)

Moodle offers several tools to help teachers administer and deliver courses. It keeps detailed access logs that enable teachers to see exactly what content students accessed, and when they did so. It also allows teachers to establish custom grading scales, which are available site-wide or for a single course. Student grades can be accessed online and also downloaded to a spreadsheet program. Finally, teachers can collaborate in special forums (bulletin boards) reserved just for them.

The Moodle philosophy

Moodle is designed to support a style of learning called *Social Constructionism*. This style of learning is interactive. The social constructionist philosophy believes that people learn best when they interact with the learning material, construct new material for others, and interact with other students about the material. The difference between a traditional class and a class following the social constructionist philosophy is the difference between a lecture and a discussion.

Moodle does not require you to use the social constructionist method for your courses. However, it best supports this method. For example, Moodle allows you to add several kinds of static course material. This is course material that a student reads, but does not interact with:

- Web pages
- Links to anything on the Web (including material on your Moodle site)
- A directory of files
- A label that displays any text or image

However, Moodle also allows you to add interactive course material. This is course material that a student interacts with, by answering questions, entering text, or uploading files:

- Assignment (uploading files to be reviewed by the teacher)
- Choice (a single question)
- Lesson (a conditional, branching activity)
- Quiz (an online test)

Moodle also offers activities where students interact with each other. These are used to create social course material:

- Chat (live online chat between students)
- Forum (you can have zero or more online bulletin boards for each course)
- Glossary (students and/or teachers can contribute terms to site-wide glossaries)
- Wiki (this is a familiar tool for collaboration to most younger students and many older students)
- Workshop (this supports the peer review and feedback of assignments that students upload)

In addition, some of Moodle's add-on modules add even more types of interaction. For example, one add-on module enables students and teachers to schedule appointments with each other.

The Moodle experience

Because Moodle encourages interaction and exploration, your students' learning experience will often be non-linear. Moodle can be used to enforce a specific order upon a course, using something called conditional activities. Conditional activities can be arranged in a sequence. Your course can contain a mix of conditional and non-linear activities.

In this section, I'll take you on a tour of a Moodle learning site. You will see the student's experience from the time that the student arrives at the site, through entering a course, to working through some material in the course. You will also see some student-to-student interaction, and some functions used by the teacher to manage the course. Along the way, I'll point out many of the features that you will learn to implement in this book, and see how the demo site is using those features.

The Moodle Front Page

The Front Page of your site is the first thing that most visitors will see. This section takes you on a tour of the Front Page of my demonstration site.

 Probably the best Moodle demo sites are http://demo.moodle.net/ and http://school.demo.moodle.net/.

Arriving at the site

When a visitor arrives at a learning site, the visitor sees the Front Page. You can require the visitor to register and log in before seeing any part of your site, or you can allow an anonymous visitor to see a lot of information about the site on the Front Page, which is what I have done:

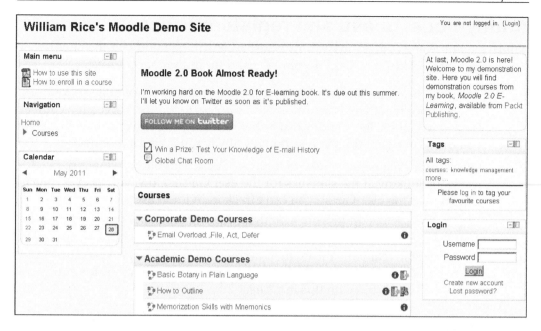

One of the first things that a visitor will notice is the announcement at the top and centre of the page, **Moodle 2.0 Book Almost Ready!**. Below the announcement are two activities: a quiz, **Win a Prize: Test Your Knowledge of E-mail History**, and a chat room, **Global Chat Room**. Selecting either of these activities will require to the visitor to register with the site, as shown in the following screenshot:

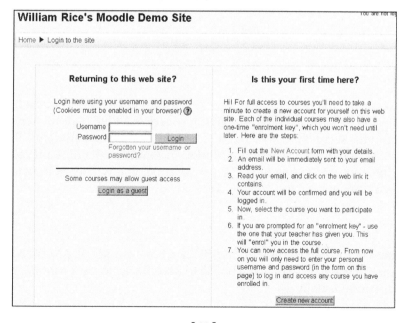

Anonymous, guest, and registered access

Notice the line **Some courses may allow guest access** at the middle of the page. You can set three levels of access for your site, and for individual courses:

- **Anonymous** access allows anyone to see the contents of your site's Front Page. Notice that there is no Anonymous access for courses. Even if a course is open to Guests, the visitor must either manually log in as the user Guest, or you must configure the site to automatically log in a visitor as Guest.

- **Guest** access requires the user to login as Guest. This allows you to track usage, by looking at the statistics for the user Guest. However, as everyone is logged in as the user Guest, you can't track individual users.

- **Registered** access requires the user to register on your site. You can allow people to register with or without e-mail confirmation, require a special code for enrolment, manually create their accounts yourself, import accounts from another system, or use an outside system (like an LDAP server) for your accounts. There's more on this in *Chapter 2*.

The Main menu

Returning to the Front Page, notice the **Main menu** in the upper-left corner. This menu consists of two documents that tell the user what the site is about, and how to use it.

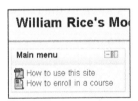

In Moodle, icons tell the user what kind of resource will be accessed by a link. In this case, the icon tells the user that the first resource is a PDF (Adobe Acrobat) document, and the second is a web page. Course materials that students observe or read, such as web or text pages, hyperlinks, and multimedia files are called **Resources**. In *Chapter 5, Adding Static Course Material*, you will learn how to add Resources to a course.

Blocks

In the side bars of the page, you will find Blocks. For example, the **Main menu**, **Calendar**, and **Tags** blocks. You can choose to add Blocks to the Front Page and to each course, individually.

Other Blocks display a summary of the current course, a list of courses available on the site, the latest news, a list of the people who are online, and other information. In the lower-right corner of the Front Page you will see the **Login** Block. *Chapter 9* tells you how to use these Blocks.

> **Your site's Front Page is a course!**
> You can add Blocks to the Front Page of your site because the Front Page is essentially a course. Anything that you can add to a course — such as Resources or Blocks, can be added to the Front Page.

Site Description

On the rightmost side of the Front Page you can see a **Site Description**. This is optional. If this were a course, you could choose to display the **Course Description** here.

The Site or Course Description can contain anything that you can put on a web page. It is essentially a block of HTML code that is put onto the Front Page.

Available courses

You can choose to display available courses on the Front Page of your site. In the demonstration site, I've created a category for **Free Courses** and another for **Wild Plants**. **Free Courses** allow Guest users to enter. Courses in other categories require users to register.

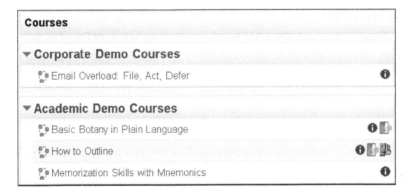

Clicking on the **Information** icon ❶ next to a course displays the **Course Description**. Clicking on a course name takes you to the course. If the course allows anonymous access, you are taken directly into the course. If the course allows guest access, or requires registration, you are taken to the Login screen.

Inside a course

Now let us take a look inside a course.

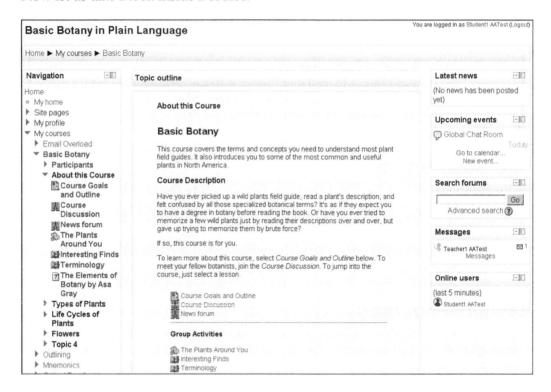

Breadcrumbs

In the preceding screenshot, the user has logged in as **student1** and entered the **Basic Botany** course. We know this from the breadcrumbs trail in the upper-left corner of the screen, which tells us the name of the site and the name of the course. In the upper-right corner of the screen, we see a confirmation that the user has logged in.

Blocks

Like the Front Page, this course uses various Blocks. The most prominent is the Navigation Block on the left. Let's talk more about navigation.

Navigation Block

The Navigation Block shows you where you are, and, where you can go in the site. In the demonstration, you can see that the student has access to several courses: **Email Overload**, **Basic Botany**, **Outlining**, **Mnemonics**, and **Critical Reading**. Right now, the student is in the **Basic Botany** course, in the topic labeled **About this Course**. Under that topic, you can see a variety of resources and activities.

With just a few clicks, the student can open another course and jump to a place in that course.

Earlier in this chapter, I commented on the non-linear nature of many Moodle courses. Notice that all of the resources for this course are available to the user at all times. Later, we'll discuss features that allow you to set conditions for when activities or resources become available to the student.

At the top of the Navigation Block is a link to the site's **Home** page. Below that, is a link to the student's home page, **My home**. The student's home page lists the courses that the student is enroled in, and the work that the student performs in those courses.

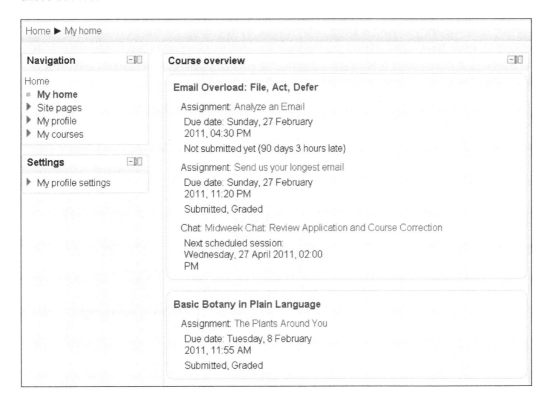

Also on the Navigation Block is a link to the student's profile, **My profile**. The name gives the impression that you will find information such as contact information, interests, and maybe a picture of the student, under this link. But there's actually much more under that link:

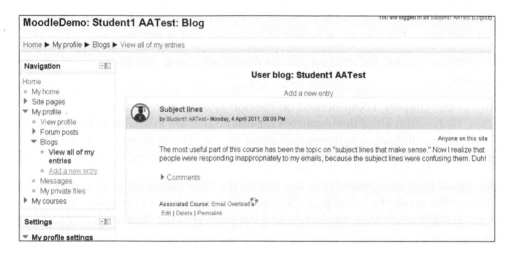

Notice that we are viewing a **Blog** entry made by the user. At the bottom of the blog entry, Moodle tells us what course the user made this blog entry in: **Email Overload**. In Moodle, when a user makes a blog entry or forum posting in a course, that entry/post appears both in the course and in the user's profile.

The user's **Messages** are also collected under this link. Here the user can see both received and sent messages.

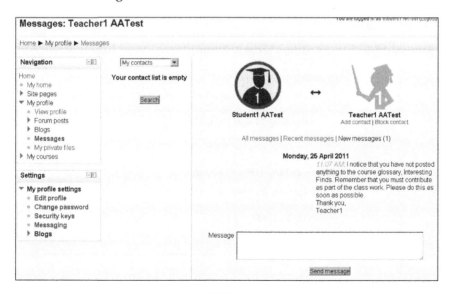

The drop-down list lets the user filter messages by person or by course.

The user's profile also contains a link to any personal files uploaded into Moodle by this user:

Unlike **Forum posts** and **Blog** entries, the **My private files** page doesn't display files that the student has uploaded to specific courses. The files here are, literally, private. However, when the student submits a file to a course, the student can select a private file and submit it to the course.

Topics

Moodle also allows you to organize a course by Week, in which case each section is labeled with a date instead of a number. Or, you can choose to make your course a single, large discussion forum. Most courses are organized by Topic, like the one shown in the following screenshot:

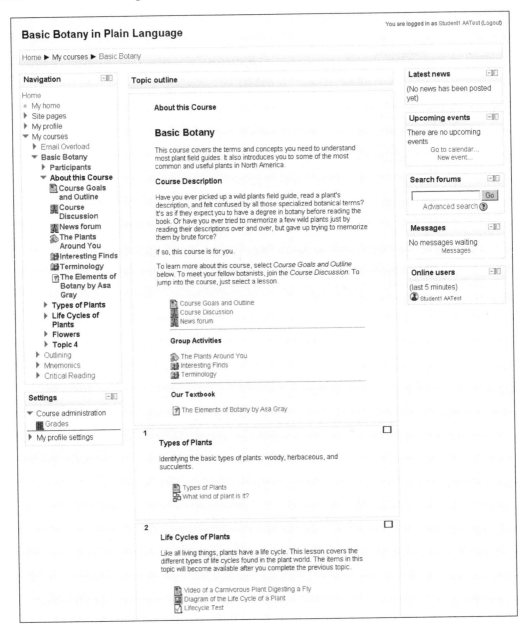

Notice that the first topic, which I've labeled **About this Course**, is not numbered. Moodle gives you a Topic 0 to use as the course introduction.

Teachers can hide and show topics at will. This enables a teacher to open and close resources and activities as the course progresses.

Topics are the lowest level of organization in Moodle. The hierarchy is: **Site | Course Category | Course Subcategory (optional) | Course | Topic**. Every item in your course belongs to a Topic, even if your course consists of only Topic 0.

Joining a discussion

Clicking on **Course Discussion**, under **Group Activities**, takes the student to the course-wide forum. Clicking on a topic line opens that thread. You can see in the following screenshot that the teacher started with the first post. Then a student replied to this post:

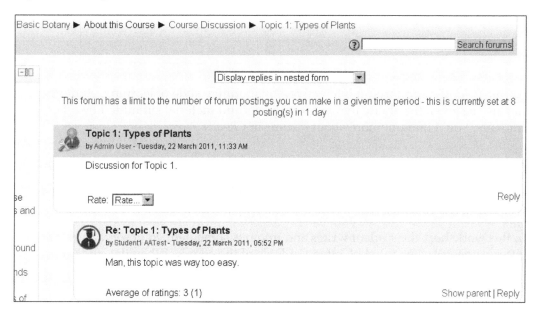

That Student's message doesn't serve our students. Fortunately, the teacher has editing rights to this forum, and so he or she can delete posts at will. The teacher can also rate posts for their relevance, as shown in the following screenshot:

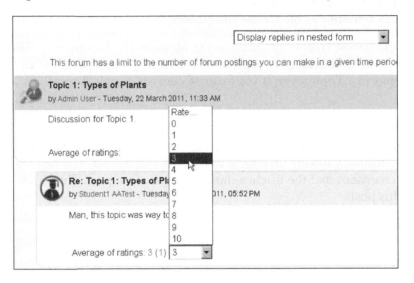

Because Moodle supports an interactive, collaborative style of learning, students can also be given the ability to rate forum posts and material submitted by other students. You'll find out more about forums in *Chapter 7*.

Completing a workshop

Now in our demonstration course, the student will enter a workshop called **Observing the Familiar**.

In this workshop, the student writes and updates some defined observations. These observations are then rated by other students of the course. When the student first enters the workshop, he or she sees instructions for completing the workshop, as shown in the following screenshot:

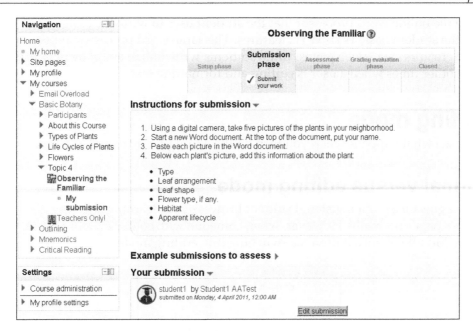

After reading these instructions, the student continues to the workshop submission form:

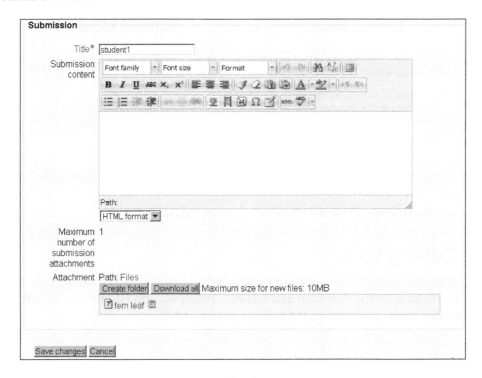

Notice the online word processor that the student uses to write the assignment. This gives the student basic WYSIWYG features. The same word processor appears when course creators create web pages, when students write online assignment entries, and at other times when a user is editing and formatting text.

Editing mode

Let us see what happens when you turn on the editing mode to make changes.

Normal versus editing mode

When a guest user or a registered student browses your learning site, Moodle displays pages normally. However, when someone with course creator privilege logs in, Moodle offers a button for switching into editing mode:

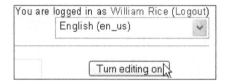

Clicking on **Turn editing on** puts Moodle into **Editing mode**:

Normal Mode   **Editing Mode**

Let's walk through the icons that become available in editing mode.

The Editing icon

Clicking the Edit icon allows you to edit whatever that icon follows. In this example, clicking on the Edit icon that follows the paragraph allows you to edit the announcement, as shown in the following screenshot:

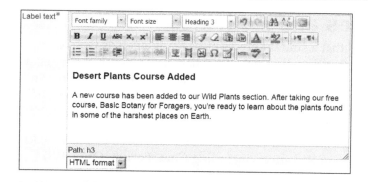

Clicking on the Editing icon next to the quiz **Win a Prize** takes you into the editing window for that quiz. In that window, you can create, add, and remove quiz questions, change the grading scheme, and apply other settings to the quiz.

The Delete icon

Clicking on the Delete icon ✖ deletes the item that the icon follows. If you want to remove an item from a course, but you're not sure if you'll want to use it later, don't delete the item; instead, hide it from view. Hiding and showing items is explained in the following section.

The Hidden/Shown icons

I call these the Hidden/Shown icons ⚊ / ⚊ instead of Hide/Show because the icons indicate the current state of an item, instead of indicating what will happen when you click on them. The Hidden icon indicates that an item is hidden from the students. Clicking on it shows the item to the students. The Shown icon indicates that an item is shown to the students. Clicking on it hides the item from the students.

If you want to remove an item from a course while keeping it for later use, or if you want to keep an item hidden from students while you're working on it, hide it instead of deleting it.

The Group icons

The ⚊ ⚊ ⚊ icons indicate what Group mode has been applied to an item. Groups are explained in a later chapter. For now, you should know that you can control access to items based upon what Group a student belongs to. Clicking on these icons allows you to change this setting.

Resources and Activities

Course material that a student observes or reads, such as web or text pages, hyperlinks, and multimedia files—are called Resources. Course material that student interacts with, or that enables interaction among students and teachers, are called **Activities**. Now let us see how to add some Resources and Activities to your Moodle site.

In Editing mode, you can add Resources and Activities to a course. Moodle offers more Activities than Resources, including **Chat**, **Forum**, **Quiz**, **Wiki**, and more.

Adding Resources and Activities

You add Resources and Activities by using the drop-down lists that appear in **Editing Mode**:

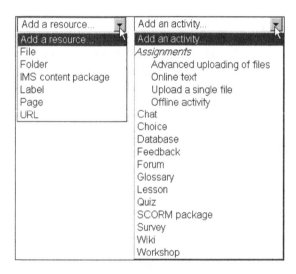

Selecting an item brings you to the Editing window for that type of item. For example, selecting **URL** displays the window to the right. Notice that you can do much more than just specify a hyperlink. You can give this link a user-friendly name, a brief description, open it in a new window, and more.

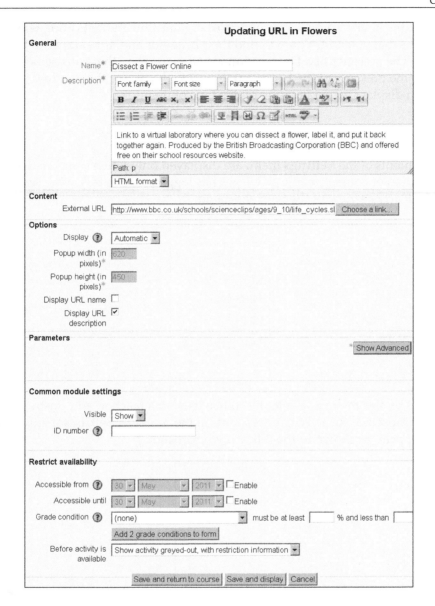

Almost every Resource and Activity that you add to Moodle has a **Description**. This **Description** appears when a student selects the item. Also, if the item appears in a list (for example, a list of all the Resources in a course), the **Description** is displayed in the list.

When building courses, you will spend most of your time in the Editing windows for the items that you add. You will find their behavior and appearance to be very consistent. The presence of a **Description** is one example of that consistency. Another example is the presence of the Help icon ⓘ next to the title of the window. Clicking on this icon displays an explanation of this type of item.

The Settings menu

The full contents of the **Settings** menu are displayed only when someone with administration or course creator privileges has logged in. The following screenshot shows the teacher's view of the **Settings** menu:

The choices on this menu apply to the course itself. If a teacher, administrator, or course creator selects an activity or resource in the course, a **Settings** menu for that item will appear, as shown in the following screenshot:

Notice that the items that used to be under the course settings menu are now under a **Course administration** menu.

And much more

This short tour introduced you to the basics of the Moodle experience. The following chapters take you through installing Moodle and creating courses. If you work through these chapters in order, you will discover many features that were not mentioned in this tour. Also, because Moodle is open source, new features can be added at any time. Perhaps you will be the one to contribute a new feature to the Moodle community.

The Moodle architecture

Moodle runs on any web server that supports the PHP programming language, and a database. It works best, and there is more support, when running on the Apache web server with a MySQL database. These things, Apache, PHP, and MySQL are common to almost all commercial web hosts, even the lowest cost ones.

The Moodle learning management system resides in three places on your web host:

- The application occupies one directory, with many subdirectories for the various modules.
- Data files that students and teachers upload—such as photos and assignments—reside in the Moodle data directory.
- Course material that you create with Moodle (web pages, quizzes, workshops, lessons, and so on), grades, user information, and user logs reside in the Moodle database.

The Moodle application directory

The screenshot below shows you my Moodle application directory. Without even knowing much about Moodle, you can guess the function of several directories. For example, the admin directory holds the PHP code that creates the administrative pages, the lang directory holds translations of the Moodle interface, and the mod directory holds the various modules:

Location: /www/moodle/moodle							
Select	Type	Permission	User	Group	Size	Date	Filename
«BACK							..
☐	📁	drwxr-xr-x	williamr	williamr	4096	Sep 05 22:05	admin
☐	📁	drwxr-xr-x	williamr	williamr	4096	May 24 02:03	auth
☐	📁	drwxr-xr-x	williamr	williamr	4096	Sep 29 22:05	backup
☐	📁	drwxr-xr-x	williamr	williamr	4096	Sep 29 22:05	blocks
☐	📁	drwxr-xr-x	williamr	williamr	4096	Sep 29 22:05	calendar
☐	📁	drwxr-xr-x	williamr	williamr	4096	Sep 23 22:05	course
☐	📁	drwxr-xr-x	williamr	williamr	4096	Jun 18 22:11	doc
☐	📁	drwxr-xr-x	williamr	williamr	4096	Sep 29 22:05	enrol
☐	📁	drwxr-xr-x	williamr	williamr	4096	May 24 02:04	error
☐	📁	drwxr-xr-x	williamr	williamr	4096	Sep 29 22:05	files
☐	📁	drwxr-xr-x	williamr	williamr	4096	Sep 29 22:05	filter
☐	📁	drwxr-xr-x	williamr	williamr	4096	Sep 27 22:05	grade
☐	📁	drwxr-xr-x	williamr	williamr	4096	Sep 29 22:05	lang
☐	📁	drwxr-xr-x	williamr	williamr	4096	Sep 29 22:05	lib
☐	📁	drwxr-xr-x	williamr	williamr	4096	Sep 23 22:05	login
☐	📁	drwxr-xr-x	williamr	williamr	4096	Sep 07 22:04	message
☐	📁	drwxr-xr-x	williamr	williamr	4096	Oct 19 14:47	mod
☐	📁	drwxr-xr-x	williamr	williamr	4096	May 24 02:07	pix
☐	📁	drwxr-xr-x	williamr	williamr	4096	Sep 29 22:05	rss
☐	📁	drwxr-xr-x	williamr	williamr	4096	Aug 01 22:25	sso
☐	📁	drwxr-xr-x	williamr	williamr	4096	Sep 29 22:05	theme
☐	📁	drwxr-xr-x	williamr	williamr	4096	Sep 28 22:04	user
☐	📁	drwxr-xr-x	williamr	williamr	4096	May 24 02:07	userpix
☐	PHP	-rw-r--r--	williamr	williamr	15087	Jul 04 22:13	config-dist.php
☐	PHP	-rw-r-----	williamr	williamr	724	Sep 30 13:24	config.php
☐	PHP	-rw-r--r--	williamr	williamr	5931	Jul 12 22:16	file.php
☐	PHP	-rw-r--r--	williamr	williamr	4893	May 24 02:03	help.php
☐	PHP	-rw-r--r--	williamr	williamr	7529	May 24 02:03	index.php
☐	PHP	-rw-r--r--	williamr	williamr	23503	May 24 02:03	install.php
☐	📄	-rw-r--r--	williamr	williamr	943	May 24 02:03	README.txt
☐	📄	-rw-r--r--	williamr	williamr	2923484	Jul 06 02:09	tags
☐	PHP	-rw-r--r--	williamr	williamr	515	Sep 10 22:05	version.php

The `index.php` file is the Moodle home page. If a student were browsing my Moodle site, the first page that the student would see is the file `http://moodle.williamrice.com/index.php`.

On my site, the free course **Basic Botany for Foragers** happens to be course number 4. Only the Moodle system knows it as course number 4; we know it as **Basic Botany for Foragers**. When a student enters that course, the URL in the student's browser reads `http://moodle.williamrice.com/moodle/course/view.php?id=4`. In the preceding screenshot, you can see that `/course` is one of the directories in my Moodle installation. As the user navigates around the site, different `.php` pages do the work of presenting information.

As each of Moodle's core components and modules is stored in its own subdirectory, the software can be easily updated by replacing old files with newer ones. You should periodically check the `http://www.moodle.org` website for news about updates and bug fixes.

The Moodle data directory

Moodle stores files uploaded by the users in a data directory. This directory should not be accessible to the general public over the Web. That is, you should not be able to type in the URL for this directory and access it using a web browser. You can protect it either by using an `.htaccess` file or by placing the directory outside of the web server's documents directory.

In my installation, the preceding screenshot shows you that the web document directory for `moodle.williamrice.com` is `/www/moodle`. Therefore, I placed the data directory outside of `/www/moodle`, in `/www/moodledata`:

Location: /www						
Select	Type	Permission	User	Group	Size	Date	Filename
	📁	drwxrwxr-x	root	williamr	4096	Oct 24 14:45	moodle
	📁	drwxrwxr-x	williamr	williamr	4096	Jul 11 16:45	moodledata
	📁	drwxrwxr-t	williamr	williamr	4096	Mar 28 2005	www
	📄	-rw-rwxr--	williamr	williamr	24	Aug 22 2003	.bash_logout
	📄	-rw-rwxr--	williamr	williamr	191	Aug 22 2003	.bash_profile
	📄	-rw-rwxr--	williamr	williamr	124	Aug 22 2003	.bashrc
	📄	-rw-rwxr--	williamr	williamr	3511	Aug 22 2003	.screenrc

On my server, the directory `/www/moodledata` corresponds to the subdomain `www.moodledata.williamrice.com`. This subdomain is protected from open access by an .htaccess file. The directory `/www/www` corresponds to the root domain, `www.williamrice.com`.

The Moodle database

When the Moodle data directory stores files uploaded by students, the Moodle database stores most of the information in your Moodle site. The database also stores objects that you create using Moodle. For example, Moodle enables you to create web pages for your courses. These web pages' actual HTML code is stored in the database. Links that you add to a course, the settings and content of forums and Wikis, and quizzes created with Moodle, are all examples of data stored in the Moodle database.

The three parts of Moodle: the *application*, *data directory*, and *database*, work together to create your learning site. However, knowing how the three parts work together is also helpful when upgrading, troubleshooting, or moving your site between servers.

Summary

Moodle encourages exploration and interaction between and among students and teachers. As a course designer and teacher, you will have most of the tools at your disposal if you work with this tendency in mind, and make your learning experiences as interactive as possible. Creating courses with forums, peer-assessed workshops, surveys, and interactive lessons is more work than creating a course from a series of static web pages. It is also more engaging and effective, and you will find it worth the effort to use Moodle's many interactive features.

When teaching an online course in Moodle, remember that Moodle allows you to add, move, and modify course material and grading tools on-the-fly. If it's permitted by your institution's policies, don't hesitate to change a course in response to student needs.

Finally, learn the basics of Moodle's architecture, and at least read over the *Installation and configuration* section in *Chapter 2*. Don't be afraid of the technology. If you can master the difficult art of teaching, you can master using Moodle to its full potential.

2
Installing Moodle

Even if you don't install Moodle yourself, you should skim this chapter for information that will be helpful to you as a course manager and/or creator. That is because the choices made during Moodle's installation can affect how the system works for people who create, teach, and/or take courses on that system.

Installing Moodle consists of the following activities:

- Obtaining space and rights on a web server that has the capabilities needed to run Moodle
- Creating the subdomains and/or directories needed for Moodle and its data
- Getting and unpacking Moodle, and uploading it to your web server
- Creating the data directory
- Creating the Moodle database
- Activating the installation routine and specifying settings for your Moodle site
- Setting up the cron job

All of these activities are covered in the following sections.

The publisher and the author of this book have provided Moodle installation instructions on `installationwiki.org`. On that site, you will find the latest installation instructions for Moodle and many other open source applications.

Installation Step 1: The web server

Moodle is run from a web server. You upload or place Moodle in your directory on the server. Usually, the server is someone else's computer. If you're a teacher, or are in the corporate world, your institution might have their own web server. If you're an individual or have a small business, you will probably buy web-hosting services from another company. In either case, we are assuming that you have an account on a web server that offers Apache, PHP, and MySQL.

If you must install your own Apache web server and MySQL software, the easiest way to do so is to use another open source tool: XAMPP from `http://www.apachefriends.org`. Apache Friends is a non-profit project that promotes the Apache web server. XAMPP is an easy, all-in-one installer that installs Apache, MySQL, PHP, and Perl. It is available for Linux, Windows, Mac, and Solaris. If you would like to create a test environment for Moodle, then installing XAMPP onto your computer will install the web server with the components required to support a Moodle installation.

You can also download a package containing Moodle and the other software needed to make it run: Apache, MySQL, and PHP. Go to the official Moodle website and under **Downloads** look for **Packages**.

What level of hosting service do you need?

With only a few dozen students, Moodle runs fine on a modest web-hosting service. At the time of writing, many hosting companies offer services that can run a small Moodle installation for less than $10 a month. Base your decision upon the following factors discussed.

Disk space

A fresh Moodle 2.0 installation will occupy less than 100MB of disk space, which is not much. The content that is added as users create and take courses will probably grow larger than that. Base your decision on how much space to obtain upon the kinds of courses that you plan to deliver. If the courses will contain mostly text and a few graphics, you'll need less space than if they contain music and video files. Also, consider the disk space occupied by the files that the students will upload. Will students upload small word processing files? Large graphics? Huge multimedia files? When determining how much disk space you will need, consider the size of the files that your courses will serve and that your students will submit. The size of files that can be uploaded is controlled by the site administrator, using a setting under **Security | Site Policies | Maximum Uploaded File Size**.

Bandwidth

Moodle is a web-based product, so course content and assignments are added over the Web. Whenever a reader or user connects to a website, they're using bandwidth. When a user reads a page on your Moodle site, downloads a video, or uploads a paper, he or she uses some of your bandwidth. The more courses, students, activities, and multimedia that your Moodle site has, the more bandwidth you will use. Most commercial hosting services include a fixed amount of bandwidth in their service. If your account uses more bandwidth than allowed, some services cut off your site's access. Others keep your site up, but automatically bill you for the additional bandwidth. The second option is preferable in case of unexpected demand. When deciding upon a hosting service, find out how much bandwidth they offer and what they do if you exceed that limit.

Are you serving videos with your course?

If your course includes many videos, or if you'll be serving video to many users, that can use up a lot of the bandwidth that your hosting company provides. Instead of hosting those videos on your Moodle server, consider hosting them on a dedicated video hosting site like vimeo.com or youtube.com. Then, you can just embed them in your Moodle page. Vimeo, YouTube, or whoever hosts the video will take care of the bandwidth.

Memory

If you're using a shared hosting service, your account will be sharing a web server with other accounts. All accounts share the memory, or RAM, of that server. During times of high demand, only a small amount of memory will be available for each account. During times of low demand, your account might be able to use more memory.

Moodle runs fine on most shared hosting services. However, when you have a large number of courses, or large courses on shared hosts with low memory limits, Moodle's automated backup routine often fails. Site administrators can get around this limitation by manually backing up their site one course at a time, or by moving to a different host.

If your site will have more than a few courses, or any courses whose size is measured in tens of megabytes, and you want to use automated backup, check your possible web hosts carefully. In particular, search the forums on Moodle.org to find out if any other customers of that host have complained about automated backups failing due to a lack of memory. In general, Moodle's automated backup routines are inefficient and you might want to consider alternatives for a large site.

In general, 1GB of RAM on your server will serve 50 simultaneous users. Note that your memory needs will be determined not by the number of total users, but the number of simultaneous users.

Ensuring minimum prerequisites

Check with your hosting service to ensure that you will be given the following minimum prerequisites:

1. Enough **disk space** for the Moodle 2.0 software, your course material, and the files that students will upload.

2. Enough **bandwidth** to serve your course files, and for students to upload their files.

3. **PHP** version 5.2.8.

4. The ability to create at least one MySQL **database**, or to have it created for you.

5. The ability to create at least one MySQL database **user**, or to have it created for you.

6. Enough shared or dedicated **memory** to run Moodle's automated backup routines. You might not know how much that is until you've tried it.

When you confirm that you have those items, you are ready to proceed with the installation.

Many hosting services also offer automated installation of Moodle. Search for hosting services using the terms "fantastico" and "moodle", or "one-click install" and "moodle". These are usually shared hosting services, so you will have the same performance limitations as if you installed Moodle yourself on a shared host. However, such hosting services simplify the installation and thus provide a fast, inexpensive way to get a Moodle site up and running. Automated installations are not always the latest version. Check with your hosting company to determine when they roll out new versions.

You should also research the services offered by the official Moodle Partners. You can find out more about Moodle partners on moodle.com (notice the "dot com" and not "dot org" address).

Installation Step 2: Subdomain or subdirectory?

A subdomain is a web address that exists under your web address, and acts like an independent site. For example, my website is `www.williamrice.com`. This is a standard website, not a Moodle site. I could have a subdomain, `http://www.moodle.williamrice.com`, to hold a Moodle site. This subdomain would be like an independent site. However, it exists on the same server, under the same account, and they both count towards the disk space and bandwidth that I use. In the following screenshot, notice that I have one subdomain, in addition to my normal website:

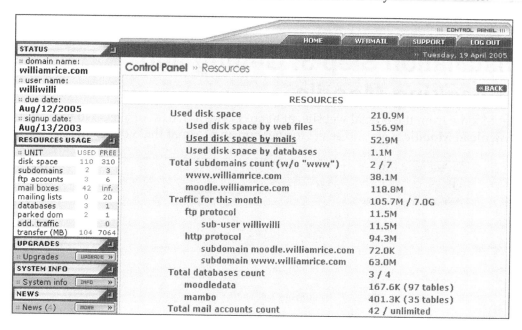

In this example, Moodle is installed in the subdomain `http://www.moodle.williamrice.com`.

Using a subdomain offers me several advantages. As you can see, I can manage them both from the same interface. Second, I can use a subdomain as a test site for my Moodle installation. I can install and test Moodle in the subdomain, and then copy it over to my main site when it's ready. Having a site to test updates and add-ons may be helpful if uninterrupted service is important to you. Later, you'll see how easy it is to copy a Moodle installation to a different location, change a few settings, and have it work. If you want to do this, make sure that the hosting service you choose allows subdomains.

If you want to keep things simpler, you can install Moodle into a subdirectory of your website. For example, `http://www.williamrice.com/moodle` or `http://www.info-overload.biz/learn`. In the next step, you will see how Moodle can automatically install itself into a subdirectory called `/moodle`. This is very convenient, and you'll find a lot of websites with Moodle running in the `/moodle` subdirectory.

Decide if you want to install Moodle into a **subdirectory** or a **subdomain**. If you choose a subdomain, create it now. If you choose a subdirectory, you can create it later, when uploading the Moodle software.

Installation Step 3: Getting and unpacking Moodle

Get Moodle from the official website, at `http://www.moodle.org/`. Go to the **Download Moodle** page and select the version and format that you need:

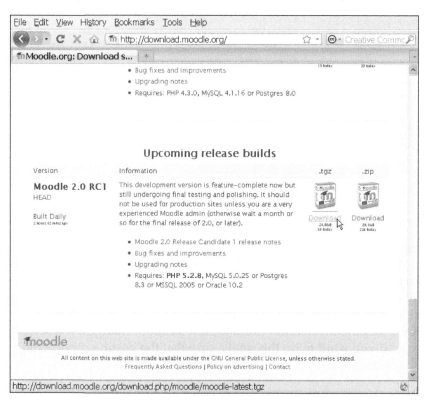

Which Version?

For a new installation, the **Latest Stable Branch** is usually your best choice. The **Last build:** information tells you when it was last updated with a bug-fix or patch. This is usually irrelevant to you; the version number determines which features you get, not the build time.

For a production server, do not use the standalone packages mentioned above; they are insecure. Instead, use the latest stable branch.

The quick way: Upload and unzip

Moodle is downloaded as a single, compressed file. This compressed file contains the many small files and directories that constitute Moodle. After downloading the compressed file, you could decompress (or unzip) the file. Unzipping it on your local PC will extract many files and directories that you must place on your server.

If you're using a hosting service, they might have the ability to decompress the file on the server. If so, you can just upload the entire ZIP file, tell the server to decompress it, and all of your Moodle files will be in place. This is much faster than decompressing the ZIP file on your computer and then uploading the many files that it creates.

Upload and decompress the ZIP file on the server

1. Go to `http://www.moodle.org/` and download the Moodle package (ZIP or TAR file) to your local hard drive.

2. Upload the file to your hosting service. My hosting service uses the popular cPanel control panel, so uploading a file looks like this:

3. In your hosting service's control panel, select the compressed file. If you're given a choice to unzip the file, then you can use this method. In the following example, I have selected the compressed file, **moodle-latest.tgz**. When I click on the **Extract** icon, the file will decompress:

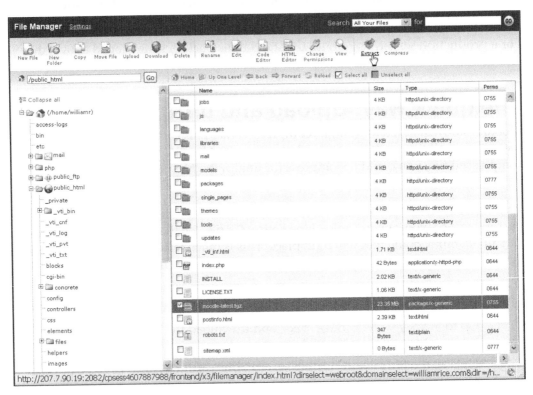

4. If your hosting service gives you the option to create a new directory for the unzipped files (**Create Subdirectory** in the preceding example), you can select not to. Moodle's compressed file will automatically create a subdirectory called moodle for the unzipped files. On my server, you can see the result. The directory /moodle is created, and the files are placed in that directory:

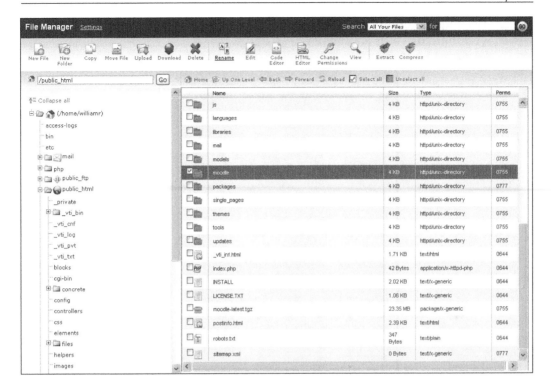

The long way: Decompress the ZIP file locally and upload files

If you cannot decompress the ZIP file on the server, you must decompress the file on your PC and then upload the extracted files to the server. If you're using a hosting service, you will probably need to carry out the following steps:

1. Download the Moodle package (ZIP file) to your local hard drive.

2. Decompress or unzip, the package. This will create many folders and files on your hard drive, as shown here:

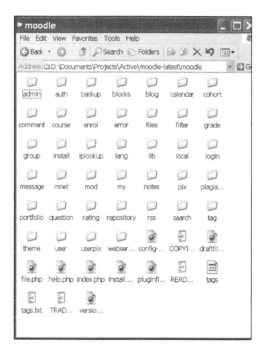

3. Upload the files to your web server. You'll need to use an FTP program to upload the files. Two of the most popular ones are FileZilla and WinSCP. Select all of the folders and copy them to your server. Uploading this many small files will be much slower than uploading a single, large `.zip` or `.tgz` archive. So, be prepared to wait for the upload to finish:

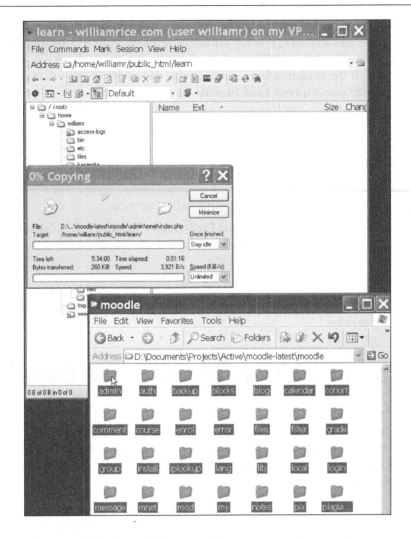

Whether you're using Windows, Mac, or a Linux personal computer, you can find a decompression program that will unzip `.zip` files. If your system doesn't have a decompression program that works with `.zip` files, and you're using Windows, try `http://www.nonags.com` for freeware unzip programs. If you're using a web page editor like Dreamweaver or Microsoft FrontPage, then your program has the ability to upload files to the server. If you're not using a web page editor that can upload files, you'll need an "FTP client". Again, try `http://www.nonags.com`, for freeware FTP clients.

If your school or company has given you space on their web server, you might have access to the directory just as if it were another folder on your PC. In that case, you can download the .tgz file, put it into your directory on the web server, and then decompress it. Tell the system administrator who gave you access what you want to do, and ask how to decompress a file in your directory.

You can decompress the file by carrying out the following steps:

1. Go to http://moodle.org and download the version of Moodle that you want to install. You will download a compressed file, in either .zip or .tgz format.

2. Upload the compressed file to your hosting service.

3. Using the control panel that your host gives you, select the compressed file. If it automatically decompresses, you're in luck. Go ahead and decompress it in place.

   Or

   Decompress the file on your local PC, and upload the resulting files to your hosting service.

Installation Step 4: The Moodle Data Directory

When you run the Moodle install script, the installer asks you to specify a directory in which to store course material. This is the Moodle data directory. It holds material that is uploaded to the courses. You will need to have this directory created before you run the install script. That is what you will do in this step.

For security, the Moodle data directory should be outside of the main Moodle directory. For example, suppose you are creating a learning site called www.info-overload.biz/learn. You will install Moodle into /learn, and create the Moodle data directory somewhere outside of /learn.

Preferably, you will put the data directory somewhere that is not accessible over the Web. For example, on my hosting service, anything put into the directory /public_ html is served over the Web. Anything outside of that directory cannot be seen over the Web.

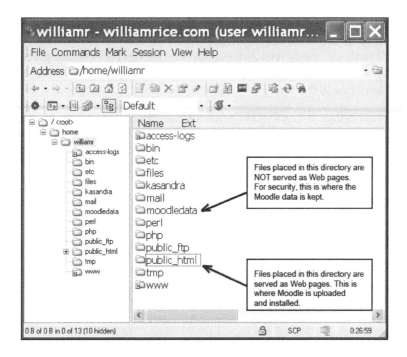

You should check with your hosting service's technical support group to see if you can create a directory that is not accessible via the Web.

 On your server, create a directory in which to hold the Moodle data. This can be a directory outside of the Moodle directory, or a subdirectory of the Moodle directory.

Installation Step 5: Creating the Moodle database and user

While the Moodle **data directory** stores files uploaded by students, and some larger files, the Moodle **database** stores most of the information for your Moodle site. By default, the installer uses the database name `moodle` and the username `moodleuser`. Using these default settings gives any hacker a head start on breaking your site. When creating your database, change these to something less common. At least make the hackers guess the name of your database and the database username.

You should also choose a strong password for the Moodle database user. Here are some recommendations for strong passwords:

- Include at least one number, one symbol, one uppercase letter, and one lowercase letter.
- Make the password at least 12 characters long.
- Avoid repetition, dictionary words, letter or number sequences, and anything based on biographical information about yourself.

You will need to create the Moodle database, and the database user, **before** you run Moodle's installation routine. Otherwise, the installation process will stop until you have created the required database.

Creating the database

Moodle can use several types of database. The recommended type is MySQL. There are many ways to create a database. If you are using a shared hosting service, you might have access to `phpMyAdmin`. You can use this to create the Moodle database and the database user.

The following is a screenshot of database creation using `phpMyAdmin`.

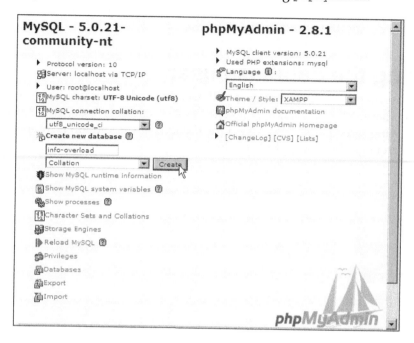

If your hosting service uses the cPanel control panel, you might use cPanel to create a database, as shown in the following screenshot::

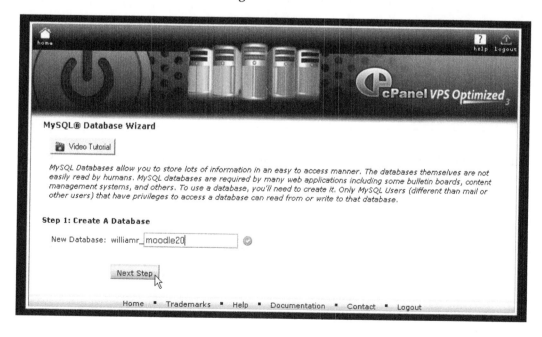

This process will create a blank database. Moodle will add the necessary database tables during the installation routine. So unless the installation routine fails, you don't need to do anything more to the database.

Creating the database user

Whatever username you use, that user will need the following privileges for the Moodle database: SELECT, INSERT, UPDATE, DELETE, CREATE, DROP, INDEX, and ALTER. In the following screenshot, I've created the database user and am now specifying the user's privileges by using phpMyAdmin.

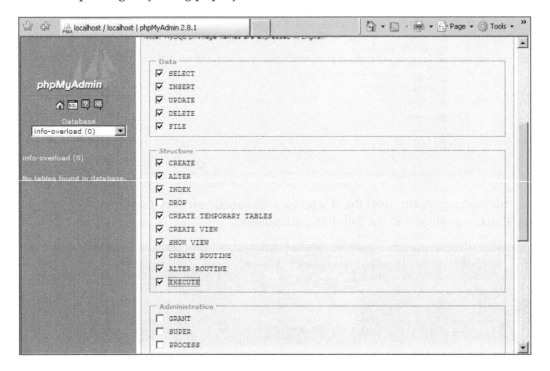

Alternatively, if your hosting service uses cPanel, you might use that to create the database user , as shown in the following screenshot:

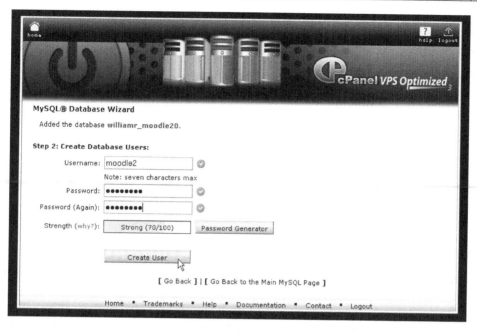

Later, during the installation routine, you will enter the name of the database, the database user, and the database user's password. If you're not creating these yourself, you will need to get them from your system administrator, or whoever creates them.

At this point, you should create the Moodle database and database user by carrying out the following steps:

1. Create the Moodle database. Moodle works best with a MySQL database, but you have a variety of choices.

2. Create a **database user** with the privileges that we saw some time back. Take note of the user's password.

3. Take note of the following information:

   - The name of the server that holds your database. If the database and Moodle are on the same server, this will probably be localhost. If you're not sure, ask your system administrator for the path that your Moodle software would use to access the database server:_____ _____

   - The name of the database:_____

   - The name of the database user:_____

   - The database user's password:_____

Installation Step 6: The installer script

At this point, you have:

1. Uploaded the Moodle software to your Web server.
2. Created a data directory outside of the directory that Moodle is served from.
3. Created a database for Moodle to use.
4. Created a user for the Moodle database.

You are now ready to run the installation routine. Moodle's installer script walks you step-by-step through how to set some of the configuration settings, and the creation of Moodle's database tables. But first, some background information.

Configuration settings and config.php

Configuration variables are settings that tell Moodle where the database is located, what the database is called, the database user and password, the web address of the Moodle system, and other necessary information. All of these configuration settings must be correct in order for Moodle to run. These variables are stored in a file called config.php in Moodle's home directory.

Stepping through the install routine creates the config.php file, among other things. Here's the config.php file for www.info-overload.biz/learn:

```php
<?php  /// Moodle Configuration File

unset($CFG);

$CFG->dbtype    = 'mysql';
$CFG->dbhost    = 'localhost';
$CFG->dbname    = 'info-overload';
$CFG->dbuser    = 'info-overload';
$CFG->dbpass    = 'badpassword';
$CFG->dbpersist =  false;
$CFG->prefix    = 'mdl20_';

$CFG->wwwroot   = 'http://info-overload.biz/learn';
$CFG->dirroot   = '/home/info-overload/www/learn';
$CFG->dataroot  = '/home/info-overload/www/info-overload-data';
$CFG->admin     = 'admin';

$CFG->directorypermissions = 00777;  // try 02777 on a server in Safe
Mode
require_once("$CFG->dirroot/lib/setup.php");
// MAKE SURE WHEN YOU EDIT THIS FILE THAT THERE ARE NO SPACES, BLANK
LINES,
```

```
// RETURNS, OR ANYTHING ELSE AFTER THE TWO CHARACTERS ON THE NEXT
LINE.
?>
```

This site uses a mysql database. On most servers, the hostname will be localhost. In an earlier subsection we covered the creation of the Moodle database. We also created a database user, with the proper privileges. Note that the configuration file stores the password for the Moodle database, which in this example is badpassword.

Database tables

Database tables are sections of your database, like miniature databases. Each table in your database stores information that is for a different purpose. For example, the table user stores the names, passwords, and some other information about each Moodle user. The table wiki_pages stores the name, content, date modified, and other information about each wiki page in your system. A standard Moodle installation creates over 200 tables in the database.

By default, the prefix mdl_ is added to the beginning of each table that Moodle creates in your database. I changed this to mdl20_ because I'm using version 2.0. If I upgrade to version 2.1, I want to be able to use the same database. You could use the same database for Moodle and something else, or for two Moodle installations, if each program used its own tables with its own prefix. The different prefixes would prevent the two programs from becoming confused and reading each other's tables. If you're running more than one copy of Moodle, you might consider using the same database and different tables. You could then back up the data for both copies by backing up the one database.

In the following subsections, I will walk you through the Moodle installation routine.

Step 6a: Run install.php

In the Moodle directory, a script called install.php creates the Moodle configuration file when the script is run. You run the script simply by launching your browser and pointing it to wherever you've placed the Moodle software. The script creates config.php.

In the following screenshot, I've pointed my browser to the home page of my Moodle installation. Moodle begins the install routine by asking you to select the language for the installation. This is the language that the installer script will use. It is not the language that your site will use; you can specify that later.

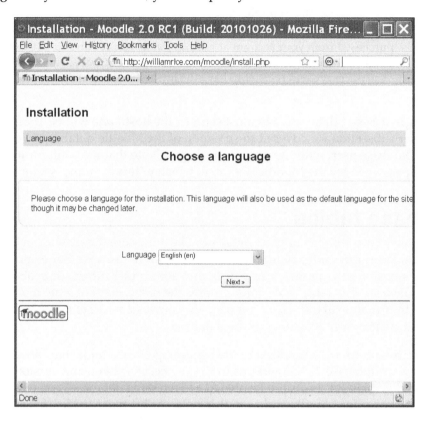

After selecting the language that you want to use during the installation, click on the **Next** button.

Step 6b: Specify the web address and directories

Next, the installation routine asks for the web address of your Moodle system, and the names of the directories for the software and data.

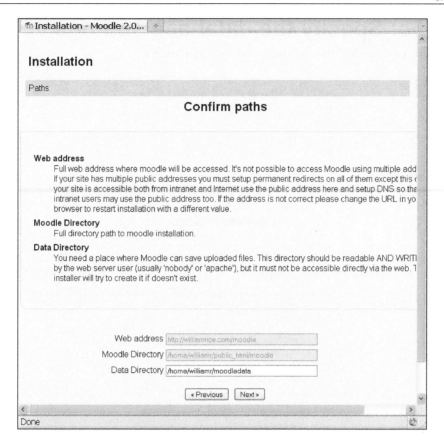

The **Web address** is the URL that browsers will use to access Moodle. The **Moodle Directory** is filled in for you. This is the directory on your server into which you uploaded the software. The **Data Directory** is the directory that you created in Step 4.

Fill in these values, and then continue to the next step.

Step 6c: Specify the database settings

In this step, you specify the database that Moodle uses.

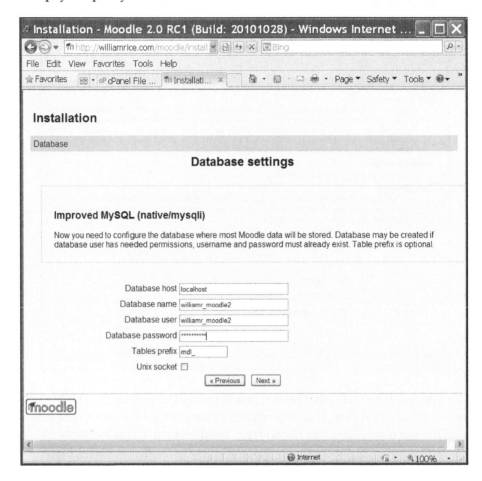

The **Host Server** is the address of the computer that serves the database. On most servers, the hostname will be `localhost`. Think of it this way: Moodle and its database are on the same server, so they are "local" to one another. So from Moodle's point of view, the database server is a local host. If the database existed on another server, you would enter the IP address or web address of that server.

Fill in the **Database name**, **Database user**, and **Database password** that you defined in Step 5.

The table prefix will be added to the beginning of the name of every table that Moodle creates. If you use the same database for Moodle and something else, you can easily spot the tables used by Moodle by their prefix (`mdl_user`, `mdl_courses`, and so on). Also, if you upgrade Moodle, you can use the same database for the old and new versions by using different prefixes for their tables (for example, `mdl20_user` **versus** `mdl21_user`).

Step 6d: Copyright

For this step, you just need to click on the **Continue** button to advance to the next step:

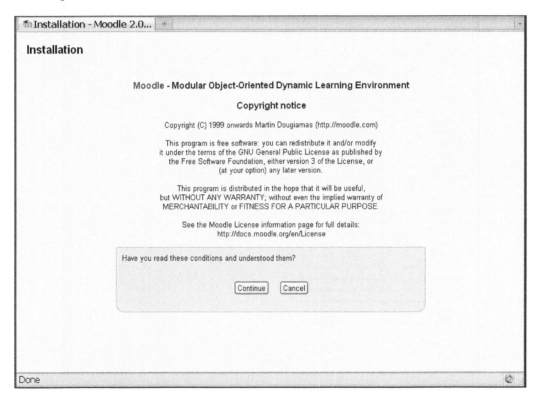

Step 6e: Check server

Moodle is written in a programming language called PHP. PHP is the most popular programming language for web applications. It is most likely already installed on your web server. Some of PHP's capabilities are turned off and on using settings that you, or your system administrator, control. Moodle's installation routine will check some of these settings to ensure that they are compatible with Moodle.

In the preceding screenshot, you can see that I have received a warning message. I need a certain PHP extension to be installed. My next task is to ask my web hosting service if this is installed, and if not, ask them if they will install it.

One common problem with the server is having the memory that PHP is allowed to use set too low. This is a common cause of the installation "hanging", or stalling. If you see a message indicating this problem, then you might want to cancel the installation and fix the situation right away.

The PHP installed on your server uses a file called `php.ini` to store its settings. The memory limit that caused the warning above is set in `php.ini`. If you have your own server, you can edit the `php.ini` file and increase this limit. On my server, I changed this limit to 128 megabytes by editing the following line in the `php.ini` file:

```
memory_limit = 128M
```

If you're using someone else's server, you will need to contact the support group and find out how to increase the limit. Sometimes it will be necessary to put a file in your Moodle directory called `.htaccess`, and include the memory limit in that file, by including the following line:

```
php_value memory_limit = 128M
```

For more information, search `http://moodle.org` for the term "php memory limit". Usually, 128 megabytes works fine. Start with that setting and increase it if necessary.

Whether you're using your own server or someone else's server, I recommend that you fix this situation before continuing with the installation.

Step 6f: Database tables created by install.php

Next, `install.php` creates the tables in your Moodle database. You don't need to do anything during this part of the installation except to click to on **Continue** see progress to next screen. The installation script tells you when the table creation is complete:

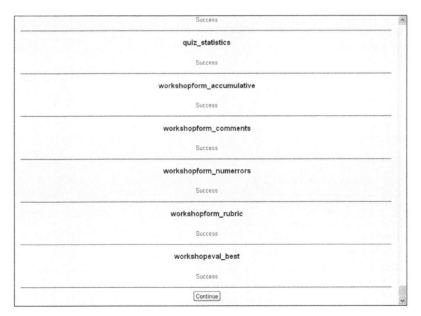

When you click on the **Continue** button, you will be taken to a page where you need to enter the details for your site's administrative user.

 Launch your browser and point it to the home page of your Moodle installation (where you uploaded the software). Step through the installation, using the subsections above as a guide. If you have all of the information ready to enter, it will probably take less than 10 minutes.

Installation Step 7: Create the administrative user

The Admin user has ultimate power on your Moodle site. This user can do anything to the site, including creating other users. When you enter the details for this user, keep them in a safe place! The fields (with an asterik besides it) are required. All others are optional:

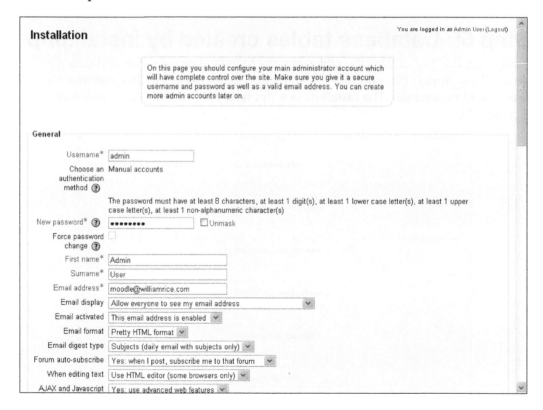

Oh no! I forgot the password to my Admin user!

Don't panic! There are ways to deal with the loss of your Admin user's password. You can still get it back, if you can get to the Moodle database. The frequently asked questions page on the Moodle website will tell you more: http://docs.moodle.org/en/Administration_FAQ#I_have_forgotten_the_admin_password.

After filling in the required details for the Admin user, scroll down and save your work. The install routine will advance to the next step.

Installation Step 8: Front page settings

The **Full site name** that you enter in this step will be displayed on the front page of your Moodle site. The **Short name** will be displayed in the navigation menu. The **Front page description** will be displayed on the front page of your site. You can easily change all of these, later. If getting them perfect slows you down, just enter the best information that you have, and continue:

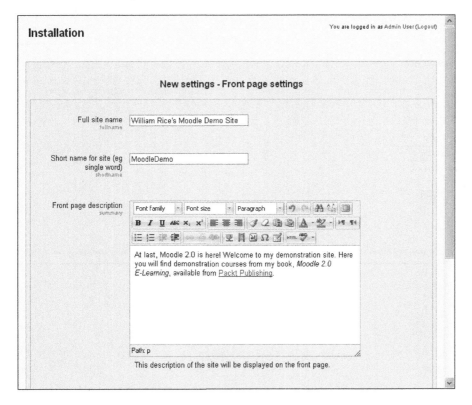

At the bottom of this page, you can choose whether to allow email-based self-registration. This capability is turned off by default. Unless you have a good reason for allowing people to register themselves, you should leave this turned off.

After you save the page, the install routine advances to the next step.

Installation Step 9: Success!

Moodle displays the front page of your new site. You're ready to start developing courses!

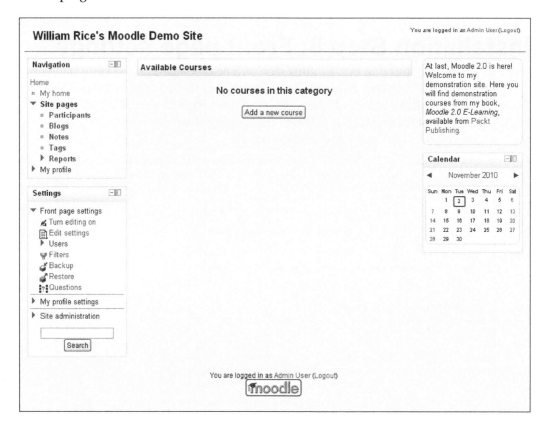

Summary

You have now created your Moodle site. From here, you can continue with any or all of the following:

- Create user accounts
- Configure your site
- Add content to your site's front page
- Create courses

You can do these in any order, but I usually use the order presented here. And don't be intimidated into thinking that you must get all of these "correct" or "right" the first time. They can be changed and edited at any time. So start with whatever you're most comfortable with, develop some momentum, and let's build your learning site.

3
Configuring Your Site

Many configuration choices that are made after the installation process affect the students' and teachers' experience when they use your Moodle site. This chapter's focus is on helping you create the user experience that you want, by making the right configuration choices.

Many of the configuration choices that you make will be easy to decide. For example, will you allow your users to select their own time zone? Other configuration choices are not so obvious. You could spend a lot of time trying different settings to see what effect a setting has on your user's experience. These are the settings that we will focus on in this chapter. The goal is to save you time by showing you the effects that key configuration choices will have on your site.

 If your system administrator or webmaster has installed Moodle for you, you might be tempted to just accept the default configuration and skip this chapter. *Don't!*

Even if you did not install Moodle, we encourage you to read the configuration sections in this chapter. If you want, you can work with your system administrator to select the settings that you want. Your administrator can create a site administrator account that you can use for configuring Moodle, or, can make these configuration settings for you.

Prepare to experiment

Although this chapter describes the effects of different configuration choices, there is no substitute for experiencing them yourself. Don't be afraid to experiment with different settings. You can try this method:

1. When installing Moodle, you created an account for the site administrator. Now, create test accounts for at least one teacher and three students.

2. Install three different browsers on your computer. For example, **Firefox**, **Opera**, and **Internet Explorer**.

3. In the first browser, log in as an **administrator.** Use this account to experiment with the settings that you read about here.

4. In the second browser, go to your site as a **teacher**. Each time you change a configuration setting, refresh the teacher's browser and observe the change to how the teacher works.

5. In the third browser, go to your site as a **student**. Each time you change a configuration setting, refresh the student's browser and observe how it changes the student's experience.

Instructions for each of these tasks are discussed in detail in the following sections.

Creating test accounts for teacher and students

These instructions begin where the installation ended: with you at the home page of your new site, logged in as the administrative user.

Create test accounts for your site

To create test accounts for your site, carry out the steps shown below:

1. Before you go into Moodle, launch your word processor or create a blank e-mail. You'll use this to take notes.

2. If you're not logged in as the administrative user, log in now. Use the **Login** link in the upper-right corner of the page.

3. You should be looking at the home page of your new Moodle site.

4. From the **Settings** menu on the leftmost side of the page, click on **Site administration**. This expands the **Site administration** menu.

5. Click on **Users**, then on **Accounts**.

6. Click on **Add a new user**. Moodle displays the **Add a new user page**.

7. The following table gives information to help you decide how to fill out each field on this page. The fields in red are required.

Field	Notes
Username	For the username, you might find it easiest to use the role that you are testing. So create usernames like teacher1, teacher2, student1,...student4, and so on.
Choose an authentication method	For your test accounts, this should be set to **Manual accounts**.
New password	Refere to your institution's password policy. To ensure that you type the password correctly, click on the **Unmask** checkbox. This enables you to see the password as you type it.
Force password change	For your test accounts, leave this blank.
First name and Surname	By default, when Moodle lists users, it sorts them by name. Often, it is convenient to have your test accounts appear next to each other in the list of users. Also, if they are at the top of the list, then you don't need to scroll or search to find them. For your test users, consider using a last name like AATest, which will put them at the top of the list with just one click.
Email address	The e-mail address of each user in Moodle must be unique. So if you are creating six test accounts, you will need six different e-mail addresses. At some institutions, the IT department won't give you multiple e-mail addresses. In that case, ask them for multiple aliases that you can use for your e-mail address.
Email display	Do you want other users on your site to see the e-mail address for this test account? For a test account, set this to **Hide my email address from everyone**, unless you have a good reason for your students to know the e-mail address of your test accounts. Also, you don't want a real student to get confused and e-mail a test Teacher account, instead of their real teacher.
Email activated	You want your test account to receive e-mail while you are developing courses, so set this to **This email address is enabled**.
Email format	To test how your site sends e-mail, you can set your odd numbered users to **Pretty HTML format** and your even numbered users to **Plain text format**.
Email digest type	When a user is subscribed to a forum, Moodle usually sends that user e-mails about new forum postings. This setting determines how often those e-mails are sent, and what they contain. For testing, leave this to **No digest**. That way, you'll know within a few minutes if a forum is sending out messages the way it should. If your test user starts getting a lot of messages from a forum, you might want to set this to a daily e-mail.
Forum auto-subscribe and Forum tracking	For testing, you can leave these settings to **Yes**. If your test user starts getting a lot of messages from a lot of forums, you might want to set one or both of these to **No**, and then unsubscribe the test user from those forums.
When editing text	To test the behavior of Moodle's HTML editor, you can leave this to **Use HTML editor**.

Field	Notes
AJAX and **Javascript**	You should find out from your IT department if the users in your organization have these enabled in their browsers.
Screen reader	For some functions, Moodle offers an interface that is more accessible for sight-impaired users. If you are testing your site for a visually impaired user, set this to **Yes** for one of your test accounts.
City/town and **Select a country**	These fields are required. If you use names for your test accounts that sound real, consider giving your test accounts a fictional city, like "Testville". It might make it easier to find the test accounts later.
Timezone	This determines what time is displayed to the user.
Preferred language	This determines what language Moodle uses for its interface. There is a site-wide setting that allows or forbids users from selecting their own language. If you plan to allow users to select their own language, their selection will overwrite what you choose here.
Description	Most sites allow users to enter their own **Description** in their user profile. You can enter a starting description here.

8. The remainder of the user fields are self-explanatory. Usually, they are filled out by the user.

9. In your word processor, take note of the user's username, password, and email address. You'll need these later.

10. At the bottom of the page, click on the **Update profile** button. This saves the profile.

11. Repeat this for each of your test users. When you finish, you will see them listed under **Settings | Site administration | Users | Accounts | Browse list of users**, as shown i the example below:

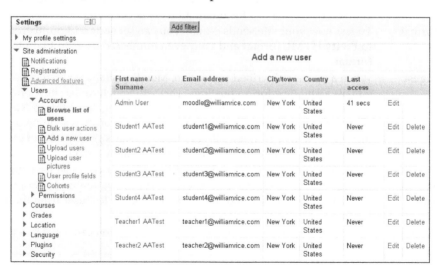

Installing several browsers

You cannot log in to Moodle with two different usernames, from the same browser, at the same time. For example, if you want to log in as both **teacher1** and **student1**, you can't do that from the same browser. You need two separate browsers.

Consider installing several browsers on your computer, to enable you to log in as several different users at once. For example, you could install:

- **Firefox**, and use this as the site administrator.
- **Opera**, and use this as a teacher.
- **Chrome**, and use this as a student.

And, don't forget that Safari and Internet Explorer are also available.

Telling you how to install these browsers is beyond the scope of this book. Here are the websites where you can get these browsers. If your organization has your computers secured so that you cannot install your own software, you will need their help to install additional browsers.

To get this browser...	Go to...	And it works on...
Firefox	http://www.mozilla.com	Windows Macintosh Linux
Opera	http://www.opera.com/	Windows Macintosh Linux
Chrome	http://www.google.com/chrome	Windows Macintosh Linux
Safari	http://www.apple.com/safari/	Windows Macintosh
Internet Explorer	http://www.microsoft.com/windows/ internet-explorer/	Windows

Exploring the site administration menu

After installing Moodle, I like to set some basic configuration options. Some of these settings determine how the site functions, such as how users are authenticated, what statistics the site keeps, and which modules are turned off or on. Other settings just affect the user experience, such as which languages are available, the color scheme, and what is displayed on the front page. All of these settings are available through the **Site Administration** menu.

To access the **Site Administration** menu, you must be logged in as an administrative user. Under the **Settings** menu, click on **Site Administration** to expand the menu:

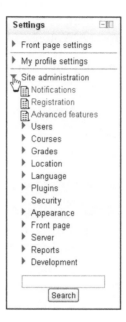

In this chapter on configuring your site, we'll cover some of the settings under the **Site Administration** menu. Others will be covered as we build our courses, teach, calculate grades, and update our site.

 The important idea here is this: Unlike many other applications, in Moodle, the **Site Administration** menu isn't something that you "set and forget". You return to the configuration settings as your site develops.

In early versions of Moodle, the Site Administration menu appeared only on the front page of the site. In Moodle 2, if you have access to **Site Administration**, it is available to you on every page of your site.

Now let's go through the settings that you can use to configure your site for the kind of user experience that you want to create.

Configuring authentication methods

Authentication and login are different. Authentication is what happens when a new user signs up for your site, and creates a new Moodle account. Login is when an authenticated user logs into Moodle.

Moodle offers a variety of ways to authenticate users. You'll find them under **Settings | Site Administration | Plugins | Authentication | Manage Authentication**. Each of the options is briefly explained by clicking on **Settings** for that option:

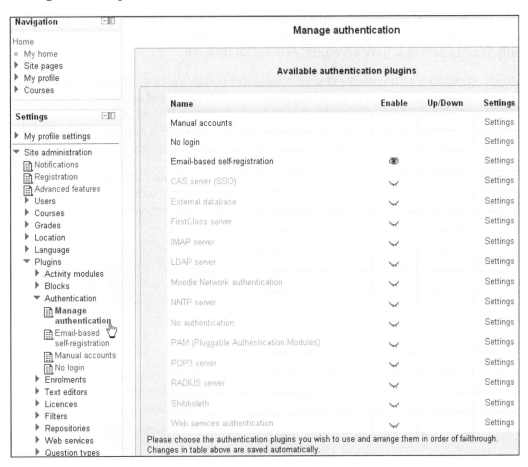

This subsection fills in some key information, in order to make it easier for you to work with these authentication methods.

Manual accounts and no login methods

In the preceding screenshot, which shows the authentication methods, notice that two methods cannot be disabled: **Manual accounts** and **No login**. These methods are always available to the site administrator.

Manual accounts enables the administrator to create user accounts. You used this method to create your test users.

Even if you are authenticating against an external database, you can still use this method to create users. For example, suppose your company or school uses Moodle, and authenticates against your organization's IMAP e-mail server. Because everyone in your organization has an e-mail account, this ensures that your colleagues, and only your colleagues, have accounts on your Moodle site.

However, what if you have a guest or consultant teach one of your courses? If your organization doesn't want to give that person an official e-mail address at your organization, then the guest teacher won't have an entry on the IMAP server. In that case, you can manually create the guest's account in Moodle. Their account will exist only in Moodle, and will not be written back to the IMAP (or other) server.

No login enables the administrator to suspend a user's account. **Suspending** a user takes away that person's ability to log in, but keeps all of the work that person did in the system, such as their blog and grades. **Deleting** a user removes the account and the user's data.

Manually creating a new user:

If you created test accounts at the beginning of this chapter, you manually created user accounts. Follow the instructions under *Preparation Task 1: Create test accounts for teacher and students* of this chapter

To suspend a user's account:

1. From the Settings menu on the leftmost side of the page, click on **Site administration | Users | Accounts | Browse list of users**. The **Users** page displays. On this page, you will search for the user.

2. In the **New filter** area, enter all or part of the user's name:

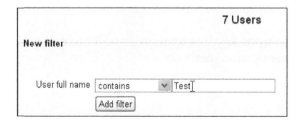

3. Click on the **Add filter** button. The user appears in the list at the bottom of the page.

4. Next to the user's name, click on the **Edit** link. This displays the **Edit profile** page for that user.

5. For **Choose an authentication method**, select **No login**.

> Be careful that you do not select **No authentication** instead. In the drop-down list, it is next to **No login**, but they are very different options!

6. At the bottom of the page, click on the **Update profile** button. This saves the change.

Enabling e-mail-based self-registration

This method enables people to register themselves for your site. When someone fills out the new user form, Moodle sends them an e-mail to confirm creation of their account.

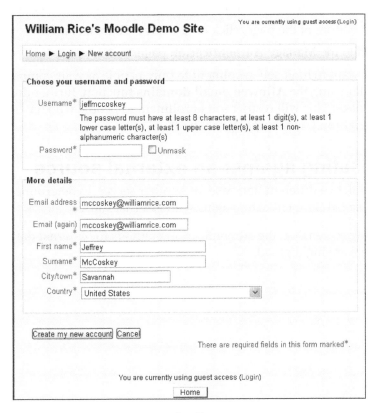

You must turn on e-mail-based self-registration in two places.

Enable e-mail-based self-registration

1. Under **Settings | Site Administration | Plugins | Authentication | Manage Authentication**, click to open the eye for **Email-based self-registration**, as shown in the example below:

Available authentication plugins			
Name	**Enable**	**Up/Down**	**Settings**
Manual accounts			Settings
No login			Settings
Email-based self-registration	👁		Settings

2. On the same page, further down, for the **Self registration** drop-down list select **Email-based self-registration**.

3. If you want to increase the security of your site, under the **Settings** for **Email-based self-registration**, enable the reCAPTCHA function.

4. At the bottom of the page, click on the **Save Changes** button.

5. Return to the **Manage Authentication** page.

6. If you want to limit self-enrolment to only people at your company or school, consider using the **Allowed email domains** function, further down on the same page. This will restrict self enrollment to people who have an e-mail address from your company or school.

Authenticating against an external source

Moodle can look to a different database, or another server, to determine if a user can log in. This is called "authenticating against an external source".

In the following screenshot, the authentication methods for external databases and external servers are highlighted.

Available authentication plugins			
Name	**Enable**	**Up/Down**	**Settings**
Manual accounts			Settings
No login			Settings
Email-based self-registration	👁		Settings
CAS server (SSO)	👁		Settings
External database	👁		Settings
FirstClass server	👁		Settings
IMAP server	👁		Settings
LDAP server	👁		Settings
Moodle Network authentication	👁		Settings
NNTP server	👁		Settings
No authentication	👁		Settings
PAM (Pluggable Authentication Modules)	👁		Settings
POP3 server	👁		Settings
RADIUS server	👁		Settings
Shibboleth	👁		Settings
Web services authentication	👁		Settings

External databases and external servers have some things in common. We'll look at these common features and how to use them for authenticating your users.

Connecting to an external database or server

When you choose to authenticate against an external source, you must tell Moodle how to connect to that source. To get to these settings, click on the **Settings** link for the source.

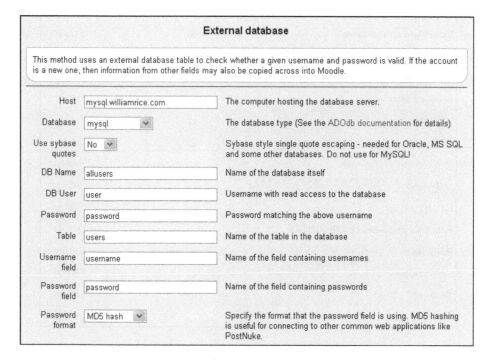

The exact settings that you need to connect are a little different for each type of authentication. The best way to obtain the information that you need is to ask the administrator of the database that you want to authenticate against. You could take a screenshot of the **Settings** page for the authentication method, and send it to the database administrator for their input.

What happens when users are deleted from the external database?

When you authenticate with an external source, each time that a person logs in, Moodle looks to the external source for that person's username and password. If the username is removed from the external source, Moodle will take one of the following actions:

- **Keep the user active in Moodle**: This means that although the person was removed from the external source, they can still log in, because their profile and login information is still in Moodle's database.
- **Suspend the user in Moodle**: The person's records will still be in Moodle, but they cannot log in.
- **Delete the user from Moodle**: The person's records will be completely deleted from Moodle.

This is controlled by the **Removed ext user** setting:

 This is an important decision, because you are deciding how Moodle will handle people who have left your organization.

For example, suppose you are authenticating Moodle users against your company's e-mail server (**LDAP server**). When a person leaves your organization, that person is removed from the e-mail server. Do you still want that person to be able to log in to Moodle? Do you want to suspend their account, but keep a record of everything they did in Moodle? Or, do you want to completely delete that person's records from Moodle? You should work with your system administrator to make this decision, and then select the appropriate option for your organization.

What happens when usernames are changed in the external database?

After Moodle checks an external source, and determines that a user has access, Moodle creates an account for that user in Moodle's database. Although, Moodle looks at the external source for the username and password, records for the user's activity are kept in Moodle. The user's grades, blog entries, history, and so on are all kept in Moodle, under that person's username.

If the username changes in the external source, there will be no connection between the old username in Moodle and the new username in the external source. For example, if you changed a person's username in your LDAP server from jsmith1 to jsmith2, how would Moodle know that jsmith2 is the old jsmith1? When user jsmith2 logs in to Moodle for the first time, Moodle will create a new account for that username. The account for jsmith1 will still be in Moodle, but it will not be used.

When you change a person's username in your external source, if you want to keep their records in Moodle synchronized with their new username, you should also change their username in Moodle.

Changing a username in Moodle

To change a username in Moodle, carry out the steps shown below:

1. From the **Settings** menu on the leftmost side of the page, click on **Site administration | Users | Accounts | Browse list of users**. The **Users** page is displayed. On this page, you will search for the user.

2. In the **New filter** area, enter all or part of the user's name:

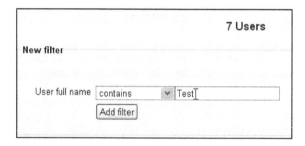

3. Click on the **Add filter** button. The user appears in the list at the bottom of the page.

4. Next to the user's name, click on the **Edit** link. This displays the **Edit profile** page for that user.

5. In the **Username** field, enter a new user name for the person.

6. At the bottom of the page, click on the **Update profile** button. This saves the change.

If the user wants to change his or her password, it usually must be done in the external source, and not in Moodle.

When you authenticate users against an LDAP server, you can allow them to change their passwords through Moodle. You can also make Moodle use the LDAP server's password expiration feature, forcing users to change their passwords periodically. These are two features that you get when authenticating against LDAP, and that you don't get when authenticating against an external database. Each type of server offers unique advantages and disadvantages.

Granting access to courses with enrolment choices

Enrolment is different from authentication. In authentication, you grant a user access to your site. In enrolment, you grant a user access to a course. That is, authentication answers the question, "Are you a member of this site?". Enrolment answers the question, "Are you enrolled in this course?".

You have several options for managing student enrolment. They are found under **Settings | Site Administration | Plugins | Authentication | Manage Authentication**, and are shown in the following screenshot:

Available course enrolment plugins					
Name	Instances / enrolments	Enable	Up/Down	Settings	Uninstall
Manual enrolments	1 / 0	👁	↓	Settings	Uninstall
Guest access	1 / 0	👁	↑ ↓	Settings	Uninstall
Self enrolment	1 / 0	👁	↑ ↓	Settings	Uninstall
Cohort sync	0 / 0	👁	↑	Settings	Uninstall
Category enrolments	0 / 0	👁		Settings	Uninstall
External database	0 / 0	👁		Settings	Uninstall
Flat file (CSV)	0 / 0	👁		Settings	Uninstall
IMS Enterprise file	0 / 0	👁		Settings	Uninstall
LDAP enrolments	0 / 0	👁		Settings	Uninstall
Course meta link	0 / 0	👁		Settings	Uninstall
MNet remote enrolments	0 / 0	👁		Settings	Uninstall
PayPal	0 / 0	👁		Settings	Uninstall

Notice the column labels across the top of the list. Let's discuss the meaning of each label, and then discuss each enrolment method.

Name

This is the name of the enrolment method.

Instances / enrolments

The number for **Instances** tells you how many courses have this enrolment method assigned to them. In the preceding screenshot, you can see that only one course has the first three enrolment methods assigned to it. However, just because a course has an enrollment method added to the course, this doesn't necessarily mean that course is using that enrolment method. For example, the **Scientific Method** course has three enrolment methods assigned to it, as shown in the following screenshot:

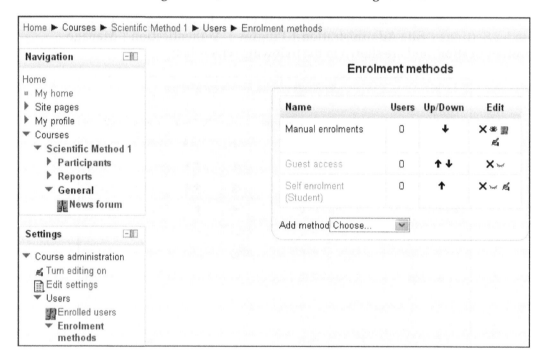

Notice that although **Guest access** and **Self enrolment** are assigned to this course, they are not available. That is, they are not being used. The teacher or administrator would need to enable those enrolment methods for this course.

> Note that self enrolment is not the same as self registration. Self registration enables a person to join your site. Self registration enables a person who has joined your site, to enroll in a course.

Remember that when we configured our site, we turned off guest access and self registration for the site. That is why these methods are disabled in this course. They can be enabled for just this course, but that will not change the settings for the rest of the site.

The specific overrides the general

In Moodle, as in most systems, settings for a specific scope override settings for a more general scope. Many settings that apply to your whole site can be overridden by settings for a specific course, and, many settings that apply to an entire course can be overridden by settings for a specific activity within that course.

Enable

This setting determines if the enrolment method is available to your courses. To make a method available, click on the eye to open it. To make it unavailable, click on the eye to close it.

Up/Down

Use the up and down arrows to put the enrolment methods in the order that you want Moodle to use them. The first enrolment method that contains the username of the user who is trying to log in, will determine if the user is authorized.

For example, suppose the username **jsmith1** is in Moodle's internal database, and also in an external database. In the following screenshot, the password and profile from Moodle's internal database would be used, because **Manual enrolments** is listed above **External database**:

Available course enrolment plugins			
Name	**Instances / enrolments**	**Enable**	**Up/Down**
Manual enrolments	1 / 0	👁	↓
Guest access	1 / 0	👁	↑ ↓
Self enrolment	1 / 0	👁	↑ ↓
Cohort sync	0 / 0	👁	↑ ↓
External database	0 / 0	👁	↑

The other, non-interactive enrollment methods are external databases or servers that are managed outside of Moodle.

Settings

Many enrolment methods have a separate page for settings, where you configure that method. For example, the following screenshot shows the settings for the **Self enrolment** method:

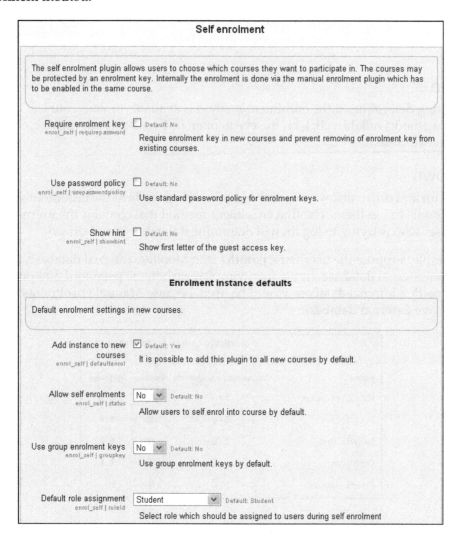

If you enable an enrolment method, then you should at least look at the **Settings** page for that method and determine if you need to change any of the enrolment method's settings.

Manual enrolments

Manual enrolment is the default form of enrolment. When this is selected, a teacher or administrator can enrol the student.

To manually enrol a student in a course:

1. Enter the course as a teacher or an administrator.

2. From within the course, select **Settings | Users | Enrolled users**.

3. In the upper right corner of the page, click on the **Enrol users** button. The **Enrol users** window is displayed:

4. To find a user, enter any part of the user's name into the **Search** field and then press *Enter* or *Return* on your keyboard. A list of possible matches is displayed, as shown in the following example:

5. To enrol a user, click on the **Enrol** button next to the user's name. The display of that user's name will change to indicate that (s)he is enrolled.

6. When you finish enrolling users, click on the close box for this window. You will return to the **Enrolled users** page, and see the user added to the list of enrolled users.

 Remember: Teachers can enrol users in a course, but they can't create new users.

Unless you override Moodle's default settings, teachers cannot create new users. They can only enrol existing users. By default, only a site administrator can manually create new users. In the following screenshot, the site administrator is logged in to the browser on the left. Notice that **Site administration | users | Accounts | Add a new user** is available for the administrator. A teacher is logged in to the browser on the right. Notice that the **Site administration** menu is not available to the teacher.

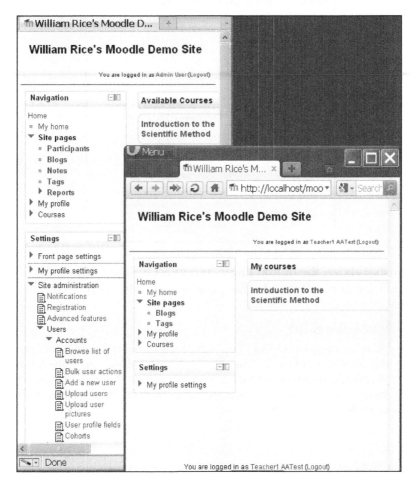

Guest access

Your Moodle site has a special user called "Guest". This user can be used to grant access to courses, without requiring the user to be enrolled. Essentially, you are allowing anonymous users to access your site and/or course.

In the screenshot above, the button **Login as a guest** indicates that guest access has been enabled for this site. If you disable guest access, this button does not appear.

Who is this guest?

Who is your guest visitor? You will probably never know! That's because the guest account can be used by anyone. Therefore, you won't know the guest's name. When you look at your site logs and see the activity for the guest, you are looking at the activities performed by every visitor who used the guest account.

The **Settings** page for the guest access method contains some settings for a password:

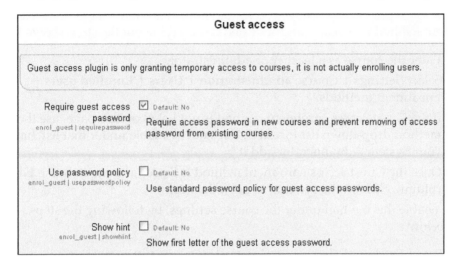

It might seem odd to set a password for an anonymous guest. However, there is a good reason for requiring a password for the guest user. That prevents automated software, such as web crawlers and spam harvesters, from entering your course. Requiring a password for the guest ensures that the user entering the course is a human and not a piece of software.

If you require a password for guest access, you'll need to tell your guests what the password is. You could add that to the course description that visitors see on the front page of your site, as shown in the following screenshot:

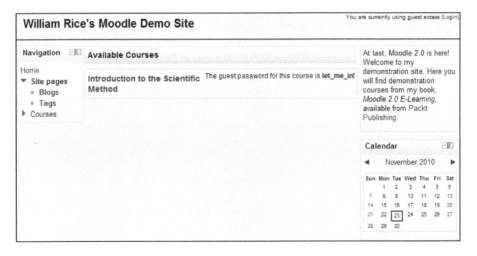

We'll talk about the course description later, when we create new courses.

Enabling guest access for a course

To enable guest access for a course, you should first, make sure that the Guest access enrollment method is available and activated , by carrying out the steps shown below.

1. Enter the course as a teacher or administrator.
2. Select **Settings | Course administration | Users | Enrolled users | Enrolment methods**.
3. If the Guest access enrolment method is not listed on this page, use the **Add method** drop-down list to add it. If it's not available under that list, have your System Administrator add it.
4. Once the Guest access enrolment method is listed, activate it. In the **Edit** column, click on the eye icon to open the eye.

Second, enable this method under the course settings, by following the steps shown below:

1. Select **Settings | Course administration | Edit settings**. The **Course settings** page is displayed.
2. From the **Allow guest access** drop-down list, select **Yes**.
3. If you require a password for guest access, enter this password into the **Password** field.
4. At the bottom of the page, click on the **Save Changes** button.

Self enrolment

The Self enrolment method allows users to enrol themselves in courses. As with guest access, you must enable this method under **Site administration** for your entire site, and also activate it for the specific course.

On the **Settings** page for **Self enrolment**, you can choose to require an enrolment key:

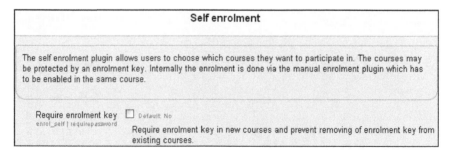

An enrolment key is a code that the user must enter when enrolling in a course. After the user is enrolled, the enrolment key is no longer needed.

You can allow self registration on your site, and then require users to have an enrolment key for a course. The self registration removes the burden of creating accounts for users from you. The enrolment key ensures that only those to whom you give the key can enter your course.

Cohort sync

In a Moodle course, you can add students to a Group. Then, you can manage that group's access to activities and resources in the course, instead of managing the students one at a time. In previous versions of Moodle, a Group existed only in the course in which it was created. Now, Moodle enables you to create site-wide groups. These are called Cohorts.

The Cohorts sync enrolment method enables you to enroll a Cohort to a course. This enrolls everyone who is a member of that Cohort in the course at the same time.

Inside a course, a Teacher can create a Group. But because a Cohort is a site-wide group, by default, only your site's Administrator can create a Cohort and enable Cohort sync in the enrolment methods.

Creating a Cohort

To create a Cohort, follow the steps shown below:

1. Log in to your site as an Administrator.
2. Select **Settings | Site administration | Users | Cohorts**. The Cohorts page is displayed.
3. Click on the **Add** button. The **Edit Cohort** page is displayed.
4. Give the Cohort a **Name** and **ID**. You will probably leave the **Context** set to **System**, so that you can use the Cohort throughout your site.
5. Optionally, add a **Description**.
6. Click on the **Save Changes** button. You are returned to the Cohorts page, where your new Cohort is now listed.

To enrol a Cohort in a course

To enrol a Cohort in a course, follow the steps shown below:

1. Access the course definition as an Administrator.
2. Select **Settings | Course administration | Users | Enrolled users**.

3. Click on the **Enrol cohort** button (by default, this button doesn't appear for Teachers, only for Administrators). A pop-up window appears. This window lists the Cohorts defined to the site.

4. Next to the Cohort that you want to enrol, click on **Enrol users**. The system displays a confirmation message.

5. At the confirmation message, click on the **OK** button. You are taken back to the Enrolled users page.

Notice that although you can enrol all of the users in a Cohort all at once, there is no button to unenrol them all at once—you will need to remove them from your course, one at a time.

Category enrolments

If you used a previous version of Moodle, and enrolled students in courses using Category roles, then activating this enrolment method will enable you to import those enrolments into the new version of Moodle. If you're not importing Category roles from a previous version, you can leave this enrolment method deactivated.

Flat file

A "flat file" is a text file that contains information in a simple text format. The flat file method of student enrolment causes Moodle to read in a text file, and use that as the source for enrolment information. The flat file method is especially useful if you need to enrol a large group of people who have records in another system.

For example, suppose that all of the nurses at your hospital need to be trained in patient privacy laws. We can assume that the nurses have records in the hospital's human resource or payroll system. Or, suppose all of the teachers at your school need to be trained on new educational standards. These teachers will probably have records in the school's e-mail or human resources system. If you can get a flat file, or text file, containing a list of everyone who needs to be trained, and that file contains their ID Numbers, you are well on your way to enrolling them all at once. You might want to speak to the system administrator of the other system, and ask them for an "extract" from their system.

The file

The flat file has the following format:

```
operation, role, ID number of user, ID number of course
```

Where:

- `operation` is `add` or `del`, which enrol the user to the course, or unenrol the user from the course, respectively.

- `role` is role, or function that the user will have in the course. For example: **student** or **editingteacher**.

- `ID number of user` is a unique identifier for the user.

- `ID number of course` is a unique identifier for the course.

Moodle periodically reads in this file, and modifies its enrollment data according to what the file says. For example, the following line will add the **student** with an **ID number** of **007** to the course with an **ID number** of **EM102**:

```
add, student, 007, EM102
```

Place this file in a directory that is accessible to your web server. For example, you can put it inside the Moodle data directory.

Student ID number required

Before you can enrol a person in a course, that person needs to be a member of your site. That is, the person needs to be authenticated. In this case, your first step is to authenticate the users using one of the methods discussed in the section on *Authentication*.

If you use a flat file to enrol students in a course, the file will identify each student by their ID number. Whatever method you use to authenticate your users, it should include a unique ID number for each user. This number should consist of only digits, and be up to ten characters in length. On the user profile page, you can see that **ID number** is an optional field, as shown in the screenshot below:

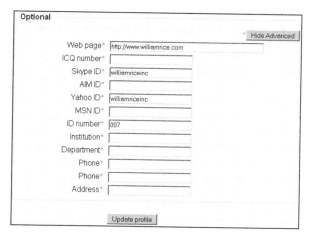

This ID number will match the student in Moodle to a record in the enrolment file. For example, the following line from the file enrolls student **007** into the course with an ID of **EM102**:

```
add, student, 007, EM102
```

In the Moodle database, you will find the student's **ID number** in the table **mdl_user**, in the field **idnumber**:

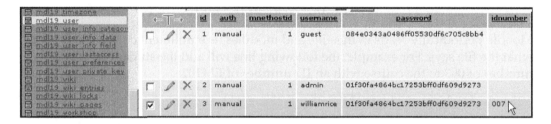

If you want to use a flat file to mass enrol a group of students, and your users don't have ID numbers, speak to your administrator about loading those numbers directly into the Moodle database. They might be able to use a database command to populate that field.

If your database administrator cannot add ID numbers for your users, you will need to edit each user's profile manually and add the ID numbers to each user's record.

Course ID required

If you use a flat file to enrol students in a course, the file will identify each course by its ID number. The example that we saw earlier was:

```
add, student, 007, EM102
```

This ID can consist of any alphanumeric characters, not just digits, and can be up to 100 characters in length. On the **Edit course settings** page, you can see that **Course ID number** is an optional field, as shown in the following screenshot:

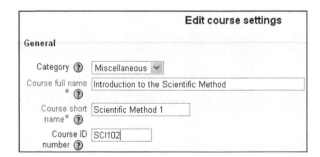

In the Moodle database, you will find the **Course ID number** in the table **mdl_course**, in the field **idnumber**:

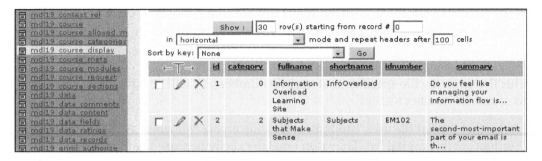

If you want to use a flat file to mass enrol a group of students, and your courses don't have ID numbers, you can add them in the **Edit course settings** page for each course. If you need ID numbers for a lot of courses, your database administrator might be able to use a database command to populate that field.

Role

A user's role in a course determines what the user can do in that course. Later in the book, we'll discuss Moodle's built-in roles in detail, how to customize roles, and how to create new ones. For now, let's look at the built-in roles that Moodle gives you as part of a standard installation:

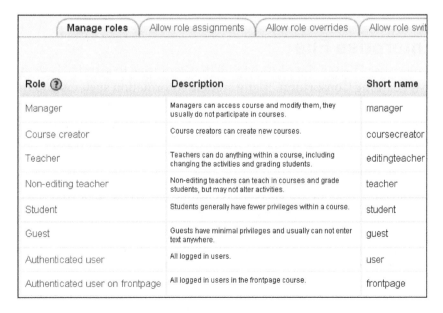

A user can have a role in the site, and a role in a course. The most permissive role wins.

When you use a flat file to enrol students in a course(s), the file specifies what role each user will have in the course. Let's return to our example:

```
add, student, 007, WP102
```

This line from the file specifies that user ID number `007` will be added as a `student` to course ID number `WP102`.

Notice that the flat file uses "student" with a lowercase "s", whereas the role is called "Student" with a capital "S". They don't match exactly because the flat file uses the "short name" of the role. To find out the short name of a role, go to **Settings | Site Administration | Users | Permissions | Define roles**.

Flat files: Summary

A flat file provides an effective way to mass enrol a large group of students into one or more courses at once. Remember that this method requires you to have a student ID number and a course ID number, both of which are optional by default. You'll need to populate those fields in your student records and course settings either manually or automatically, before you can use the flat file to batch enrol students. If you're authenticating users against an external system that has ID numbers, such as your school's LDAP server, consider mapping the student ID number field to your server's ID numbers.

IMS Enterprise File

An IMS Enterprise File is a flat file (text file) that conforms to standards set by the IMS Global Learning Consortium. Many student information systems and human resource information systems can both export an IMS-compliant file. For example, PeopleSoft and Oracle can export IMS files. These standards enable human resources systems and learning management systems to exchange data. Just like many Word processors can read and write `.rtf` files, many human resources and learning systems can read and write IMS files.

If your organization uses an HR system that can produce IMS files, you can use this method to enrol and unenrol students. You can also use this method to create new courses. This would be especially useful for a school that wanted to offer teachers the option of an online work space for every course. Each semester, the school could export an IMS file from their enrolment system, read this into Moodle, and use it to create an online course for every class that the school offers.

Let's return to an example used in the *Flat file* section. Suppose that all of the nurses at your hospital need to be trained in patient privacy laws. We can assume that these nurses have records in the hospital's human resource system. The human resource system might also be used to track the courses and certifications that the nurses need. You could export the nurses' information from the HR system, including the courses and certifications that they need. When you import the IMS file into Moodle, it will create the required courses, and enroll the nurses in them.

You can find the *IMS Enterprise Best Practice and Implementation Guide* at `http://www.imsglobal.org/enterprise/enbest03.html`. From that document:

> *Corporations, schools, government agencies, and software vendors have a major investment in their systems for Training Administration, Human Resource Management, Student Administration, Financial Management, Library Management and many other functions. They also have existing infrastructure and systems for managing access to electronic resources. To be effective and efficient, Instructional Management systems need to operate as an integrated part of this Enterprise system environment.*

> *The objective of the IMS Enterprise specification documents is to define a standardized set of structures that can be used to exchange data between different systems.*

LDAP

Remember that authentication is when a user logs into your site, and enrolment is when a user is made a student of a specific course. LDAP can be used for both authentication and/or enrolment. If you use LDAP for one, you do not need to use it for the other.

LDAP, External Database, and IMS Enterprise File are all able to create new courses as they enrol students. All of the other methods can only enrol students in existing courses.

External database

You can use an external database to control student enrolment. In this case, Moodle looks in the designated database and determines if the student is enrolled.

 As of version 2.0, Moodle will not write back to the external database. All changes in the external database are made by another program. So to enrol and unenrol students, you will need to change the external database.

In addition to using an external database, you can also allow Moodle's normal enrolment routine. If you enable manual enrolments in addition to the external database, Moodle checks two databases when a student tries to enter a course: the external one, and its own internal one.

External database connection

In the **External database connection** settings, you enter information that enables Moodle to connect to the external database. You should get this information from the administrator of the external database.

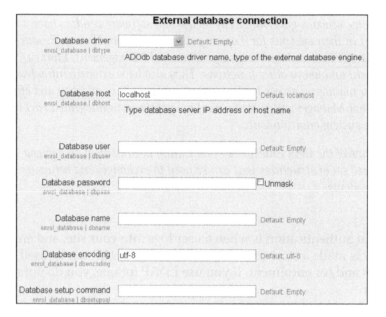

Local field mappings

In the **Local field mapping** settings, you answer the question, "What name does the external database use for the course?". In the following screenshot, you can see that you have three choices:

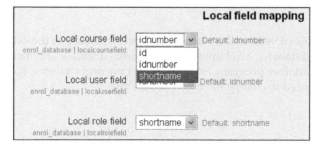

In Moodle, every course has an ID. The front page of your Moodle site is always course number 1. The next course that you create is course number 2, and so on. In your external database, you can use this ID to specify your courses. However, I recommend against using the ID in an external database. Here is why:

Suppose you install a new version of Moodle. You export your courses out of your old Moodle installation and you import them into your new Moodle installation. The first course that you import will have an ID of 2. The second course that you import will have an ID of 3, and so on. These course IDs might be different from those in the external database. Therefore, when you connect your new Moodle site to the external database, the course IDs will no longer match.

Consider using the **idnumber** or **shortname** of the course in the external database. One advantage of using the **shortname** is that this is a required field for every course, so you know that every course will have one.

The **shortname** is used in the navigation bar at the top of the page. In the following screenshot, the **shortname** of the course is **Scientific Method 1**.

The **idnumber** of a course is optional. Students will not see the **idnumber**; only administrators and teachers will see it.

Remote enrolment sync and creation of new courses

In the **Remote enrolment sync** settings, you tell Moodle where in the external database the course identifiers and students are stored. In the **Creation of new courses** settings, you tell Moodle where in the external database to find information for creating new courses. In both areas, you are entering the names of the tables and fields in the external database that hold the data that Moodle needs.

Paypal

The Paypal option enables you to set up paid access to the site, or to individual courses. When you select this option, you enter a value into the field **Enrol Cost**. This becomes the fee for joining the site. If you enter zero into **enrol_cost**, students can access the site for free. If you enter a non-zero amount, students must pay to access the site.

Selecting this option also puts an **Enrol Cost** field into each of the **Course Settings** pages. Again, entering zero into **Enrol Cost** for a course enables students to access it for free. Entering a non-zero amount requires students to pay to access the course.

The Paypal payment screen displays a notice that this course requires a payment for entry:

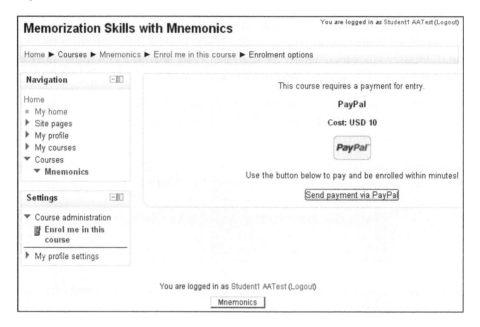

Mnet Remote Enrolments (formerly Moodle Networking)

The official Moodle documentation describes Moodle Networking as:

The network feature allows a Moodle administrator to establish a link with another Moodle, and to share some resources with the users of that Moodle.

The initial release of Moodle Network is bundled with a new Authentication Plugin, which makes single-sign-on between Moodles possible. A user with the username Jody logs in to her Moodle server as normal, and clicks on a link that takes her to a page on another Moodle server. Normally, she would have only the privileges of a guest on the remote Moodle, but behind the scenes, single-sign-on has established a fully authenticated session for Jody on the remote site.

If you need to authenticate users across Moodle sites that are owned by different people, then Moodle Networking is an obvious choice. However, if all of the sites are owned by the same person or institution, you need to weigh the advantages and disadvantages of using Moodle Networking versus some kind of central login. For example, suppose several departments in your university install their own Moodle sites. If they want to authenticate students on all of their sites, they could use Moodle Networking to share student login information. This would make sense if the university's IT department could not, or would not, let them authenticate students against the university's LDAP server or student database. But if all of the departments could authenticate against a central database maintained by the university, it would probably be easier for them to do so.

Language

The default Moodle installation includes many language packs. A language pack is a set of translations for the Moodle interface. *Language packs translate the Moodle interface, not the course content.* Here's the front page of a site when the user selects Spanish from the language menu:

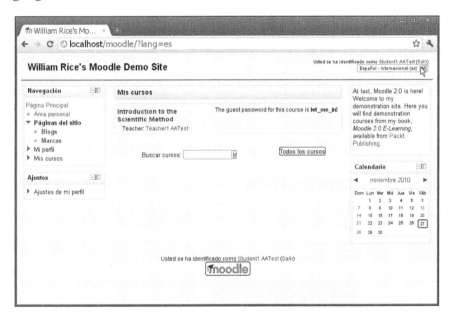

Notice that the interface is being presented in Spanish: menu names, menu items, section names, buttons, and system messages. Now, let's take a look at the same front page when the user selects **Tagalog** from the language menu:

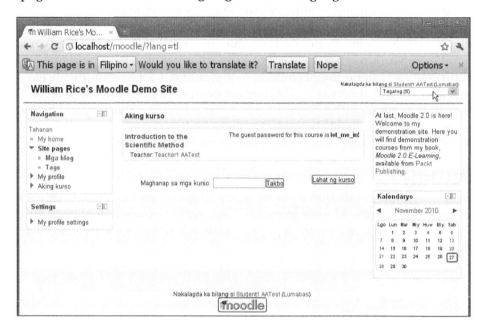

Notice that some of the interface has not been translated. For the example, the month name in the calendar and some of the links under **Navigation** are still in English. When a part of Moodle's interface is not translated into the selected language, Moodle uses the English version.

About the language files

When you install an additional language, Moodle places the language pack in its home directory, under the subdirectory /lang. It creates a subdirectory for each language's files. The following screenshot shows the results of installing the International Spanish and Romanian languages language packs:

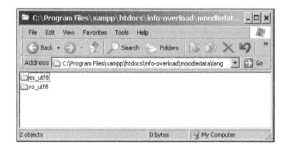

For example, the subdirectory /lang/en_us holds files for the U.S. English translation, and /lang/es_es holds the files for traditional Spanish (Espanol / Espana).

The name of the subdirectory is the "language code". Knowing that code can be useful. In the example above, es_utf8 tells us the language code for International Spanish is es.

Inside a language pack's directory, we see a list of files that contain the translations:

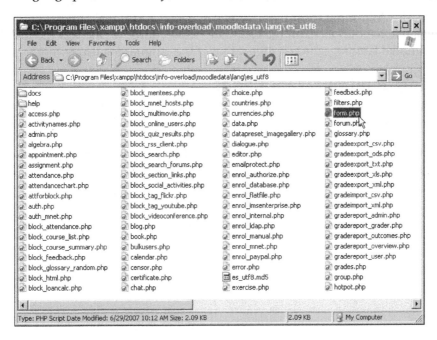

For example, the file /lang/es_utf8/forum.php holds text used on the forum pages. This includes text that is displayed to the course creator when creating the forum, and text that is displayed to the students when they use the forum. Here are the first few lines from the English version of that file:

```
$string['addanewdiscussion'] = 'Add a new discussion topic';
$string['addanewtopic'] = 'Add a new topic';
$string['advancedsearch'] = 'Advanced search';
```

And here are the same first three lines from the Spanish version of that file:

```
$string['addanewdiscussion'] = 'Colocar un nuevo tema de discusión
aquí';
$string['addanewtopic'] = 'Agregar un nuevo tema';
$string['advancedsearch'] = 'Búsqueda avanzada';
```

The biggest task in localizing Moodle consists of translating these language files into the appropriate language. Some translations are surprisingly complete. For example, most of the interface has been translated to **Irish Gaelic**, even though this language is used daily by only about 350,000 people. This is the nature of open source software: it's not always the largest group of users who get what they want, but often the most active group.

Installing and enabling additional languages

Using the **Site Administration** menu, you can install additional languages and make them available to your users. In the following subsections, we'll cover the installation of an additional language and configuration of the language settings.

Installing additional languages

To install additional languages, you must be connected to the Internet. Then, follow the steps shown below:

1. Select **Settings | Site Administration | Language | Language packs**. A list of all available language packs is displayed:

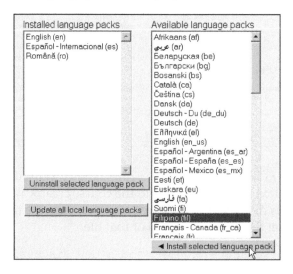

2. From the list of available languages on the right, select the language that you want to install.

3. Click on the button for **Install selected language pack**. Moodle retrieves the most recent version of the language pack from the Web and installs it. This is why Moodle must be connected to the Web to use this feature. If Moodle is not connected, you will need to manually download the language pack and copy it into the /lang directory yourself.

If you don't see the language that you want in the list of **Available language packs**, it's not available from the official Moodle site.

Configuring language settings

The settings covered in this subsection are found under **Settings | Site Administration | Language | Language settings**.

The **Default language** setting specifies which language users will see when they first encounter your site. If you also select **Display language menu**, a language menu is displayed on your Front Page, and users can use this to change the language.

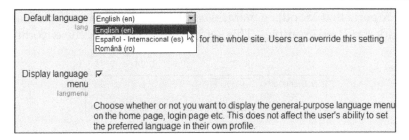

The setting **Languages on language menu** enables you to specify which languages users can pick from the language menu. The directions tell you to enter "language codes". These codes are the names of the directories that hold the language packs. In the subsection on Language Files above, you saw that the directory `es_utf8` holds the language files for International Spanish. If you wanted to include that language in the list, you would use the specification shown in the following screenshot:

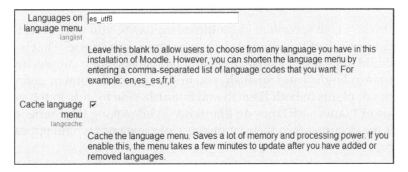

Leaving this field blank will enable your students to pick from all available languages. Entering the names of languages in this field limits the list to only those entered.

Sitewide locale

Enter a language code into this field, and the system displays dates in the format appropriate for that language.

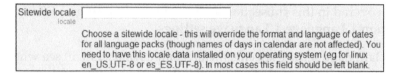

Excel encoding

Most of the reports that Moodle generates can be downloaded as Excel files. User logs and grades are two examples. This setting lets you choose the encoding for those Excel files.

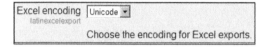

Your choices are **Unicode** and **Latin**. The default is **Unicode**, because this character set includes many more characters than **Latin**. In many cases, Latin encoding doesn't offer enough characters to completely represent a non-English language.

Offering courses in multiple languages

The settings on the **Language Settings** page apply to translating the Moodle interface. However, they do not apply to translating course content.

If you want to offer course content in multiple languages, you have several choices. First, you could put all of the different languages into each course. That is, each document would appear in a course in several languages. For example, if you offered a botany course in English and Spanish, you might have a document defining the different types of plants in both English and Spanish, side by side in the same course: **Types of Plants** and **Tipos de Plantaras**. While taking the course, students would select the documents in their language. Course names would appear in only one language.

Second, you could create separate courses for each language, and offer them on the same site. Course names would appear in each language. In this case, students would select the course in English or Spanish: **Basic Botany** or **Botánica Básica**.

Third, you could create a separate Moodle site for each language. For example, `http://moodle.williamrice.com/english` and `http://moodle.williamrice.com/spanish`. In the Home Page of your site, students would select their language and be directed to the correct Moodle installation. In this case, the entire Moodle site would appear in the students' language: the site name, menus, course names, and course content. These are things you should consider before installing Moodle.

Fourth, and most elegantly, you could use the Multi-Language Content filter described later in this chapter to display course content in the language selected by your user.

And fifth, you could use groupings to hide the different languages from different users.

Security settings

You will find the security settings under **Site administration | Security**. This section will not cover every option under that menu. Instead, it will focus on the options that are not self-explanatory, and describe how they affect your users' experience.

IP blocker: Limiting access from specific locations

This page enables you to block or allow users accessing your site from specific IP addresses. If you want to limit access to your Moodle so that users must be on campus, this is especially useful.

Site policies

The Site policies page contains a variety of security settings that you should either set yourself, or work with your administrator to set.

Protect usernames

If you forget your password, Moodle can display a page that enables you to retrieve it. If you enter your username or e-mail address, Moodle will send an e-mail with your login information to the e-mail address for that user:

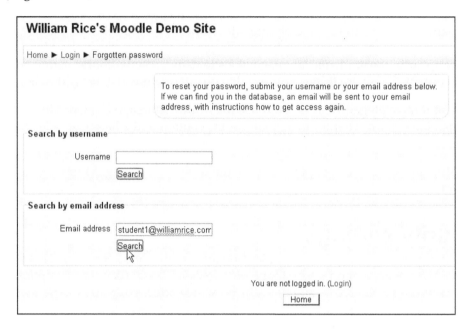

When Moodle sends this e-mail, it confirms that the e-mail has been sent but does not display the e-mail to which the message was sent:

The e-mail address is hidden to protect the user's privacy. Many countries have laws that forbid the disclosure of personal information. If someone could guess a usernames (which is often the case in large institutions), they could enter them into the lost password page and harvest the e-mail addresses for abuse.

Forcing users to log in

As stated in the directions, setting this to **Yes** causes the Front Page to become hidden until a visitor logs in to Moodle. When visitors first hit your Moodle site, they see the Moodle Login Page.

Setting this to **Yes** means that you cannot use Moodle's Front Page as an information and sales tool. You can customize the text on the Login Page, but you won't be able to add all of the features available on the Front Page.

Setting this to **No** enables you to use a non-Moodle page as your introduction to the site. If you want your Front Page to be something that cannot be created in Moodle, this is a good option. For example, we could make `moodle.williamrice.com/index.htm` into a flash presentation about our site. Visitors then click on an **Enter** link and are taken to the Moodle Login Page at `moodle.williamrice.com/moodle/index.php`. Notice that this requires us to put Moodle into its own subdirectory. If you want a non-Moodle introduction page that leads to a Moodle Login Page, put Moodle into its own subdirectory or subdomain.

Force users to log in for profiles

What the directions don't state is that setting this to **No** enables anonymous visitors to read not only teachers' profiles, but also the profiles of any students enrolled in courses that have guest access. This may be a privacy issue.

The effect of enabling **Force users to login for profiles** is that anonymous visitors cannot read the profiles for the teachers in a course that accepts guest access. They must register as a student before being able to read student and user profiles. This may be a drawback if your teachers' profiles are a selling point for the course.

Consider enabling this to force people to register before reading student or teacher profiles. Then, if your teachers' profiles are a selling point, you can add a section to the Front Page for "About Our Teachers".

Open to Google

This setting lets the Google indexing robot into courses that allow guest access. If you want to know more about the **Googlebot**, see `http://www.google.com/bot.html`.

It seems that everyone with a website wants their site to be ranked high in Google's search results. However, you should consider whether you really want Google to add each of your guest-enabled courses to its search engine. There are several disadvantages:

- If your course content changes frequently, Google might index out-of-date information for your courses.

- Your students and teachers might not want their names and materials indexed and available to the public.

- If Google indexes all of your guest-enabled courses, you have less control over what information about your site appears in Google. Everything on the pages that the Googlebot searches is used in indexing your site. There might be items on those pages that don't accurately represent your site. For example, a negative forum posting or an off-topic discussion could become associated with your site. Also, if the focus or structure of your Moodle site changes, it may take a while before all of the Google references to all those pages are corrected.

If you want strict control over what information about your site appears in Google, then set **Open to Google** to **No**. Put only the information that you want to appear in Google on the Front Page of your site, and do not allow teachers or students to modify anything on the Front Page. This way, Google will index only your Front Page.

You should also request that anyone who links to your site links only to the Front Page (for example, "Please link only to http//www.williamrice.com/moodle, not directly to a course page."). Google and other search engines use links to your site to calculate your ranking. If all of those links point to the same page, you can better control your site's public image. By disabling **Open to Google**, and requesting that people link only to the Front Page, you are trading away some of your search engine presence in exchange for greater control over your site's public image.

For the ultimate in control of what information about your site is indexed, consider this plan: Disable **Open to Google** and enable **Force users to login** to keep search engine robots out of Moodle completely. Under **Users | Authentication**, set **Guest login button** to **Hide** to eliminate the possibility that any other search engine's robots crawl your guest courses. Now you've locked out all but registered users.

Put Moodle into a subdirectory of your site. Link to Moodle from the index page at the root of your site. In the demo site, we would put Moodle into `moodle.williamrice.com/moodle/` and link to it from `moodle.williamrice.com/index.htm`. Then, we can use `index.htm` as an introduction to the site. Ensure that `index.htm` contains exactly the kind of information that you want the public to know about your site, and optimize it for the best search engine placement.

Maximum uploaded file size

Also on the **Security** page, you will find a setting to limit the size of files that users and course creators can upload:

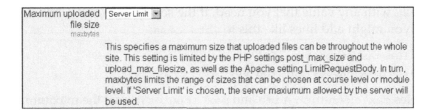

This setting affects students, teachers, and course creators. If you're creating a course that has a large file, such as a video, and Moodle forbids you from uploading the file, this setting might be the cause.

As stated in the directions on the page, there are three other settings that limit the size of a file that can be uploaded on your server. The first two are PHP settings and the third is an Apache setting. To see the PHP settings on your server, go to **Site Administration | Server | PHP info**. Scroll down until you see the `post_max_size` and `upload_max_filesize` settings.

The Apache setting `LimitRequestBody` also sets a limit on the size of uploaded files. From the official Apache 2 documentation:

> *This directive specifies the number of bytes from 0 (meaning unlimited) to 2147483647 (2GB) that are allowed in a request body.*

> *The `LimitRequestBody` directive allows the user to set a limit on the allowed size of an HTTP request message body within the context in which the directive is given (server, per-directory, per-file or per-location). If the client request exceeds that limit, the server will return an error response instead of servicing the request. The size of a normal request message body will vary greatly depending on the nature of the resource and the methods allowed on that resource. CGI scripts typically use the message body for retrieving form information. Implementations of the* PUT *method will require a value at least as large as any representation that the server wishes to accept for that resource.*

Changing the limit on uploaded file size in PHP

If you have your own server, you can change the values for `post_max_size` and `upload_max_filesize` in the file `php.ini`. You will usually find this file in `/apache/bin`.

If you are using someone else's server (such as a hosting service), you probably can't change anything in `php.ini`. Try creating a file called `.htaccess` that contains these lines:

```
php_value post_max_size 128M
php_value upload_max_filesize 128M
```

Replace 128M with any value that you need. If the server times out while uploading large files, you might add lines like this to .htaccess:

```
php_value max_input_time 600
php_value max_execution_time 600
```

The variables max_execution_time and max_input_time set the maximum amount of time allowed for a page in order to upload and process the files to be uploaded. If you will be uploading several megabytes of data, you may want to increase this setting. The execution time is specified in milliseconds (thousandths of a second). You can check your host's settings for these under **Site Administration | Server | PHP info**.

Next, place .htaccess into the directory that contains the PHP scripts that you want to run. For example, the script for uploading files is in the directory /files.

Your hosting service can disable .htaccess, which would make this solution impossible. In this case would need to ask your hosting service to change these values for you.

Changing the limit on uploaded file size in Apache

Just like you might be able to use .htaccess to override PHP settings, you also might be able to use the same file to override Apache settings. For example, placing the following line in .htaccess changes the limit on uploaded files to 10 megabytes:

```
LimitRequestBody 10240000
```

Notice that the limit is specified in bytes, not megabytes. Setting it to zero will make the setting unlimited. The highest number that you can specify is 2147483647, or two gigabytes.

Allow EMBED and OBJECT tags

By default, you cannot embed a Flash or other media file in a Moodle page. Instead, the media file plays in Moodle's built-in media player. However, many course developers do not like to use Moodle's built-in media player. Instead, they prefer that their media plays on the course page in the player designed for that media. One example of this is embedding a YouTube video in a web page.

If you allow users to embed objects on a Moodle page, then users can embed objects only in pages where they have editing rights. For example, a Teacher can embed a YouTube video on a page in the Teacher's course. But a Student cannot, because the Student cannot edit course pages.

However, every user has a profile that they can edit. In the following example, Student1 has embedded a video in his profile:

HTTP Security

The HTTP Security page has several options that you can use to further secure your site.

Use HTTPS for logins

This setting is found under **Security | HTTP security**. If you enable this setting, but your server doesn't have HTTPS enabled for your site, you will be locked out of your site. Moodle will require that you use HTTPS when you log in, but you won't be able to comply. If that happens to you, then you must go into the Moodle database and change this setting to No.

The following screenshot shows an administrator using the web-based product **phpMyAdmin** to edit this setting in Moodle's database. Notice the setting for logging in via HTTPS is in the table `mdl_config`. The administrator is clicking on the **Edit** icon. If this cell contains a 0, HTTPS login is not required. If it contains a 1, HTTPS login is required. *If you're locked out because of HTTPS login, change the contents of this cell to 0. Then try logging in again.*

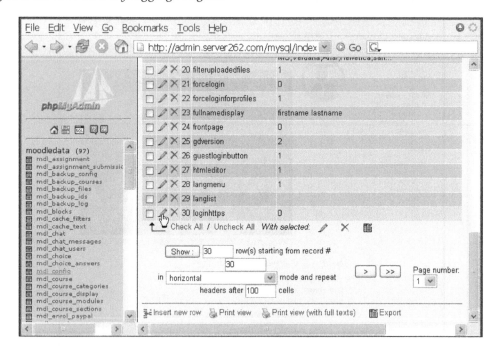

Running Moodle entirely from HTTPS

Although this is not a setting on the HTTP security page, we should note at this point that you can run Moodle entirely from a secure connection. You can do this by configuring your Web server to serve Moodle's address using a secure connection. You will need to speak to your web server administrator to set this up.

Note that using this setting greatly increases the amount of memory and processing time that your server will use when serving Moodle. Your system administrator will need to closely monitor the performance of the server to ensure that it gives your users acceptable performance.

Filters

Moodle's Filters read text and media that users put on the site. The Filters can then do three things with that material: **link**, **interpret**, and/or **restrict**.

In Moodle 2.0 and above, these filters can be enabled site-wide by the administrator, disabled-sited wide, or turned off by default, with the option of the Teacher enabling them for individual courses.

First, a filter can automatically link words and phrases to items in your site. For example, suppose you create a **Glossary** that contains the phrase "self-determination". If you activate the **Glossary Auto-linking** filter, whenever that phrase appears on your site, it will be highlighted and will link to this glossary entry. When a reader clicks on the phrase, the reader is taken to the glossary entry.

Second, a filter can interpret what you have uploaded. For example, you could upload a document that is written in the markup language call TeX (think HTML on steroids). The TeX Notation filter would interpret this document and enable Moodle to display it correctly. There's also an Algebra Notation filter that interprets a special markup language for writing math formulas.

Third, a filter can restrict the kind of content that a user can place on the site. For example, the Word Censorship filter can filter out a list of "bad words" that you don't want to appear on your site. Every time that text is uploaded or entered, it is checked against the list of forbidden words.

You'll find the **Filters** settings under **Site Administration | Plugins | Filters**. Read the following descriptions for detailed information about what each filter can do for your site.

Activity names and Glossary Auto-linking filters

The Auto-linking filters search the text on your site, and automatically link to items when they find the item mentioned in the text. For example, **Glossary Auto-linking** looks for terms that are in any glossary, and when it finds them links the term to the glossary entry. The term is highlighted, and when a user clicks it, the user is taken to the glossary.

Activity Names Auto-linking searches course text for the names of course activities. When it finds the name of an activity, it links to the activity. This means whenever a student sees the name of an activity, wherever the student is in the course, the student can just click on the name of the activity and be taken to this activity.

Math filters

Algebra Notation and **TeX Notation** search the text for special characters used to describe mathematical formulas. For example, if you enter `@@cosh(x,2)@@` the **Algebra Notation** filter will display it as:

$$\cosh^2 (x)$$

If you enter `$$\Bigsum_{i=\1}^{n-\1}$$`, the **TeX Notation** filter will display it as:

$$\sum_{i=1}^{n-1}$$

Algebra Notation and **TeX Notation** are standard markup languages. The `http://www.moodle.org` site contains more information about **Algebra Notation**. For more information about **TeX**, see the **TeX Users Group** at `tug.org`. TeX is more mature and complete than **Algebra Notation**. If you plan on writing more complex equations, I suggest making the **TeX Notation** filter active and leaving the **Algebra Notation** filter inactive.

E-mail protection filter

Activating this filter makes email addresses on the site unreadable to search engines, while keeping them 'human-readable'. If you set **Open to google** to **No**, or require users to log in, then you probably don't need to worry about search engines automatically picking up your students' email addresses. If your site is open to search engines and anonymous users, then you might want to use this filter to protect the users' email addresses.

Multimedia plugins

If you leave the multimedia plugins filter inactive, then multimedia content will usually play in a separate window. For example, without this filter, when a user clicks on a video, that video might open and play in a separate **Windows Media Player** or **RealPlayer** window. By activating this filter, you cause multimedia to play in Moodle's multimedia player.

Multi-language content

Earlier, you might have used the setting **Display language menu** to give your users a list of languages for the site. When a user selects one of these languages, only the Moodle interface is translated; the course content remains in whatever language you created it in. If you want your site to be truly **multi-lingual**, you can also create course content in several languages. Activating the **Multi-Language Content** filter will then cause the course material to be displayed in the selected language.

To create course content in multiple languages, you must enclose text written in each language in a `<span>` tag, like this:

```
<span lang="en">Basic Botany</span>
<span lang="es">Botánica Básica</span>
```

This requires that you write course material in HTML. This can be done for headings, course descriptions, course material, and any other HTML document that Moodle displays.

Word censorship

When this filter is activated, any word on the offensive list is blacked out. You can enter a list of banned words under the **Settings** for this filter. If you don't enter your own list, Moodle will use a default list that is found in the language pack.

Tidy

This filter checks HTML that is written or uploaded to Moodle, and attempts to "tidy" it by making it compliant with the XHTML standard. If your audience is using a wide variety of browsers (or browser versions), or a screen reader for the blind, making your pages compliant with this standard could make the pages easier to render.

Configuring the Front Page

Your site's Front Page welcomes the world to your learning site. Moodle treats your Front Page as a special course. This means that you can do everything to the Front Page that you can do for a normal course, plus a few additional settings.

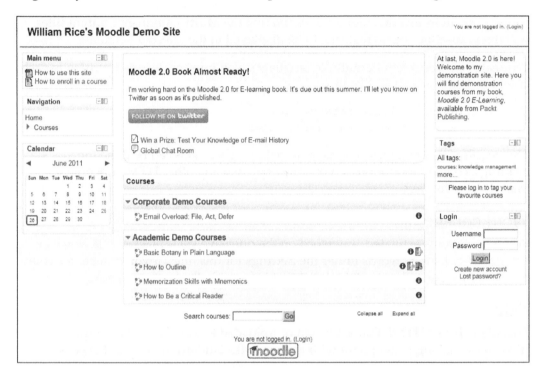

How to use this section

Early in the process of building your site, you can make some decisions about how your Front Page will look and function. This section deals with the settings that it makes sense to select when you're first building your site. **Some configuration settings on the Front Page won't make sense until you've created some courses, and seen how Moodle works.** You will find these settings covered in the chapter on "Welcoming Your Students".

If you have already created courses for your site when you read this, consider working your way through this section, and then working through the chapter "Welcoming Your Students". These two will give you a fairly complete process for configuring the Front Page of your site.

Front Page Settings Page

The settings for the Front Page of your site are found under **Site Administration |
Front Page | Front Page Settings**:

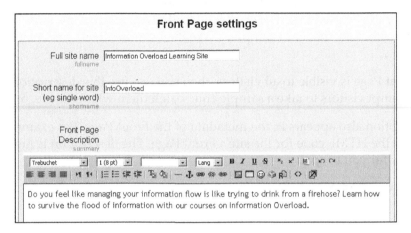

Full Site Name

The **Full site name** appears at the top of the Front Page, in the browser's title bar,
and also on the page tab when browsing using tabs.

The **Full site name** also appears in the metadata for the Front Page. Here's the first
few lines of HTML code from the Front Page. The line containing the **Full site name**
is in bold:

```
<html dir="ltr">
<head>
<meta http-equiv="content-type" content="text/html; charset=iso-8859-
1" />
<style type="text/css">@import url(http://moodle.williamrice.com/lib/
editor/htmlarea.css);</style>
<meta name="description" content="
Welcome to the Wilderness Skills site. If you have an interest in
primitive living/survival skills, you're at the right place. This site
offers courses in basic botany (just enough for a beginning forager),
shelter building, firestarting without matches, orienteering, and
other wilderness skills.The first course, Basic Botany for Foragers,
is free. It covers the terms and concepts you need to know to
understand most field guides and to talk about wild plants. Try the
free course, and if you like it, you can join us for other courses for
a low fee.">

<title>Wilderness Skills</title>
<meta name="keywords" content="moodle, Wilderness Skills " />
```

Front Page Description

This description appears in the left or right column of your site's Front Page. If you require visitors to register and log in before seeing the Front Page, remember that visitors will see this description **after** they have logged in. In that case, the Front Page description can't be used to sell your site. Instead, it can instruct students on how to get started with your site. For example, "Take the Introduction course to learn how to use this site…".

If your Front Page is visible to all visitors, then you can use this description to sell your site, tempt visitors to take a sample course, tell them what's inside, and so on.

This description also appears in the metadata of the Front Page. For example, below you can see the HTML code for the site's Front Page. The description is highlighted so it's easier for you to spot:

```
<html dir="ltr">
<head>
<meta http-equiv="content-type" content="text/html; charset=iso-8859-
1" />
<style type="text/css">@import url(http://moodle.williamrice.com/lib/
editor/htmlarea.css);</style>
<meta name="description" content="
Welcome to the Wilderness Skills site. If you have an interest in
primitive living/survival skills, you're at the right place. This site
offers courses in basic botany (just enough for a beginning forager),
shelter building, firestarting without matches, orienteering, and
other wilderness skills.The first course, Basic Botany for Foragers,
is free. It covers the terms and concepts you need to know to
understand most field guides and to talk about wild plants. Try the
free course, and if you like it, you can join us for other courses for
a low fee.">

<title>Wilderness Skills</title>
<meta name="keywords" content="moodle, Wilderness Skills " />
```

A page's metadata is used by search engines to help place it in the correct search results. So even if you decide to hide the box that displays the Front Page description, enter the description into the Front Page settings. It will make your site more findable on search engines.

Front Page items

Two settings determine whether the center column of the Front Page shows news items, a list of courses, and/or a list of course categories. These settings are **Front Page** and **Front page items when logged in**, as shown in the following screenshot:

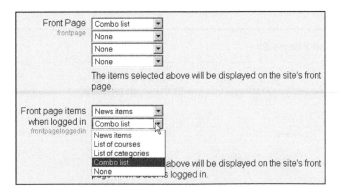

Notice that the Front Page settings apply to visitors who are not logged in. In the example above, we want to entice visitors with a list of the courses that we offer. However, since site news would probably not be of interest to anonymous visitors, we will show site news only to logged in users. Each choice has its unique advantages. The screenshot below shows an example of using a Combo list on the Front Page:

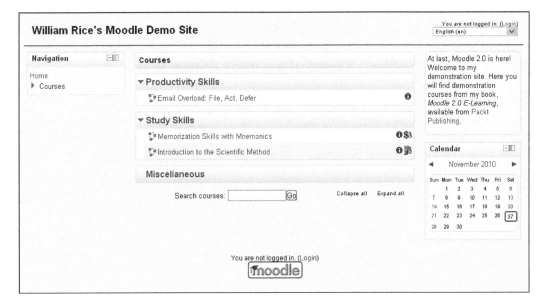

Using a Topic Section on the Front Page

Remember that the Front Page description always appears in the left or right column of the Front Page. It does not appear in the center column. If you want your site description (for example, **Welcome to the**....) to appear top and center, you'll need to include a topic section, which always appears in the center of your Front Page:

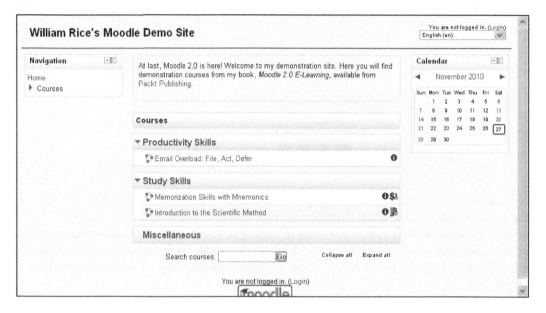

You could make your site description the first topic. In this example, we turned the **Front Page Description** off. We are using the first topic to introduce the site, instead. That puts the site description top and center, where it's most noticeable.

Show News items

The **Show News items** setting is useful if the content of your site changes frequently, and you want to keep visitors informed. If one of the primary purposes of your Front Page is serving repeat customers, showing news items on the Front Page is a good idea.

Backup

You'll find the backup settings under **Site Administration | Courses | Backups**. Most of these settings enable you to choose the type of data that gets backed up. You can also choose which days of the week the backup will automatically run, and the hour the backup job will start. Usually, you want to choose a time when there are few users on the site. The backup is activated by the cron job routine.

Seting up the Cron Job

Some of Moodle's functions occur on a regular, timed schedule. The most visible example is mailing out notices to the subscribers of a forum that a new message has been posted. A script called `cron.php` checks periodically to see if new messages have been posted to any forum. If so, the script causes the notice to be emailed to the members of that forum.

The cron job also triggers routines that clean up old data and back up your courses.

The script `cron.php` must be triggered at regular intervals. You can set this interval. The mechanism that triggers the script is called a **cron job.** Directions for setting up the cron job are in the Moodle installation guide, available from `http://moodle.org/`.

Some web-hosting services allow you to set up cron jobs. If you're buying hosting services, look for a host that allows you to set a cron job to run every hour, or even every few minutes. Some hosting services allow you to run a cron job only once a day. This means that Moodle will perform those functions that depend on `cron.php` only once a day.

If you've been given space on your school's or company's web server, speak to the system administrator about setting up the cron job. Moodle's `cron.php` uses very little memory and few system resources. Most servers could run it every 15 minutes without affecting the server's performance.

If you cannot set up the cron job on your host, then your only other option is to set up the cron job on a Windows machine that you control. The cron job will reach out over the Internet to your Moodle site, and activate the script `cron.php`. Again, directions for this are in the Moodle installation guide, available at `http://moodle.org/` installation guide. However, if you choose this option, you must keep that Windows PC running all the time, and it must also be connected to the Internet at all times. If the Windows PC goes down or offline, then the Moodle functions that require periodic triggering will also go down.

The following is a screenshot of installing the **MoodleCron** application, where we specify the location of the `cron.php` script. In this example, you can see the line **Location: /www/moodle/admin**, which on our server corresponds to `www.moodle.williamrice.com/admin`. Moodle's `/admin` directory contains the `cron.php` file.

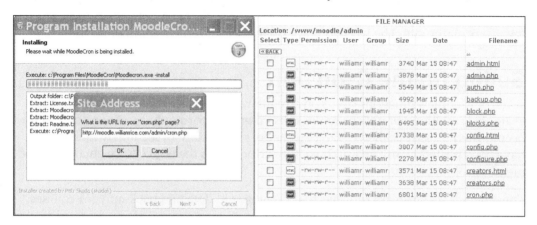

Summary

This chapter tells you how to make changes to your site's configuration. It covers the settings that, in our experience, you are most likely to change. Many of these settings affect the behaviour of the entire site. You don't need to get these choices perfect the first time, because you can return to these settings and edit them at will. As you proceed with building your site, you will probably want to experiment with some of them.

4
Creating Categories and Courses

This chapter's focus is on helping you create different categories and courses. Although someone else may have installed Moodle and made these choices for you, you can always go back and change them.

The following sections will help you to create and organize course categories. It will also tell you how to put a course into several categories. Topics covered include:

- Using course categories and the user experience
- Creating courses
- The course settings page
- Manually enrolling teachers and students
- Course completion
- Conditional activities

Using course categories and the user experience

Every Moodle course belongs to only one course category. You can set up Moodle's Front Page to display course categories, categories with courses, or a list of all available courses without their categories.

Displaying courses and categories on your front page

The list that shows both course categories and the courses is called the "combo list". It looks like this:

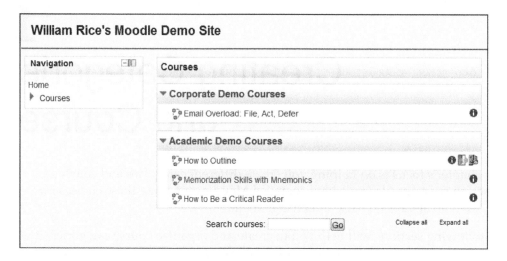

The combo list gives your front page an organized appearance. If you have a moderate number of courses, and the categories are self-explanatory for your users, this might be a good option for your front page.

If you have a lot of categories and courses, a combo list might be too long for your front page. In that case, you could display only the course categories. Then, the user would select a category and see the courses under that category:

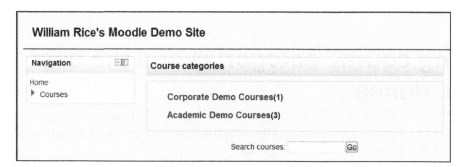

If you have too many categories to display on the front page, you can limit the number by using the setting under **Site Administration | Front page | Front page settings | Maximum Category Depth**.

First, the student must select a category. In the next example, the student selected the **Academic Demo Courses** category from the front page. Notice that unlike in the combo list, in this list, the description for each course is displayed:

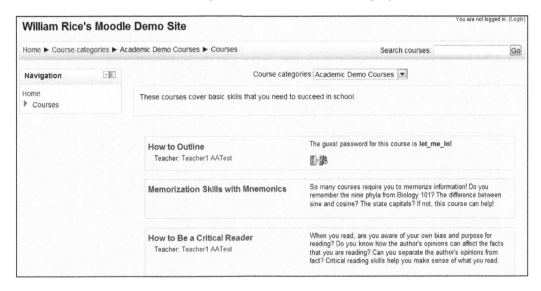

Notice that even though the student is looking at the **Academic Demo Courses** category, a drop-down list of **Course categories** enables the student to see the other categories. Typical of Moodle, this enables the student to jump to another part of the site without having to return to the front page.

 Categories provide a site-wide way to organize your courses. You can also create subcategories. The categories or subcategories become an online course catalog. Organize them in the same intuitive way that you would a printed course catalog.

The third option for showing courses on the front page is an uncategorized list of courses. This is a good option if your site has only a few courses. Some sites start out with only one course. In that case, creating a separate category for that course, and displaying a category list, doesn't make sense. For example, the following site offers a demonstration course and two courses that require payment. A simple list of courses along with their descriptions makes the most sense for this site:

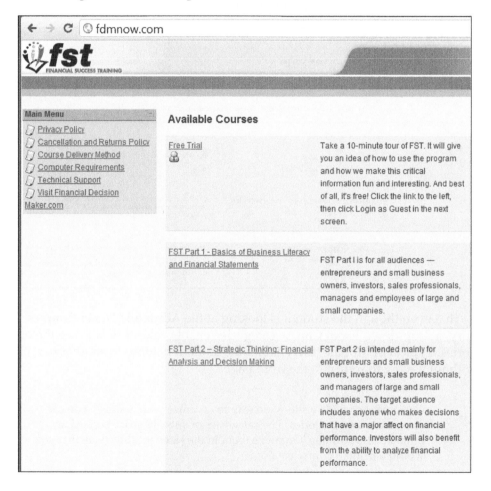

Choosing the best option for your front page

When you are deciding which option to use for your front page, try to put yourself into your student's situation.

If your students will be looking for...	...then consider using...
A specific course by name.	An uncategorized list of courses, displayed alphabetically.
A type of course.	A combo list or category list, so that the student sees the types of courses offered.
Either specific course by name, or types of courses.	A combo list. Add a notice to the front page that the student can search for courses by name (see the section *Add instructions to your front page with labels* in *Chapter 5*).
something else	An uncategorized list of courses, if you have only a few courses. You can use the course description to "sell" each course. If your list of courses is too long for the front page, you'll need to use a category list, and include information on the front page to convince visitors to explore the categories (see the section *Add instructions to your front page with labels* in *Chapter 5*).

Now that we have discussed how each option can affect how your student sees and uses the site, let's see how to implement each of these options.

Creating course categories

You must be a site administrator to create, edit, and delete course categories.

1. If you're not logged in as the administrative user, log in now. Use the **Login** link in the upper-right corner of the Front Page.

2. You should be looking at the home page of your new Moodle site.

3. From the **Settings** menu on the left-hand side of the page, click on **Site Administration | Courses | Add/edit courses**. This displays the **Course categories** page. On this page, you create new categories and courses. Here, you can also arrange the order in which the categories are displayed on the front page.

4. Click on the **Add new category** button. The **Add new category** page is displayed.

5. Select where in the hierarchy of categories this new category is to appear. In the following example, it will be a subcategory of **Critical Thinking**:

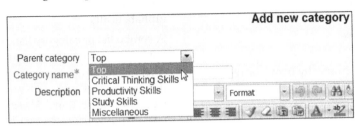

6. In the **Category name** field, enter the name for the category. Your users will see this in the category list.

7. In the **Description** field, enter the description for the category. Your users will see this name in the category list. Use this information to help your users decide if this is the category that they need.

8. Click on the **Create category** button. Moodle creates the category and displays the **Add/edit courses** page.

Rearranging course categories

You must be a site administrator to rearrange course categories. The order, in which you put them on this page, is the order in which your users will see them listed.

1. If you're not logged in as the administrative user, log in now. Use the **Login** link in the upper-right corner of the Front Page.

2. You should be looking at the home page of your new Moodle site.

3. From the **Settings** menu on the left-hand side of the page, click on **Site Administration | Courses | Add/edit courses**. This displays the **Course categories** page.

4. To move a category up or down in the list, click on the appropriate arrow button next to the category:

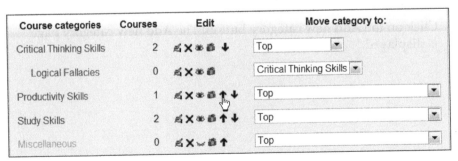

5. To move a category to a place under another category (that is, to make it a subcategory of another category), select a top-level category from the drop-down list on the right:

6. You do not need to save your changes. The changes that you make on this page are automatically saved as you make them.

Putting a course into several categories

One of Moodle's limitations is that you can put a course into only one category. In some situations, you might want to put the same course into several categories. You have several options to do this:

- You can forego the use of categories, and use direct links to the courses. In *Chapter 5*, you'll see how to add labels and links to the front page. You can use labels of your category names, and put the links below the labels. This could be a lot of maintenance for the site administrator because whenever a course is added or deleted, the list of courses will need to be manually updated.

- You can create the course in one category, and then create an identically-named course in the second category. However, you will put only one thing into the second course: a **JavaScript** that automatically redirects the user to the real course.

You can search the Web for a free JavaScript to use, or here is one from `http://javascriptkit.com/` that you can add to the course as a label:

```
<form name="redirect">
<center>
<font face="Arial"><b>You will be redirected to the script in<br><br>
<form>
<input type="text" size="3" name="redirect2">
</form>
seconds</b></font>
</center>
```

```
<script>
<!--

/*
Count down then redirect script
By JavaScript Kit (http://javascriptkit.com)
Over 400+ free scripts here!
*/

//change below target URL to your own
var targetURL="http://javascriptkit.com"
//change the second to start counting down from
var countdownfrom=10


var currentsecond=document.redirect.redirect2.value=countdownfrom+1
function countredirect(){
if (currentsecond!=1){
currentsecond-=1
document.redirect.redirect2.value=currentsecond
}
else{
window.location=targetURL
return
}
setTimeout("countredirect()",1000)
}

countredirect()
//-->

</script>
```

Creating courses

As stated before, every course belongs to a category. Don't worry if you mistakenly put a course into the wrong category. It is easy for the site administrator to change a course's category.

Creating a course and filling it with content are two different functions. In this section, we describe creating a blank course, with no content. In later chapters, we describe how to add material to a course.

To **create** a course, a user must have the role of Administrator or Course creator. To **add material** to a course, a user must have the role Administrator, Course creator, Manager, or Teacher (usually the Teacher adds material).

Creating a new, blank course

1. Log in to the site as an Administrator or Course creator.

2. Select **Site Administration | Courses | Add/Edit courses**.

3. Click on the **Add a new course** button. The **Edit course settings** page is displayed.

 The **Edit** course settings page does a good job of explaining the purpose of each setting. However, the directions do not tell you the implications of the choices that you make on this page. In the following section, I've added some commentary to help you determine how your choices will affect the operation of your site, and some information to help you decide upon the right choices for your needs.

4. From the drop-down list at the top of the page, select a Category for the course.

   You can use the drop-down list to change the category at any time. The list shows both visible and hidden categories.

   As your site grows and you add categories, you might want to reorganize your site. However, if a student logs in while you are in the middle of creating categories and moving courses, he or she might be confused. It would be best if you can perform the reorganization as quickly as possible—ideally, instantaneously.

   You can reduce the time taken for the reorganization by hiding your categories as you create them. This lets you take your time in thinking about what categories to use. Then, once you are clear on what you want, move the courses into the categories. Each course will disappear until you finally reveal the new categories.

5. Enter a **Full name** and a **Short name** for the course.

6. The full name of the course appears at the top of the page when viewing the course, and also in course listings. The short name appears in the breadcrumb, or trail, at the top of the page. In the following example, the full name is **Basic Botany in Plain Language** and the short name is **Basic Botany**:

The full name also appears in the page's title and meta data, which influences its search engine rankings. Here's the HTML code from the example above:

```
<title>Course: Basic Botany in Plain Language</title>
<meta name="keywords" content="moodle, Basic Botany in Plain
Language" />
```

Notice the full course name in the `<title>` and `<meta>` tags. Many search engines give a lot of weight to the title and keywords tags. Choose your course title with this in mind.

7. Enter a **Course ID Number**.

Chapter 2 describes how to use an external database for enrollment information. The ID number that you enter into this field must match the ID number of the course in the **External Database**. If you're not using an external database for enrollment information, you can leave this field blank.

8. Enter a **Course Summary**.

The **Course Summary** is displayed when a reader clicks on the information icon for a courser, and when the course appears in a list. In the following screenshot, the user is clicking on the information icon for a course. The user will be shown the course summary after clicking on the information icon:

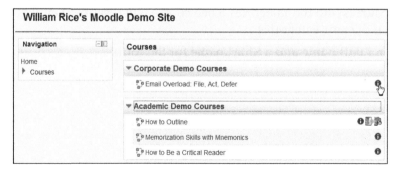

If you allow visitors to see your front page without logging in, then they will probably read your course summaries before enrolling. Consider the **Course Summary** to be a course's resume. Your course summaries need to be informative and work as a sales tool. They should offer enough information to help your visitors decide if they want to enroll, and should describe the courses in their best light.

9. Select a **Format** for the course. Among your choices are:

    ° Topics

    ° Weekly (this is the default format for a new course)

    ° Social

    ° SCORM

The *Topics format* is the most intuitive format to use for a course. As it displays each part of the course as a numbered topic, this format encourages students to proceed through the course sequentially. However, by default, Moodle does not enforce this sequence, so students are free to jump ahead and behind in the course.

You can force students to complete activities in a specific order by using conditional activities. This is covered in detail, later in the book. To use conditional activities, your system administrator must enable this feature under **System Administration | Advanced Features | Enable conditional availability**.

The *Weekly format* appears almost identical to the Topics format, except that it displays dates for each topic. As of this writing, Moodle does not automatically enforce these dates. That is, Moodle does not turn on and off weekly sections on the appropriate dates. The site administrator or teacher must do that. Alternatively, you can just allow students to access the weeks in any order.

The *Social format* turns the entire course into a discussion forum. Discussion topics are displayed on the course's Home Page. Replies to a topic are added and read by clicking on the **Discuss this topic** link.

One of the settings available for forums enables you to prevent students from creating new topics, so that they can only post replies to existing topics (later, we will cover the settings that are available in a forum). When this setting is activated, only the teacher can create new topics. Students then discuss these topics by adding replies to them. This enables you to better control the discussion, and to prevent the creation of so many topics that the course's Home Page becomes too long.

The Social format is very different from a traditional, sequential course. It lacks the organization and ability to add activities and resources that you find in the Topic and Weekly formats. However, because the Social format turns the entire course into a discussion forum, it offers you the chance to put a discussion forum right into the course listings. You can then have a discussion appear in the course listing on the front page of your site.

The SCORM format allows you to upload a SCORM-compliant activity. This activity then becomes the course.

If you want to use a SCORM package as one part of your course, then under **Add an activity** you can use **SCORM package**. If you want to use a SCORM package as your entire course, then use the SCORM format setting.

10. Select the **Number of weeks/topics**.

    You can change the number of weeks or topics in a course, on-the-fly. If you increase the number, then blank weeks/topics are added. If you decrease the number, then weeks/topics are deleted. Or, so it seems.

    One of Moodle's quirks is that when you decrease the number of sections in a course, if the topics that are dropped contain any material, they're not really deleted. They're just not displayed, even for the teacher. If you increase the number of topics so that those topics are added back to the course, they reappear with their content intact.

    Notice that this is different from hiding weeks/topics from students. When you hide topics or weeks from students, the teacher can still see those sections. When a section disappears because the number of weeks/topics in the course was reduced, the topics or weeks are hidden from for everyone, even the teacher. The only way to bring them back is to increase the number of weeks/topics.

11. Set the **Course Start Date**.

    For a Weekly course, this field sets the starting date that is shown for the course. It has no effect on the display of Topic or Social courses. Students can enter a course as soon as you display it; the course start date does not shut off or hide a course until that date. This field's only other effect is that logs for course activity begin on this date.

If you want to limit the period for which a course is available for students to enrol in, look under **Course administration | Users | Enrolment methods**. Enable the enrolment method for **Self enrolment**. Then, under the settings for **Self enrolment**, set the **Enrolment period**.

12. Select how the course will display **Hidden Sections**.

The setting **Number of weeks/topics** determines how many weeks or topics your course has. Each week or topic is a section. You can hide or reveal any individual section at will, except for Topic 0, which is always displayed. To hide or reveal a section, turn on course editing, and click on the open or closed eye icon next to the section, as appropriate. The following example shows a course creator hiding and revealing section 1 of a course:

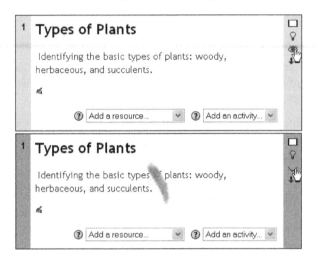

If you select **Hidden sections are shown in collapsed form** under **Hidden Sections**, then the titles or dates of sections that you have hidden will appear grayed out. The user cannot enter that section of the course, can see that it is there. This is most useful if you plan to make sections of a course available in sequence, instead of making them available all at once. If you select **Hidden sections are completely invisible**, then hidden sections are invisible to students. Course creators and teachers can still see those sections, and can access the resources and activities in them.

If you choose to make hidden sections completely invisible to students, then there is no real disadvantage of having more sections than you're using. You can keep the section that you're working on hidden, and then reveal it when you're finished. If you want to modify an existing section, you can create a hidden duplicate of the section, work on it, and then, with a few clicks in a few seconds, hide the old section and reveal the new one.

You can move resources between sections in a course. This makes a hidden section a convenient place to hold resources that you might want to use later, or that you want to archive. For example, if you find a site on the Web that you might want to use in your course later, but you're not sure, you can create a link to the site in a hidden section. If you eventually decide you want to use the site, you can just move that link from the hidden section to one of the sections in use.

13. Specify how many **News Items to Show** in the **Latest news** block.

    For **Weekly** and **Topics** course formats, a News forum automatically appears on the course's Home Page. If you want to delete this forum, set the **News Items to Show** to zero, and then delete the forum.

    The News forum is like any other forum, except that its postings appear in the **Latest news** block. Like other forums, the course creator and editor can enable or disable the ability of students to create new topics, or to reply to existing topics.

    The **Latest news** block automatically disappears if you have **News items to show** set to zero, or if there are no news items (no topics in the forum). Also, the **Latest news** block can be manually hidden, regardless of this setting or how many news items are posted.

The maximum number of news item that the block will show is 10.

14. If **Show gradebook to students** is set to **Yes**, then a student can view a list of all of their grades for the course by clicking on the **Grades** link in the **Course administration** block.

If the course allows Guest access, the Guests will not be able to earn grades. So if your site has a free sample course, and you want people to see how Moodle displays their grades, you might want to make people register for that free sample course.

15. Under your profile, you can see a report of your activity in each course that you take. Note that your personal activity report is in your profile, not in the courses. The setting for **Show activity reports** determines if a student's activity for this course will be kept in that student's profile.

For a course that allows guest access, setting this to **Yes** usually doesn't make much sense. Remember that every anonymous, unregistered user enters the course under the name Guest. So having a report that shows the grades and activities for Guest is usually not very useful. If you want to track how many people tried a sample course, and what parts of the course they sampled, allow users to create a free account to use in the fully-functioning sample course. Make this especially easy by not requiring e-mail confirmation when the student registers; instead give instant approval. Then, you can track and study individual usage in the sample course. To keep these anonymous users out of the courses requiring registration or payment, use a Login Page for such courses.

16. The setting for **Maximum upload file size** limits the size of a file that a student can upload into this course. There is also a site-wide limit set under **Site Administration | Security | Site policies**. The smaller of the two settings—site-wide or course-wide—takes precedence here.

17. The color and icons that Moodle uses are determined by its theme. Usually, you use the same theme throughout your site. However, teachers and even students can change the theme that they use. The setting **Force theme** determines whether users can choose a different theme when they are in this course, or if they are forced to use the predetermined theme.

A theme can do more than just provide a pleasant color scheme. For example, you can assign the courses a distinctive theme for each teacher, or assign the same theme to all of the courses in a particular category, and so on. For more about themes, see the official Moodle site at http://moodle.org.

18. Under **Guest access**, choose whether to allow guests to take the course. You 17.can also set a guest **Password**. This password applies only to guests, and not to enrolled students.

19. Select the **Group mode**.

Group mode applies to activities in the course. Each course can have either no groups or several groups. When set to **No**, all students assigned to the course are considered to be in one big group. When set to **Separate**, all of the students in the same group can see each other's work. However, students in different groups, even though they are taking the same course, cannot see work from another group. That is, the work done by different groups is kept separate. When set to **Visible**, students are divided into groups but can still see the other groups. Even though the other groups are visible to each other, the work done by one group's students is not visible to the other group's students.

You can change this setting for individual activities. For example, suppose you want to run groups through a course separately. However, you have one project for which you want all students, in all groups, to be able to see each other's work. You can choose **Separate** for the course, and then for that one project, override the course setting by using **Visible** for the project. Then, only for that one project, each group can see the other groups' work.

Running separate groups through a course versus having separate courses

Using **Separate** groups allows you to reuse a course for many groups, while giving the impression to each group that the course is theirs alone. However, this doesn't work well for a Weekly format course, where the weeks are dated. That's because the course home page displays the dates for each week. If you start each group on a different date, the weekly dates will become incorrect.

If you're running a Topics format course, you can easily reuse the course by separating your students into groups and running each group individually. Later, you'll see how to assign teachers to a course. You can also assign a teacher to a group, so that each teacher can see only his or her students.

If you run several groups through a course, and those groups are at different points in the course, be aware that the teacher cannot regulate the flow of students through the course by turning topics off and on. That is, you cannot reveal just Topic 1 until the group has finished it, and then reveal Topic 2 until the group has worked through it, and then Topic 3 and so on. If you tried this while running several groups who were at different points in the course, you'd be turning off topics that some groups still need.

If you really must enforce the order of topics by revealing them one at a time, create a copy of the course for each group, or use conditional activities to reveal activities after previous ones have been completed by a student.

20. Normally, the course's group mode can be overridden for each activity. When the course creator adds an activity, the teacher can choose a different group mode than the default group mode set for the course. However, when **Force group mode** is set to **Yes**, all activities are forced to have the same group mode as the course.

21. The **Default grouping** for the course determines how groups are filtered in the gradebook. This setting has no effect unless you are using groupings.

22. While you're working on a course, you may want to set **Availability** to **This course is not available to students**. This will completely hide your course from students' view. Teachers and administrators can still see the course, so you can collaborate on the course content with them.

23. Select a setting for **Force language**. Selecting **Do not force** enables a student to select any language on the pull-down list of languages.

    Remember that the languages on the pull-down list are limited by the setting you chose under **Site Administration | Language | Language Settings | Display language menu** and **Languages on menu**. Also, remember that you must have the language pack for any language that you want to use installed.

    Also remember that only Moodle's standard menus and messages are automatically translated when a student selects a different language. Course material is not translated unless the course creator entered material in another language and used the Multi-language Content filter.

24. If you want to use different terms for the roles in your course, you can use **Role Renaming**. Moodle inserts your term for teacher or student into Moodle's standard messages. For Teacher, you can substitute any term such as Instructor, Leader, and Facilitator. For Student, you could use terms such as Participant or Member.

25. At the bottom of the page, click on the **Save Changes** button.

> Congratulations! You now have a new, blank course. You're ready to start configuring it and filling it with great material.

Enrolling teachers and students

Who will teach your course? And how will students be enrolled? The settings that you choose for your course enrolment will determine these things.

Assign teachers

After a site Administrator or Course Creator has created a blank course, (s)he can assign a Teacher to build the course.

Assigning a teacher to a course

In order to assign a teacher to a course, the teacher first needs an account on your site. If you need to manually create the teacher's account, see *Preparation Task 1: Create Test Accounts for a Teacher and Students* in *Chapter 3*.

1. Enter the course as a teacher or administrator.

2. From within the course, select **Settings | Users | Enrolled users**.

3. In the upper-right corner of the page, click on the **Enrol users** button. The **Enrol users** window is displayed:

To find a user, enter any part of the user's name into the **Search** field and then press *Enter* or *Return* on your keyboard:

1. From the **Assign roles** drop-down list, select **Teacher**.

2. Next to the user's name, click on the **Enrol** button. The display of that user's name will change to indicate that (s)he is enrolled.

3. When you finish enrolling users, click on the close box for this window. You will return to the Enrolled user's page, and see the user added to the list of enrolled users.

How to set enrolment methods

In *Chapter 3*, in the section *Enrolment methods*, you enabled a list of enrollment methods for your site. For each course, you can enable or disable any or all of these enrolment methods.

The teacher can enable, disable, and arrange only the interactive enrolment methods. Interactive enrolment happens when a user tries to enrol on a course. The user must do something to be enrol, such as selecting a course and confirming that they want to enrol, or paying for a course.

Non-interactive enrolment methods are checked when a user tries to log in to a course, for example when logging in via, an external database or LDAP server. Only a Site Administrator can enable or disable a login-time enrolment method. These are not managed at the course level, but at the site level.

1. Enter the **Course** as a Site Administrator or Teacher.

2. Select **Course administration | Users | Enrolment methods**. The **Enrolment methods** page displays all of the enrolment methods that are enabled for the site.

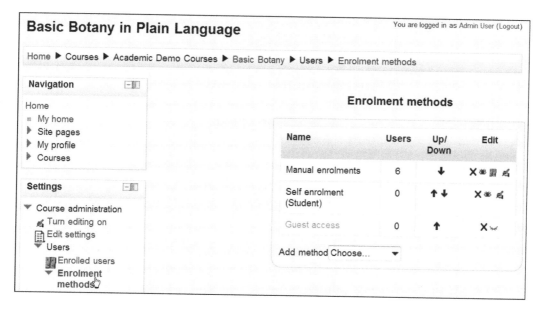

3. To enable or disable an enrolment method for this course, click on the eye icon. When the eye is open that enrolment method can be used for this course. When the eye is closed, that enrolment method is not available for this course.

4. Place the enrolment methods in the order that you want this course to use them. Do this by clicking on the up and down arrows next to each enrolment method, to move each method into the required position in the list.

Many enrolment methods have a separate page for settings, where you configure that method:

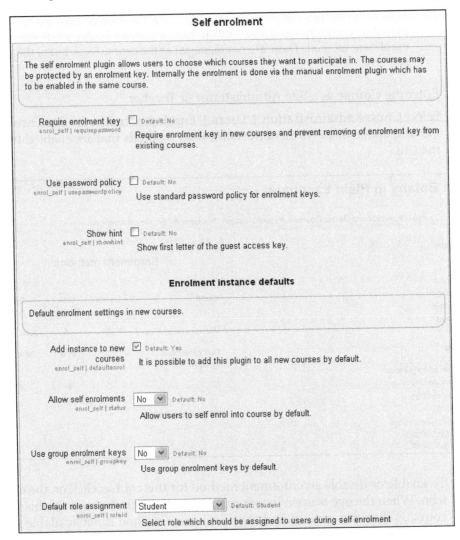

If you enable an enrollment method, you should at least look at the **Settings** page for that method and determine if you need to change any of the settings.

Summary

Just as Moodle enables students to explore courses in a non-linear fashion, it also allows you to build courses in a flexible, nonlinear manner. Once you fill out the **Course settings** page, the order in which you add material and features to your course is up to you. Don't get stuck if you don't know where to begin. For example, if you're unsure whether to use a **Weekly** or **Topics** format, just pick one and start adding material. If the course content begins to suggest a different type of course format, you can change the format later.

If your course is still under development when it's time to go live, use hidden sections to hide the unfinished portions. You can reveal them as you complete them.

When deciding which blocks to display, consider the comfort level of your students. If they're experienced web surfers, they may be comfortable with a full complement of blocks displaying information about the course. Experienced web surfers are adept at ignoring information they don't need (when was the last time you paid attention to a banner ad on the Web?). If your students are new computer users, they may assume that the presence of a block means that it requires their attention or interaction. And remember that you can turn blocks off and on as needed.

In general, make your best guesses when you first create a course, and don't let uncertainties about any of these settings stop you—continue on with the next chapter, *Adding Static Course Material*. As you add static, interactive, and social materials in the coming chapters, you can revisit the course structure and settings described in this chapter, and change them as needed.

5

Adding Static Course Material

Static course materials are resources that students read but don't interact with, such as web pages, graphics, and Adobe Acrobat documents. This chapter teaches you how to add such resources to a course, and how to make the best use of them.

In this chapter, we will cover:

- Kinds of static course material that can be added
- Adding links
- Adding pages
- Adding files for your students
- Adding media
- Organizing your course
- Restricting access by date or score

Kinds of static course material that can be added

Static course material is added from the **Add a resource** drop-down menu. Using this menu, you can create:

- Web pages
- Links to anything on the Web
- Files
- A label that displays any text or image
- Multimedia

Adding links

On your Moodle site, you can show content from anywhere on the Web by using a link. You can also link to files that you've uploaded into your course. By default, this content appears in a frame within your course. You can also choose to display it in a new window.

When using content from outside sites, you need to consider the legality and reliability of using the link. Is it legal to display the material on your Moodle site? Will the material still be there when your course is running? In this example, I've linked to an online resource from the BBC, which is a fairly reliable source:

Remember that the bottom of the window displays **Window Settings**, so you can choose to display this resource in its own window. You can also set the size of the window. You may want to make it appear in a smaller window, so that it does not completely obscure the window of your Moodle site. This will make it clearer to the student that he or she has opened a new window.

To add a link to a resource on the Web:

1. Log in to your course as a Teacher or Site Administrator.

2. In the upper-right corner of the page, if you see a button that reads, **Turn editing on**, click on this button. If it reads **Turn editing off**, then you do not need to click on this button. (You will also find this button in the **Settings** menu on the leftmost side of the page.)

3. From the **Add a resource...** drop-down menu, select **URL**.

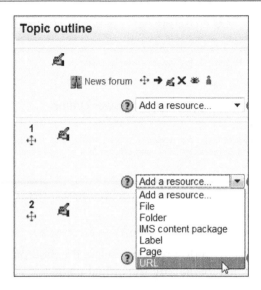

4. Moodle displays the **Adding a new URL** page.

5. Enter a **Name** for the link. This is the name that people will see on the home page of your course.

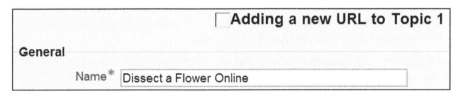

6. Enter a **Description** for the link. When the student sees the course's home page, they will see the **Name** and not the **Description**. However, whenever this resource is selected from the **Navigation** bar, the **Description** will be displayed.

   Here is a link as it appears on the home page of a course:

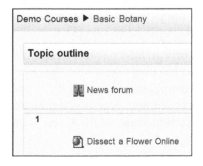

Here is the same link, as it appears when selected from the **Navigation** bar:

Demo Courses ▶ Basic Botany ▶ Topic 1 ▶ Dissect a Flower Online

Dissect a Flower Online

Link to a virtual laboratory where you can dissect a flower, label it, and put it back together again. Produced by the British Broadcasting Corporation (BBC) and offered free on their school resources website.

Click http://www.bbc.co.uk/schools/scienceclips/ages/9_10/life_cycles.shtml link to open URL.

7. In the **External URL** field, enter the Web address for this link.

8. From the **Display** drop-down menu, select the method that you want Moodle to use when displaying the linked page:

9. **Embed** will insert the linked page into a Moodle page. Your students will see the **Navigation** bar, any blocks that you have added to the course and navigation links across the top of the page, just like when they view any other page in Moodle. The center of the page will be occupied by the linked page.

    Open will take the student away from your site, and open the linked page in the window that was occupied by Moodle.

    In pop-up will launch a new window, containing the linked page on top of the Moodle page.

    Automatic will make Moodle choose the best method for displaying the linked page.

10. The checkboxes for **Display URL name** and **Display URL description** will affect the display of the page, only if **Embed** is chosen as the display method. If selected, the **Name** of the link will be displayed above the embedded page, and the **Description** will be displayed below the embedded page.

11. Under **Options**, the **ShowAdvanced** button will display fields that allow you to set the size of the popup window. If you don't select **In pop-up** as the display method, these fields have no effect.

12. Under **Parameters**, you can add parameters to the link. In a Web link, a parameter would add information about the course or student to the link. A discussion of URL parameters is beyond the scope of this book. If you have Web programming experience, you might take advantage of this feature. For more about passing parameters in URLs, see http://en.wikipedia.org/wiki/Query_string.

13. Under **Common Module Settings**, the **Visible** setting determines if this resource is visible to students. Teachers and site Administrators can always see the resource. Setting this to **Hide** will completely hide the resource. Teachers can hide some resources and activities at the beginning of a course, and reveal them as the course progresses.

Show/Hide versus Restrict availability

If you want a resource to be visible, but not available, then use the **Restrict Availability** settings further down on the page. Those settings enable you to have a resource's name and its description appear, but still make the resource unavailable. You might want to do this for resources that will be used later in a course, when you don't want the student to work ahead of the syllabus.

14. The **ID number** field allows you to enter an identifier for this resource, which will appear in the Gradebook. If you export grades from the Gradebook and then import them into an external database, you might want the course ID number here to match the ID number that you use in that database.

15. The **Restrict Availability** settings allow you to set two kinds of conditions that will control whether this resource is available to the student:

16. The **Accessible from** and **Accessible until** settings enable you to set dates for when this resource will be available.

17. The **Grade condition** setting allows you to specify the grade that a student must achieve in another Activity in this course, before being able to access this Resource. Note that adding Activities is covered in Chapters 6 and 7.

18. The setting for **Before activity is available** determines if the Resource will be visible while it is unavailable. If it is visible but unavailable, Moodle will display the conditions needed to make it available (achieve a grade, wait for a date, and so on.).

19. Click on one of the **Save** buttons at the bottom of the page to save your work.

Adding pages

Under the **Add a resource** drop-down menu, select **Page** to add a Web page to a course. A link to the page that you create will appear on the course's home page.

Moodle's HTML editor

When you add a Page to your course, Moodle displays a Web page editor. This editor is based on an open source web page editor called TinyMCE. You can use this editor to compose a web page for your course. This page can contain almost anything that a web page outside of Moodle can contain.

A full discussion of the editor's features is beyond the scope of this section. Instead, we will examine a few of the key features that are available in Moodle's HTML editor.

Pasting text into a Moodle page

Many times, we prefer to write text in our favorite word processor instead of writing it in Moodle. Or we may find text that we can legally copy and paste into a Moodle page, somewhere else. Moodle's text editor does allow you to do this.

To paste text into a page, you can just use the appropriate keyboard shortcut. Try *Ctrl* + *V* for Windows PCs and *Apple* + *V* for Macintoshes. If you use this method, the format of the text will be preserved.

To paste plain text, without the format of the original text, click on the **Paste as Plain Text** icon, as shown below:

When you paste text from a Microsoft Word document into a web page, it usually includes a lot of non-standard HTML code. This code doesn't work well in all browsers, and makes it more difficult to edit the HTML code in your page. Many advanced web page editors, such as AdobeDreamWeaver, have the ability to clean up Word HTML code. Moodle's web page editor can also clean up Word HTML code.

When pasting text that was copied from Word, use the Paste from Word icon, as shown in the image below. This will strip out most of Word's non-standard HTML code.

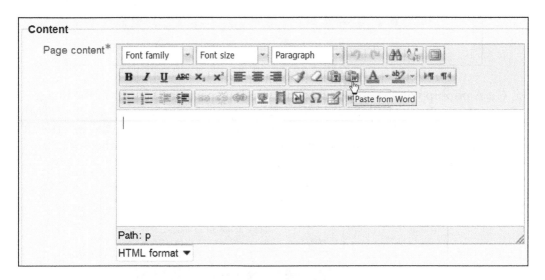

Adding images to a page

When you select an image to add to a Moodle page, you can choose images from those that you have already uploaded, or, you can upload a new image. A less obvious feature is the ability to link to a picture that is hosted on another website. For example, you could link to a picture hosted on a Flickr account, or one that appears on a non-profit educational website.

Inserting a linked picture into a Moodle Page

The following steps explain how to insert a linked image that is hosted in another location on the Web, into a Moodle page. If you want to insert an image file that you have on your computer, see *To insert an image file* in the next subsection.

1. Find the image that you want to link to.
2. In your browser, right-click on the image. A pop-up menu will appear. One of the options on this menu will enable you to copy the URL (the Web address) of the picture. For example, in Internet Explorer 8, you would select **Properties** and then copy the **Address** of the image. In Firefox 3+, you would select **CopyImageLocation**.
3. Switch back to Moodle, where you are editing the Page.
4. Click on the Page, so the insertion point is where you want the picture to appear.

5. Click on the **Insert Image** icon, as shown in the example below:

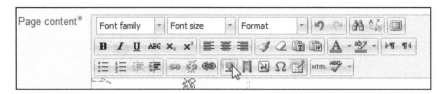

6. A pop-up window appears. In this window, paste the address of the image into the **Image URL** field. In the following screenshot, you can see the HTML editor window in the background. On top of that, you can see the **Insert/edit image** window. At the bottom of the screen is the original location of the image.

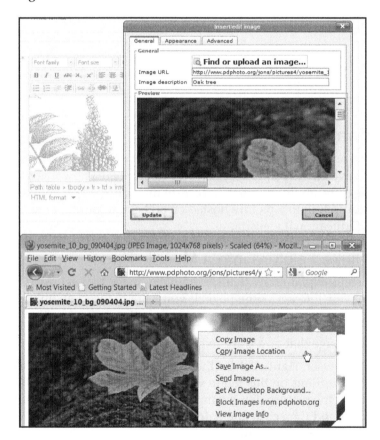

7. If needed, fill out the fields under **Appearance**. In particular, you might want to resize the picture, because Moodle will, by default, display the picture at its original size.

Inserting an image file

Follow the steps below in order to insert an image file that you have on your computer. For example, if you have a `.jpg` or `.png` file.

1. On the Moodle Page, position the insertion point where you want the image to appear.

2. Click on the **Insert Image** icon, as shown in the example below:

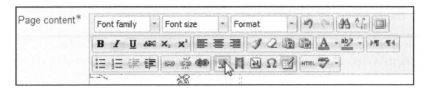

3. A pop-up window appears. In this window, click on the button labeled **Find or upload an image**.

4. The **File picker** window is displayed. In this window, click on the **Upload a file** link.

5. Click on the **Browse...** button.

6. Locate the file on your computer, and select it.

7. Click on the **Open** or **OK** button.

8. Optionally, enter the a name that you want the file to have in Moodle.

9. Click on the **Upload this file** button. The file is uploaded to your Moodle system.

10. If needed, fill out the fields under **Appearance**. In particular, you might want to resize the picture, because Moodle will, by default, display the picture at its original size.

11. Click on the **Insert** button. The picture is inserted into the page.

Composing in an HTML editor and uploading to Moodle

For long or complex HTML pages, or just for your own comfort, you might want to compose your web page in an HTML editor like **DreamWeaver** or **FrontPage**. This is especially true if you want to take advantage of these editors' ability to insert JavaScript timing, and other advanced features. How, then, do you get that page into your Moodle course? You can copy and paste the HTML code from your web page editor into the Moodle page editing window. To do this you would:

1. Select the HTML view in your web page editor. For example, in DreamWeaver you would select **View | Code**, and in FrontPage you would select **View | Reveal Codes**.

2. Select all of the HTML code, between the two body tags. That is, drag from just after the `<body>` tag near the top, to just before the `</body>` tag at the end. Copy the code by selecting menu option **Edit | Copy** or by using the keyboard shortcut *Ctrl+C*.

3. Switch over to Moodle, and create the new web page.

4. Display the HTML code by clicking on the `<>` icon.

5. Paste the code into the page by pressing *Ctrl+V*.

A second method is to publish your web page to someplace outside of Moodle, and create a link to it from your course.

Learn more about HTML

To learn more about HTML code, you can start with the organization responsible for defining the standards. The World Wide Web Consortium (W3C) maintains the complete standards for HTML online at `http://www.w3.org/TR/html4`. W3C also maintains a basic tutorial at `http://www.w3.org/MarkUp/Guide/`. Everything covered in this basic guide can be done using the WYSIWYG tools in Moodle. The advanced HTML guide at `http://www.w3.org/MarkUp/Guide/Advanced.html` covers some features that you would need to go into HTML view to add, such as defining clickable regions within images, and using roll-overs.

Adding files for your students to download

You can add files to a course, so that your students can download them onto their personal computers. Some examples of files you might want students to have are: forms, reading to complete before class, word processing files to edit, and more.

What happens when a student selects a file from the course?

When a student selects a file from your course, the student's computer will attempt to open that file. Moodle will only pass the file to the student's computer. For example, if it's a PDF file, your student's computer will try to use Adobe Acrobat to open the file. If it's a word processing file, your student's computer will attempt to use Word or some other word processor to open it.

You can override this behavior with a setting called **Force download**. When you choose that setting, your student's computer will not try to open the file. Instead, it will download the file and prompt the student to save it.

If you want the student to use a file immediately upon accessing the file, then indicate to Moodle that you want the file to open when the student selects it. If you want the student to save the file for future use, then use the **Force download** setting.

Adding a file to your course

1. Log in to your course as a Teacher or Site Administrator.
2. In the upper-right corner of the page, if you see a button that reads, **Turn editing on**, click on this button. If it reads **Turn editing off**, then you do not need to click on this button.
3. From the **Add a resource...** drop-down menu, select **File**.
4. Moodle displays the **Adding a new URL** page.
5. Enter a **Name** for the file. This is the name that people will see on the home page of your course.
6. Enter a **Description** for the file. When the student sees the course's home page, they will see the Name but not the Description. However, whenever this resource is selected from the Navigation bar, the Description will be displayed.

The Site Administrator can turn off the requirement to add a Description for each file. By default, this requirement is turned on.

7. Under **Content**, click on the **Add...** button. The **File picker** window displays.

8. If the file already exists in the system, and you have access to it, you can find it under **Server files**, **Recent files**, or **Private files**. If you don't find the file under one of these areas, then click on **Upload a file**.

9. Click on **Browse...** and select the file.

10. In the **Save as** field, enter a name for this file.

11. Click on **Upload this file**. The **File picker** window closes, and you are returned to the page where you edit the file. The options are as follows:

12. From the **Display** drop-down menu, select the method that you want Moodle to use when displaying the file:

13. **Open** and **Embed** will insert a link to the file into a Moodle page. Your students will see the Navigation Bar, any blocks that you have added to the course, and navigation links across the top of the page, just like when they view any other page in Moodle. The center of the page will have a link to the file.

    In pop-up will launch a new window on top of the Moodle page, containing a link to the file.

    Automatic will make Moodle choose the best method for displaying the linked page.

    Force download will force the file to be downloaded to your student's computer.

14. The checkboxes for **Display resource name** and **Display resource description** will affect the display of the page, only if **Embed** is chosen as the display method. If selected, the **Name** of the file will be displayed above the link to the file, and the **Description** will be displayed below the link to the file.

15. Under **Options**, the **ShowAdvanced** button will display fields that allow you to set the size of the pop-up window. If you don't select **In pop-up** as the display method, these fields have no effect.

16. Under **Common Module Settings**, the **Visible** setting determines if this resource is visible to students. Teachers and Site Administrators can always see the resource. Setting this to **Hide** will completely hide the resource.

Show/Hide versus Restrict availability

If you want a resource to be visible, but not available, then use the **Restrict Availability** settings further down on the page. Those settings allow you to have a resource's name and its description appear, but still make the resource unavailable. You might want to do this for resources that will be used later in a course, when you don't want the student to work ahead of the syllabus.

17. The **ID number** field allows you to enter an identifier for this resource, which will appear in the Gradebook. If you export grades from the Gradebook and then import them into an external database, you might want the course ID number here to match the ID number that you use in that database.

18. The **Restrict Availability** settings allow you to set two kinds of conditions that will control whether this resource is available to the student. These settings are:

19. The **Accessible from** and **Accessible until** settings allow you to set dates for when this resource is available.

    The **Grade condition** setting allows you to specify the grade that a student must achieve in another Activity in this course, before being able to access this Resource. Note that adding Activities is covered in *Chapter 6* and *Chapter 7*.

20. The setting for **Before activity is available** determines if the Resource will be visible while it is unavailable. If it is visible but unavailable, Moodle will display the conditions needed to make it available (achieve a grade, wait for a date, and so on.).

21. Click one of the **Save** buttons at the bottom of the page to save your work.

Adding media (video and audio)

If you want to add video or audio to your course, you have two choices. First, you can add it as a file. If you do that, when the student selects the file, one of two things will happen. Either the media file will be downloaded to the student's computer, and played by the software on the student's computer, or Moodle will try to play that file with its built-in media player. If multimedia plugins are enabled under **Site Administration | Plugins**, then Moodle will try to play the file in its built-in media player. If multimedia plugins are not enabled, then the file will be played using whatever media player is available on the student's computer (such as Windows Media Player or Quicktime).

Second, you can embed the media on a Moodle Page (see the section on *Adding pages*). That will cause the media to be played on the web page. By default, the media will be played using Moodle's built-in media player.

Adding video or audio to a page

Follow the steps below in order to add a video, audio, or applet to a Moodle Page. You must be in possession of the file that you are adding. That is, the file must be on your computer, and not on another website. If the file that you want to appear is on another website, see the procedure for embedding media from another website on a page, earlier in this chapter.

1. On the Moodle Page, position the insertion point where you want the media to appear.

2. Click on the **Insert Media** icon, as shown in the example below:

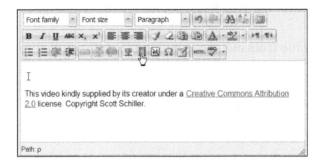

3. A pop-up window appears. In this window, click the button labeled **Find or upload a sound, video, or applet**.

4. The File picker window displays. In this window, click on the **Upload a file** link.

5. Click on the **Browse…** button.

6. Locate the file on your computer, and select it.

7. Click on the **Open** or **OK** button.

8. Optionally, give the file a name that you want the file to have in Moodle.

9. Click on the **Upload this file** button. The file is uploaded to your Moodle system.

10. If needed, fill out the fields under **Appearance**. In particular, you might want to resize the picture, because Moodle will, by default, display the picture at its original size.

11. Click on the **Insert** button. The media is inserted into the page.

To embed a video on a page:

1. Find the media that you want to link to. For example, you might find a video on `Vimeo.com`, or `Flickr.com`, that you can use.

2. Check the license for the material, to ensure that you have the right to use it as you intend.

3. Somewhere on the page, you will see a button or link that will give you the HTML code to embed the video, as shown in the example below:

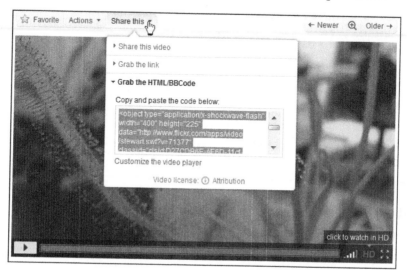

4. Copy the code for embedding the video.

5. Switch back to Moodle, where you are editing the Page.

6. On the Moodle Page, position the insertion point where you want the media to appear.

7. Click on the Edit HTML icon:

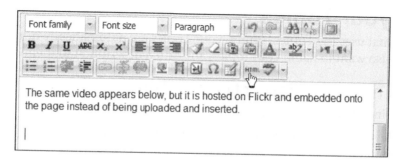

8. The **HTML Source Editor** is displayed. In this window, paste the code that you copied from the video sharing site.

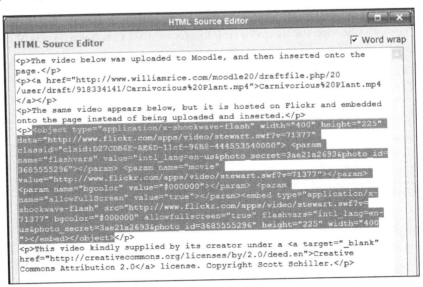

9. At the bottom of the editor window, click on the **Update** button.

10. You are returned to the editing page. Continue editing, and then save your work when you are finished.

Organizing your course

The main tools for organizing a course in Moodle are Topics and Labels. In this section, we'll look at how to use them, and how to move material around on the course page.

Name your Topics

In a course that uses the Topics format, your Topics are automatically numbered. You might also want to name your topics, and add a description to them.

To add a name and description to a Topic

1. Log in to your course as a Teacher or Site Administrator.

2. In the upper-right corner of the page, if you see a button that reads, **Turn editing on**, click on this button. If it reads **Turn editing off**, then you do not need to click on this button.

3. Next to the Topic's number, and then click the Edit button:

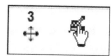

4. The **Summary** page for your Topic is displayed. You must uncheck the checkbox for **Use default section name**. If there is a checkbox in this field, then you cannot edit the name or description of the Topic.

5. In the **Section** name field, enter the name for your Topic.

6. In the **Summary** field, enter a description for your Topic. This is a full-featured Web page editor, so you can enter text, graphics, and media.

7. Save your work. You will be returned to the course home page. The Topic's name and summary are displayed.

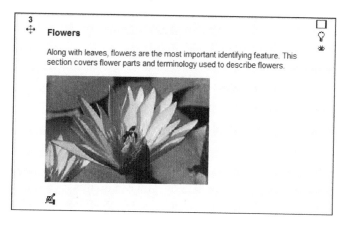

Rearrange (move) items on the course home page

As you build your course, you will be adding Resources and Activities to the course page. Moodle allows you to easily reposition these items. It's so easy to reposition them that I recommend that you don't even worry about getting them in the right place as you are creating them. Just forge ahead, create them, and then rearrange them later.

Rearranging items on the course page:

1. Log in to your course as a Teacher or Site Administrator.

2. In the upper-right corner of the page, if you see a button that reads, **Turn editing on**, click on this button. If it reads **Turn editing off**, then you do not need to click on this button.

3. Next to the item that you want to move, place the mouse pointer over the crosshairs icon:

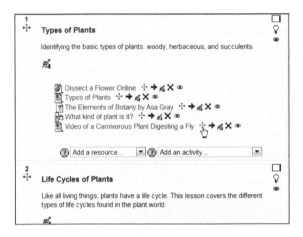

4. Drag the item to where you want it on the course page, and drop it.

You can also drag-and-drop entire Topics, if your browser has Ajax-enabled drag. You'll know you can do this if you see a crosshairs icon next to the Topic. Just click on the crosshairs icon and then drop it where you want the Topic to go.

Provide directions and organization through labels

Topic and Weekly courses are organized into sections. Labels can help you to organize material within a section, giving you another level of organization. A label can have any amount text, an image, or other content that you can put on a web page. It is essentially an HTML document. However, just because a label can handle any HTML content, you don't want to go overboard and create entire web pages in a label. A label's main purpose is to add organization to a course's Home Page. In the following screenshot you can see that the **WildPlants** course uses labels to organize course resources. The horizontal lines and **Jump to a topic**, **Group Activities**, and **Before You Start the Course: Do These Activities** headlines are labels:

Jump to a Topic

Types of Plants

Life Cycles of Plants

Leaves

Flowers

Roots

Other Identifying Features

Habitats

Group Activities

Course Discussion

Group Wiki

Before You Start the Course: Do These Activities

The Plants Around You

? Have you tried edible wild plants?

Foraging Journal

In our example, the course creators used text labels to organize the course content. A label can also hold a graphic. Adding a graphic to the beginning of each topic is a good way to add visual interest to a course. Also, a label can consist of a large amount of text. You can introduce activities by using a paragraph-long label. In the preceding screenshot, perhaps a sentence explaining each activity would help the student understand the course flow. That can be added by using a label. Make creative use of labels for organization, interest, and information.

To add a Label to the course's home page:

1. Log in to your course as a Teacher or Site Administrator.

2. In the upper-right corner of the page, if you see a button that reads, **Turn editing on**, click on this button. If it reads **Turn editing off**, then you do not need to click on this button.

3. From the **Add a resource** drop-down menu, select **Label**.

4. The **Adding a new Label page** is displayed. In the **Label** text field, you can enter anything that can appear on a Web page: text, graphics, media, and so on.

5. Save your work, and then return to the course home page.

Restricting access by date or score (restrict availability setting)

Moodle allows you to restrict access to an item, by date or by score. That is, you can make the item available only during specific dates, and/or only when the student has achieved a specific score on some specific activities).

This feature is turned on by default. If it's not enabled on your site, you will need to ask your Site Administrator to enable it for you.

You will find the **Restrict Availability** settings at the bottom of the page, when you are editing a **Resource** or **Activity**.

The **Restrict Availability** settings allow you to set two kinds of conditions that will control whether this resource is available to the student.

The **Accessible from** and **Accessible until** settings allow you to set dates for when this resource is available.

The **Grade condition** setting allows you to specify the grade that a student must achieve in another Activity in this course, before being able to access this Resource. Note that adding Activities is covered in *Chapter 6* and *Chapter 7*.

The setting for **Before activity is available** determines if the Resource will be visible while it is unavailable. If it is visible but unavailable, Moodle will display the conditions needed to make it available (achieve a grade, wait for a date, and so on).

Summary

Static course materials (text pages, web pages, links, files, and labels) form the core of most online courses. Most student/teacher interaction will be about something that the student has read or viewed. Adding static material first gives you a chance to think about how the material will be discussed and used. In later chapters, you'll see how to add more interactive material. The interactive material will allow the teacher to see student performance, and assess how well they have assimilated the static material.

6
Adding Interaction with Lessons and Assignments

Course activities enable students to interact with the instructor, the learning system, or each other. Note that Moodle doesn't categorize activities into "Static," "Interactive", and "Social" as we do in this book. In Moodle, all activities are added from the **Add an activity** menu, after selecting the option **Turn editing on**. We use the terms "Static", "Interactive", and "Social" as a convenient way to categorize the activities that Moodle offers.

In the previous chapter, we saw how to add static course material, such as web pages, links, and media. In this chapter, we will see how to add two kinds of interactive course material: Lessons and Assignments.

An **assignment** is an activity completed offline, outside of Moodle. When the student completes the assignment, they either uploads a file for the instructor's review or reports to the instructor in some other way. Regardless of whether the assignment requires a file to be uploaded, the student receives a grade for the assignment.

A **lesson** is a series of web pages displayed in a given order, where the next page displayed might depend upon the student's answer to a question. Usually, the "jump question" is used to test a student's understanding of the material. Get it right, and you proceed to the next item. Get it wrong, and you either stay on the page or jump to a remedial page. But the jump question could just as easily ask a student what they are interested in learning next, or some other exploratory question.

A lesson gives Moodle some of the branching capability found in commercial computer-based training (CBT) products. You could make a course consisting of just a summary, one large lesson, and a quiz.

Adding assignments

After logging in as a teacher, and turning on editing, you can add an assignment from the **Add an activity** menu. In the following screenshot you can see that we are adding one of the four types of **Assignments** available:

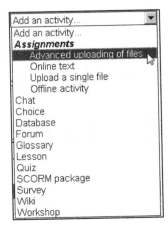

Adding different types of assignments

You can select from four types of assignments, as listed below. Each is explained in the following sections.

- **Upload a single file**
- **Advanced uploading of files**
- **Online text**
- **Offline activity**

Uploading a single file

Use the **Uploading a single file** assignment type when you want the student to submit a single file online. The following screenshot shows what the student sees before (s)he submits the file:

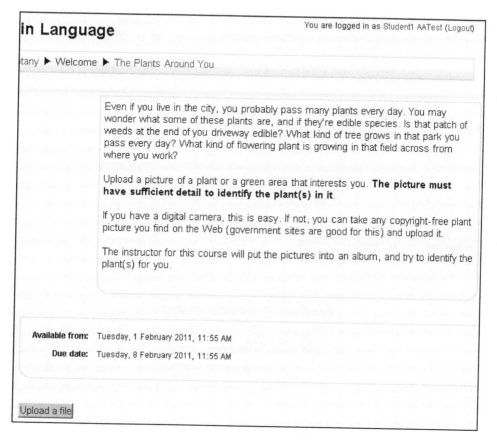

The following screenshot shows what the student sees after submitting (uploading) the file and once the submission has been graded by the teacher:

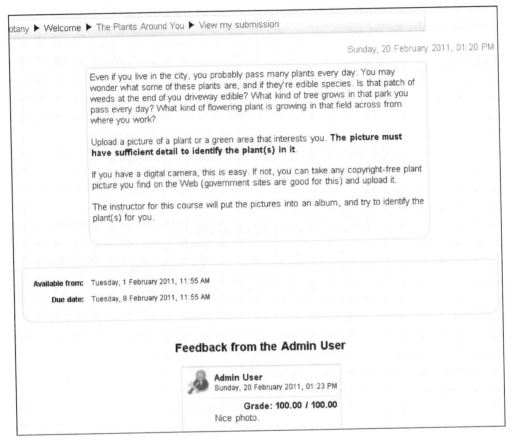

Advanced uploading of files

Just as with the **Upload a single file** assignment type, the **Advanced uploading of files** type of assignment allows each student to upload a file in any format. However, the student can upload multiple versions, or drafts, of the file. Until the student uploads the final version of the file, the submission is marked as a draft.

The teacher determines how many versions can be uploaded when (s)he creates the assignment. The student indicates that a file is the final version, up to the limit, that the teacher set.

Students can also enter notes for the submitted file. In the following screenshot, you can see that a student has uploaded a file, added a note, and that the submission is still a draft. Notice:

- The student can replace the existing file by uploading another one. That will count as another draft.

- The **Edit** button enables the student to edit the note.

- The **Send for marking** button allows the student to call this the final submission, even if they haven't submitted the maximum number of drafts allowed.

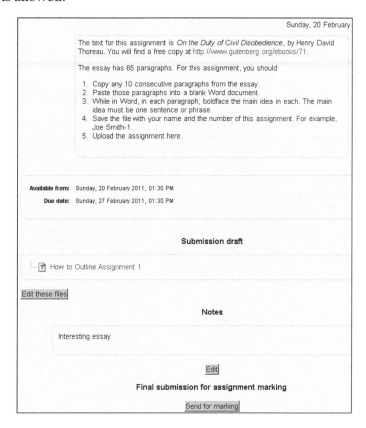

Creating an online text assignment

Select an **Online text** assignment type when you want the student to create a page online. Although it's called "Online text" assignment, note that the student can include anything on the page that you can include in a web page, such as graphics and links. That's because the student creates the page using Moodle's built-in web page editor. If you include this assignment type, consider giving your students directions on how to use the online editor to insert graphics, links, multimedia, and tables. Most of the functions of the online editor are self-explanatory, especially for a generation of bloggers, but these functions might give your students some problems if you don't explain them.

While grading the assignment, the teacher can edit the student's online text page. When the student clicks on the assignment to see their grade, the student also sees the original and edited versions of their page.

In the following screenshot, notice that the student has a full-featured online word processor in which to post their response:

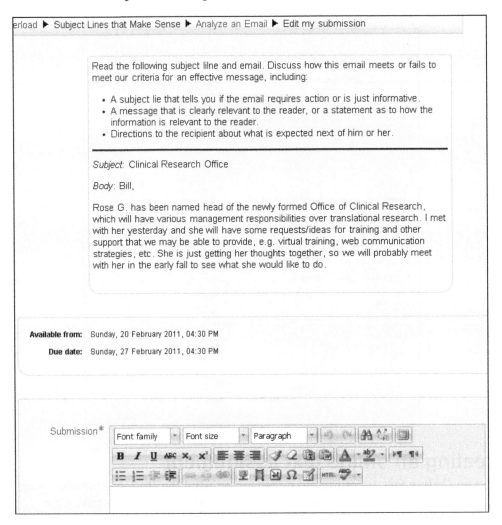

If the teacher allows resubmission of the assignment, then the back-and-forth of feedback and grading can continue until the teacher decides upon the final grade for the assignment.

Offline activity

Select the **Offline activity** when you want the student to do something outside of Moodle. Note that "outside of Moodle" doesn't have to mean "offline". The assignment could be something elsewhere on the Web. Or it could be completely offline, such as taking a photograph or visiting a museum.

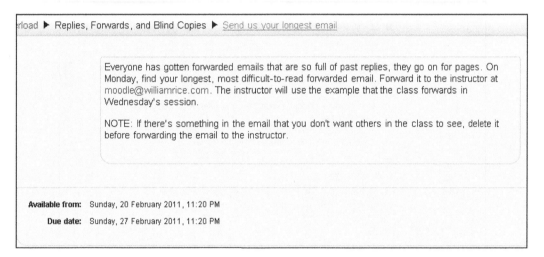

Although the work is performed outside of Moodle, the teacher still records the grade in Moodle.

Creating an assignment

Adding an assignment automatically brings up the **Editing Assignment** window, as shown in the following screenshot:

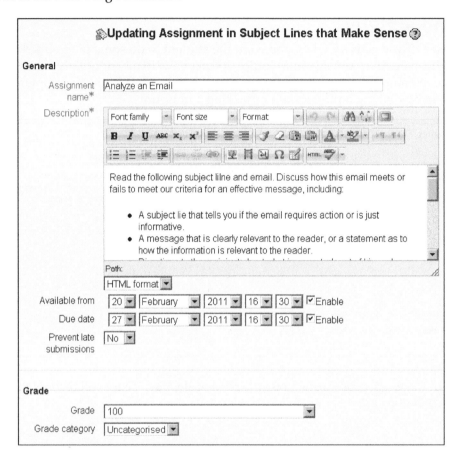

The **Assignment name** field is displayed on the course page. When a student clicks on the name, the **Description** field is displayed. The description should provide complete instructions for completing and submitting the assignment.

Assignments that are due soon will appear in the **Upcoming Events** block. If you do not set a due date, by default it will be set to the current date (the day on which you created the assignment). This will make the assignment show up in the **Upcoming Events** block, as if it's overdue. Make sure that you set an appropriate due date for the assignment.

Other settings in the **Editing assignment** window control the behavior of the assignment.

The setting for **Allow resubmitting** determines if a student can retry an assignment after (s)he has submitted it.

Selecting **Email alerts to teachers** causes an e-mail to be sent to the teacher(s) when a student submits an assignment.

 Email alerts are especially useful in courses where you allow students to proceed at their own pace, as otherwise you will not know what activities they have completed unless you check in to the course and look at the gradebook.

Comment inline is unique to online text assignments. Selecting this option makes it easier for the teacher to comment on the text that the student has submitted.

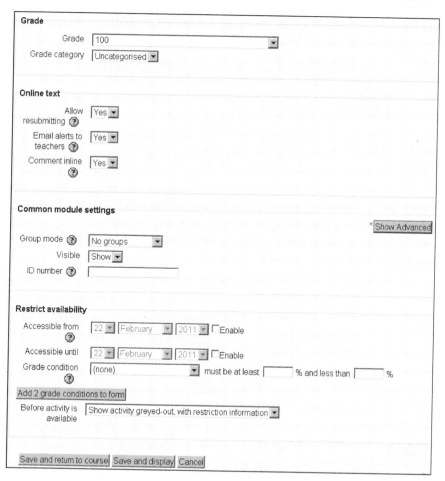

Printer-friendly directions

As assignments are completed offline, you may want the directions to be printer-friendly so that students can take the directions with them. Make sure that any graphics that you've embedded into the **Description** field are less than the width of the printed page. Alternatively, you can upload the directions as an **Adobe Acrobat** (`.pdf`) file, and use the **Description** field to instruct students to print the directions and take the directions with them.

Making it clear that assignments are mandatory

On the course's Home Page, an assignment link appears with its own icon, like this: ⬟. It is not immediately apparent to a new student that this icon means "Do this assignment." You might want to use a label to indicate that the assignment is something that the student should do. In the following example, a label instructs the student to complete the assignment and a multiple-choice survey question:

You can also label the individual activities with an imperative, such as "Read about the plants around you" or "Answer a survey question about your experience with edible plants".

Assignments are always added to the **Upcoming Events** block. Even if you have no other events planned for the course (such as a field trip, discussion, chat, and so on), if you have an assignment consider adding the **Upcoming Events** block. This will serve as an additional reminder for the students.

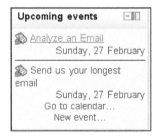

Lesson

A **Lesson** is the most complex, and most powerful, type of activity. Essentially, a **Lesson** is a series of web pages that presents information and questions.

A Moodle lesson can be a powerful combination of instruction and assessment. Lessons offer the flexibility of a web page, the interactivity of a quiz, and also provide branching capabilities.

What is a lesson?

A lesson consists of a series of web pages. Usually, a lesson page contains some instructional material, and a "jump question" about the material that the student just viewed. The "jump question" is used to test a student's understanding of the material. Get it right, and you proceed to the next item. Get it wrong, and you're either taken back to the instructional page or are taken to a remedial page. But the jump question could just as easily ask a student what he is interested in learning next, or who her favorite candidate is, or be labeled **Continue** and take the student to the next page.

The following is a screenshot of a lesson page. Its purpose is instructional. It appears like any normal web page. Indeed, you can put anything on a lesson page that you can put on any other Moodle web page.

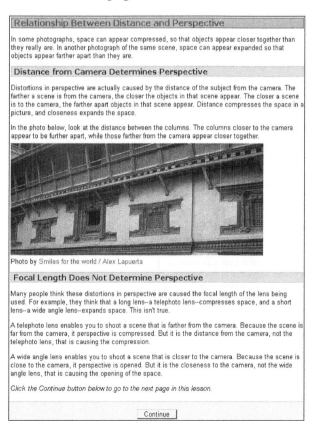

At the bottom of the lesson page is a **Continue** button. In this lesson, when the student clicks this button, (s)he is taken the question page, as shown in the following screenshot:

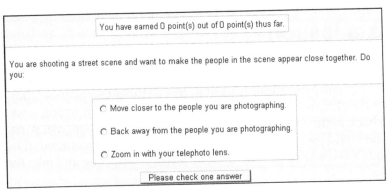

Each answer displays different feedback, just like a quiz:

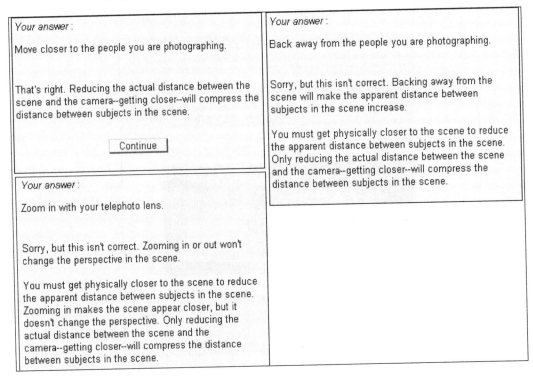

If the student answers correctly, (s)he is taken to the next instructional page. An incorrect answer takes the student to a remedial page. The following screenshot is an example of a remedial page:

Remedial: Compressing Perspective

In the photo below, the space between each of the marchers in the front row is the same:

Photo by Celeste Hutchins.

Look at the two men closest to you. You can see that the space between them is over four feet. If one of them reached out his arm, he could not touch the other:

This is the simplest sequence for a lesson in Moodle. You can also add a few, more advanced features. We'll discuss these later, after looking at the basic features.

Configuring lesson settings

When you first create a lesson, you are presented with a window where you choose settings for the entire lesson. Before you can add even a single page to a lesson, you must specify the lesson settings. If you're not sure about any of these settings, just take your best guess. You can always return to this page and change the settings later.

Remember, one of the advantages of Moodle is the ease with which you can experiment with and change your course material. Get accustomed to taking a bolder, more experimental approach to using Moodle and you will enjoy it a lot more.

The **Editing Lesson** window is broken into six areas:

- General
- Grade options
- Flow control
- Lesson formatting
- Access control
- Dependent on
- Pop-up to file or web page
- Other
- Common Module Settings

In this section, we'll go through the Editing Lesson page from top to bottom. We'll discuss most of the settings, and focus on the ones that are most useful for creating the effect of a deck of flash cards. So, by the end of this section, you will understand how most of the settings on the Editing Lesson page affect the student's experience.

General settings

Each of the **General** settings is described in the following subsection.

Name

This is the name of the lesson, which students will see on the course's home page.

Time limit

This is the time limit for the entire lesson (not for each individual page). Enabling this option displays a timer, with a countdown. The timer uses JavaScript, so to use this feature your students must have JavaScript installed and enabled in their browsers.

When the time limit is reached, the student is not ejected from the lesson. The student remains in the lesson. However, any question that the student answers after the time limit is reached does not count towards the student's grade.

Maximum number of answers/branches

At the bottom of each question page in a lesson, you can place a quiz question. **Maximum number of answers/branches** specifies the maximum number of answers that each question can have. If each answer sends the student to a different page, then the number of answers is also the number of branches possible. For True/False questions, set this to **2**. After creating question pages, you can increase or decrease this setting without affecting the questions that you have already created.

Grade options

If a lesson is being used only for practice, most of the grade options are irrelevant.

Practice lesson

If you set **Practice lesson** to **Yes**, this lesson will not show up in the Gradebook.

Custom scoring

Normally, a correct answer in a question is worth the entire point value for the question, and each wrong answer is worth zero. Enabling custom scoring allows you to set a point value for each individual answer in a question. Use this if some answers are "more right" or "more wrong" than others. You can also use this to set the point value for a question. If a specific question is more important than others in the same lesson, use custom scoring to give it more points.

Maximum grade

If you set **Maximum grade** to **0**, the lesson does not appear in any of the Grades pages, and the student's score in this lesson will not affect the student's final grade for the course.

Student can re-take

This setting determines if the student can repeat the lesson.

Handling of re-takes

This setting is relevant only if the student is allowed to repeat the lesson (the setting *Student can re-take* is set to **Yes**). When the students are allowed to re-take the lesson, the grades shown in the **Grades** page are either the average of the re-takes or the student's best grade, depending on the value of this setting.

Display ongoing score

When this is set to **Yes**, each page of the lesson displays the student's score and the number of possible points so far.

Notice that selecting this option displays the number of points that the student could have earned for the pages that , depending on the value of this setting viewed so far.

If a lesson is not linear-that is, if it branches-then the path that each student takes through the lesson can change. This means that each student can have the chance to earn a different number of points. So in a branching lesson, the "total number of points possible for the entire lesson" is not meaningful because the lesson can be different for different students. For example, you might create a lesson with many branches and pages, and then, require the student to earn at least 200 points on that lesson. This would encourage the student to explore the lesson and try different branches until (s)he has earned the required points.

Flow control

Some of the options under **Flow control** make the lesson behave more like a flash card deck. Other settings on this page become irrelevant when a lesson is used for flash cards.

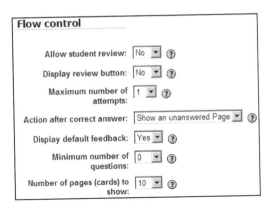

Allowing student review: Allow student review allows a student to go backwards in a lesson, and retry questions that (s)he got wrong. This differs from just using the **Back** button on the browser, in that the setting enables the student to retry questions, whereas using the **Back** button does not.

In the preceding screenshot, look at the setting for **Action after correct answer**. Notice that in this case it is set to **Show an unanswered Page**. That means that after a student answers a question correctly, Moodle will display a page that the student either hasn't seen or that (s)he answered incorrectly. The **Show an unanswered Page** setting is usually used during a flash card lesson to give the student second chances at answering questions correctly. During a practice lesson, you will usually use **Allow student review** to allow students to go back to questions that they got wrong.

Providing option to try a question again: Selecting Provide option to try a question again displays a message after the student incorrectly answers a question. The message invites the student to try the question again, but for no points:

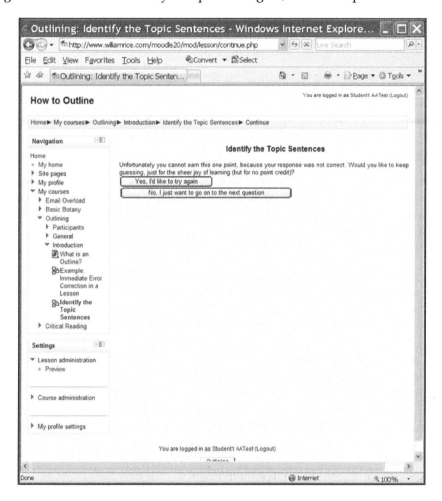

When you create a question in a **Lesson,** you can create feedback for each of the answers to that question. However, if you set **Provide option to try a question again** to **Yes,** Moodle will override the feedback that you created for the answers. Instead, it will display the message shown in the preceding screenshot.

If you created custom feedback for the answers in your **Lesson,** but Moodle is not displaying the feedback that you created, check the **Provide option to try a question again** setting. It might be set to **Yes.** Set it to **No,** and your custom feedback will be displayed.

Setting Maximum number of attempts: The **Maximum number of attempts** setting determines how many times a student can attempt any question. It applies to all questions in the lesson.

Setting Minimum number of questions: The **Minimum number of questions** setting sets the lower limit for the number of questions used to calculate a student's grade on the lesson. It is relevant only when the lesson is going to be graded. If the student doesn't answer this minimum number of questions, then the lesson is not graded.

If you don't see this setting, it is probably because you have **Practice lesson** set to **Yes**. Set **Practice lesson** to **No**, save the page, and then you should see this setting appear.

Displaying default feedback: If **Display default feedback** is set to **Yes**, if Moodle does not see any custom feedback that you created for a question, it will display a default message like "That's correct" or "That's incorrect". If you set this to **No**, and Moodle does not see any custom feedback that you created for a question, then Moodle will not display any feedback when the student answers the question.

Displaying left menu: Selecting **Display left menu** displays a navigation bar on the leftmost side of the slide show window. The navigation bar allows the student to navigate to any slide. Without this navigation bar, the student must proceed through the slide show in the order that Moodle displays the lesson pages, and must complete the lesson to exit (or the student can force the window to close). Sometimes, you want a student to complete the entire lesson, in order, before allowing him or her to move freely around the lesson. The setting for **Only display if Student has grade greater than** accomplishes this. Only if the student has achieved the specified grade will (s)he see the navigation menu. You can use this setting to ensure that the student goes completely through the lesson the first time, before allowing the student to freely move around the lesson.

Displaying Progress bar: The **Progress Bar** setting displays a progress bar at the bottom of the lesson.

The **Setting Number of pages (cards) to show** determines how many pages are shown. If the lesson contains more than this number, the lesson ends after reaching the number specified here. If the lesson contains fewer than this number, the lesson ends after every card has been shown. If you set this to zero, the lesson ends when all cards have been shown.

Flow control: Advanced settings

The settings under **Flow control**'s **Advanced** settings can be used to turn the lesson into a slide show, which appears in a pop-up window. The **Slide Show** setting creates the slide show window, when set to **Yes**. **Slide show width, height**, and **background color** set the format of the slide show. The **background color** setting uses the Web's 6-letter code for colors. This code is officially called the "Hex RGB". For a chart of these color codes, try a web search on the terms "hex rgb chart" or you can see a partial chart at http://www.w3.org/TR/2001/WD-css3-color-20010305#x11-color.

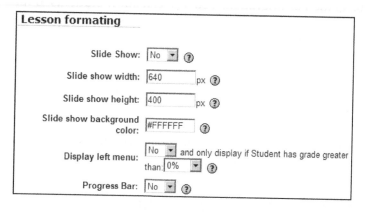

Popup to file or web page

When the student launches the lesson, you can cause a new web page or file to be launched at the same time as the lesson. This page or file will be launched in a separate window. This enables you to use the page or file as the focal point for your lesson. For example, you could launch an animation of a beating heart in a pop-up window, and use the lesson to point out parts of the heart and quiz the student on what each part does during the heartbeat.

Moodle will display the following file types in their own viewer:

MP3	Plain Text
Media Player	GIF
Quicktime	JPEG
Realmedia	PNG
HTML	

File types for which Moodle does not have a built-in viewer are launched via a download link instead.

Even if your file type is supported by one of Moodle's viewers, you might want to embed the file in a web page instead. Putting the file on a web page allows you to write an explanation at the top of the page, such as "You will refer to this graphic during the lesson. Reposition this window and the lesson window so that you can see both windows at the same time, or easily switch between the two".

If you combine this with the **Slide show** setting that we saw earlier in this chapter, you'll have the Moodle slide show displayed in one window, and the specified file displayed in another.

A lesson can be graded or ungraded. You also can allow students to retake the lesson. Even though Moodle allows you to grade a lesson, remember that a lesson's primary purpose is to teach, not to test.

 Don't use a Lesson to do the work of a Quiz or Assignment.

The lesson's score is there to give you feedback on the effectiveness of each page, and to allow students to judge their own progress.

Adding the first question page

Immediately after you save your lesson settings, Moodle presents you with the following page:

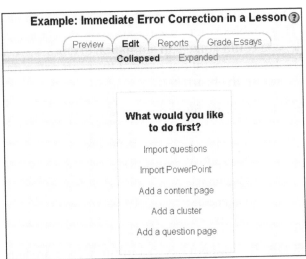

At this point, it is time to create the first question page, or import question pages from another system. Let's take a look at each of your options.

Importing questions

If you choose to **Import questions**, you can import questions created in another instance of Moodle or from other online learning systems. Some of the formats that you can import are:

GIFT and Moodle XML	These are Moodle's proprietary formats. GIFT is text only, and XML can include graphics and special characters.
Aiken	This format is used for multiple-choice questions.
Missing Word	This format is used for missing word multiple choice questions.
Blackboard	If you're converting from Blackboard to Moodle, you can export questions from Blackboard and import them into Moodle.
WebCT	This format supports multiple choices and short answers questions from WebCT.
Course Test Manager	If you're converting from Course Test Manager to Moodle, you can export questions from Course Test Manager and import them into Moodle.
Embedded Answers (Cloze)	This format is a multiple question, multiple answer question with embedded answers.

Each question that you import will create a lesson page.

Importing PowerPoint

Basic text and graphics can be imported from PowerPoint into Moodle, but advanced features are lost.

> If you've created a complex PowerPoint presentation—with animations, special text effects, branching, and other advanced features—don't expect to import those advanced features into a Moodle lesson.

Before you import your PowerPoint slideshow, you must export it as a series of web pages. This ability is built into PowerPoint, so it is not difficult and does not require additional software. But you should be aware that Moodle does not read PowerPoint files directly. Instead, it reads the web pages that PowerPoint exports.

Adding a content page

A content page consists of a page of links to the other pages in your lesson. At this point, immediately after you've finished the lesson settings page, your lesson doesn't have any pages. However, if you want to begin your lesson with a page of instructions, you can add a content page and make it jump to the next page. Creating a content page would look like this:

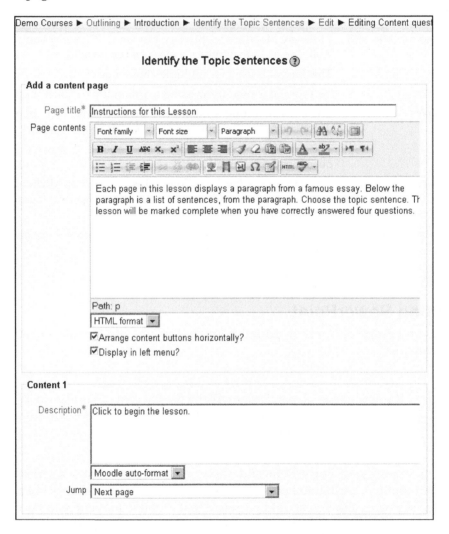

When the student runs the lesson, that content page will look like this:

▶ Introduction ▶ Identify the Topic Sentences

Identify the Topic Sentences

Instructions for this Lesson

Each page in this lesson displays a paragraph from a famous essay. Below the paragraph is a list of sentences, from the paragraph. Choose the topic sentence. The lesson will be marked complete when you have correctly answered four questions.

Click to begin the lesson.

Adding a cluster

A **cluster** is a group of question pages. Within this cluster, you can require that the student correctly answer a number of questions before being allowed to proceed out of the cluster. This enables you to test that a student understands a concept before moving on.

Alternatively, you can display a random page from the cluster, and from that page, proceed to any other page in the lesson. This enables you to send students down random pathways in the lesson, so that not all students have the same experience.

A cluster consists of a beginning cluster page, and end of cluster page, and pages in between them.

Adding a question page

This option enables you to add a question page to your lesson, using Moodle's built-in editor. The process for creating a question page is covered in the next section, *Creating the question pages*.

Try adding your question pages first. Then, put a content page with instructions at the beginning of the lesson. If necessary, organize your question pages into branches or clusters. Finally, end the lesson with a content page to say good-bye to the student.

Creating the question pages

After you fill out and save the **Settings** page, it is time to create the first question page. Even though it's called a "question page", the page can contain more than just a question. It's a web page, so you can add any content to it. Usually, it contains information and a question to test the student's understanding. You can choose from the following types of questions:

- Multiple choice
- True/false
- Short answer
- Numeric
- Matching
- Essay

You can also create feedback for each answer to the question, similar to creating feedback for the answers in a quiz question. You can also make the lesson jump to a new page, based upon the answer that the student provides.

In the following example, you can see that the question page contains some text, a graphic, and three answers to the question. Notice that for each answer, there is a **Response** that the student sees immediately after submitting the answer. There is also a **Jump** for each answer. For the two incorrect answers, the **Jump** displays the same page. This allows the student to try again. For the correct answer, the **Jump** displays the next page in the lesson.

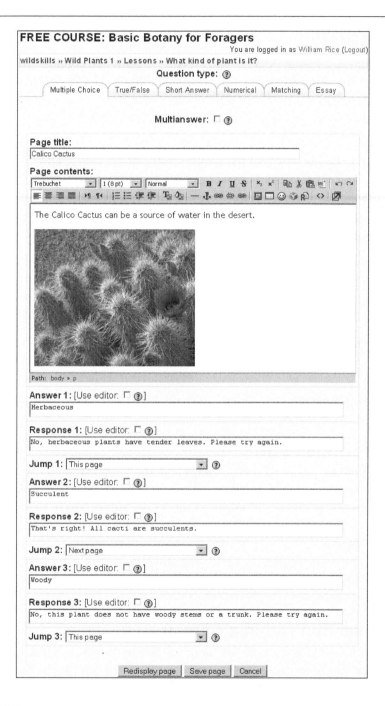

Page Title

The **Page Title** will be displayed at the top of the page when it is shown in the lesson.

Page contents

As was said before, a lesson page is really a web page. It can contain anything that you can put on any other Moodle web page. Usually, it will contain information and then a question to test the student's understanding.

Answers

The **Answers** will be displayed at the bottom of the lesson page, after the **Page Contents**. The student selects an answer in response to the question posed in the **Page Contents**.

Responses

For each **Answer** that the student selects, its **Response** is shown before the student is taken to a new page.

Jumps

Each **Answer** that a student selects results in a **Jump** to a page.

This Page

If **Jump** is set to **This page**, the student stays on the same page. The student can then answer the same question again.

Next or Previous Page

If **Jump** is set to **Next page** or **Previous page**, the student is taken to the next or previous page respectively. Be aware that this is a **relative** jump, so if. After you rearrange the pages in a lesson, this jump might give you different results.

Specific Pages

You can select a specific page to jump to. The drop-down list displays all of the lesson's pages' titles. If you select a specific page to jump to, the jump will remain the same even if you rearrange the pages in your lesson.

Unseen Question within a Cluster

Recall that a Branch Table is a table of contents, listing the pages in a lesson. When you insert a Branch Table into a lesson, you can also insert an End of Branch later in the same lesson. The pages between the Branch Table and End of Branch become a Branch. For example, a lesson with two Branches might look like this:

```
Cluster 1
Question Page
Question Page
Question Page
End of Cluster
Cluster 2
Question Page
Question Page
Question Page
End of Cluster
```

For a **Jump**, if you select **Unseen question with a branch**, the student will be taken to a question page that (s)he has not yet answered correctly in this session. That question page will be in the same cluster as the current page.

 Unseen question with a branch takes the student to a question page that (s)he hasn't answered correctly. The student might have seen the page before, but answered it incorrectly.

Random Question within a Content Page

For a **Jump**, if you select **Random question within a content page**, the student will be taken to a random question page in the same cluster as the current page.

In the **Lesson Settings** page, if **Maximum number of attempts** is set to something greater than 1, the student might see a page that (s)he has seen before, but a previously-viewed page will only be re-displayed if **Maximum number of attempts** is greater than 1. If it's set to 1, a random question page that the student has not seen before will be displayed, which has the same effect as choosing **Unseen question within a cluster**.

To restate this: When the lesson setting **Maximum number of attempts** is set to **1**, then **Random question within a content page** acts exactly like **Unseen question within a cluster**. When **Maximum number of attempts** is set to greater than 1, then **Random question within a content page** displays a truly random question.

One strategy for using this setting is to forgo the use of **Unseen question within a cluster**. Whenever you want to use **Unseen question within a cluster**, instead use **Random question within a content page** and set the **Maximum number of attempts** to 1. Then you have the option of converting all of your lessons to random jumps just by setting **Maximum number of attempts** to 2 or greater.

Creating pages and then assigning jumps

When filling out a question page, **Answer1** is automatically assumed to be the correct answer, so **Jump1** automatically reads **Nextpage**. This is because in most cases, you want a correct response to result in the next page in the lesson being displayed. However, you can select any existing page in the lesson for the jump. Note that when you are filling out the first question page, there are no other pages to jump to, so the jumps on the first page will all read **This page**. After creating more pages, you can go back and change the jumps.

 It is usually more efficient to create all of your question pages first, and then go back and assign the jumps.

The jumps that you create will determine the order in which the pages are presented to the student. For any answer, you can select a jump to the last page of the lesson. The last page displays an end-of-lesson message and, if you choose, the grade for the lesson. It also displays a link that takes the student back to the course's **Home Page**.

The flow of pages

The most obvious usag of question pages and jumps is to enforce a straight-through lesson structure. A correct answer results in a positive response, such as "That's correct!" and then jumps to the next page. An incorrect answer results in a negative response or a correction. An incorrect answer can then redisplay the page so the student can try again, as in the preceding example. (**Jump1:This page**). Alternatively, an incorrect answer can jump to a remedial page.

The order of pages that the student would follow if (s)he answered every question correctly is called the **logical order**. This is what the teacher sees when editing the lesson, and when displaying all of the pages in the same window.

Question pages without questions

In previous versions of Moodle, if you wanted a page without a question, you would need to create a question page and just not supply any answers. By omitting the answers, Moodle displayed a **Continue** link that took the student to the next page.

In Moodle 2.0, you are required to add an answer to a **Question** page. If you want an informative page without a question, then you should create a **Content** page. On the **Content** page, create just one link, which jumps to the next page.

Editing the lesson

After you've created several lesson pages, you might want to see and edit the flow of the lesson. You can do this on the **Edit** tab.

Collapsed and expanded

The **Edit** tab is where you edit the content of your lesson. From here, you add, delete, rearrange, and edit individual lesson pages.

On the **Edit** tab, when you select **Collapsed**, you see a list of all of the pages in your lesson, like the example shown in the following screenshot:

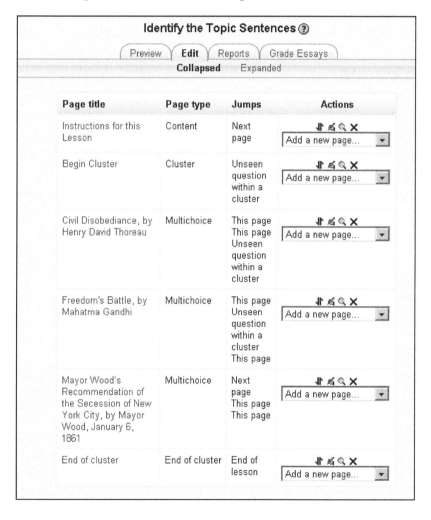

The pages are listed in their logical order, which would be the shortest path through the lesson if a student got all of the questions correct. Notice that the contents of the pages are not displayed. The purpose of this screen is not to edit individual questions, but to help you see the flow of the lesson.

Rearranging pages

To rearrange the pages, click the up/down arrow ⬍ for the page that you want to move. Note that it is the jumps that determine the order in which Moodle presents the pages. If a question is set to jump to the next page, rearranging the pages can change the jumps. A question can also be set to jump to a specific, named page. In that case the order in which the pages appear doesn't determine the landing point for the jump, so rearranging the pages here won't affect that jump.

Editing pages

From the **Edit** tab, to edit a page, click the edit icon: ✎. Clicking this takes you to the editing page for that page. The previous section in this chapter gave detailed instructions for editing a lesson page.

Adding pages

The **Add a page here** drop-down list allows you to insert a new page into the lesson. You can choose from several different kinds of pages:

- A Question page is the normal, lesson page.
- As stated before, a Content page is a page that contains links to other pages in your lesson.
- A Cluster is a group of question pages, where one is chosen at random.

Content pages

You can add a Content page, which allows students to jump to other pages in your lesson. A Content page consists of a page of links to the other pages in your lesson. This page of links can act as a table of contents. For example, suppose you're developing
a lesson on William Wallace. The traditional way of teaching about a person's life is to organize the information in a timeline. That would be easily accomplished with a straight-through lesson like the one described above. But suppose you wanted to teach about the different areas of a person's life, and they do not all fit well on a timeline.

For example, Wallace's historical achievements would fit well on a timeline. But a timeline might not be the best way to teach about Wallace's personal beliefs and religion. Wallace's family might fit well on a timeline, but background information about the culture and society in which he lived might not. A straight-through lesson might not be the best way to present Wallace's life. Instead, you might use a content page.

In this content page, each link could be an aspect of Wallace's life: historical achievements, personal beliefs, family, and the world in which he lived. At the beginning of the lesson, the student would choose a branch to explore. At the end of each branch, the student would choose between going back to the content page (beginning of the lesson), or exiting the lesson.

You can mark the end of a branch with an **End of Branch** page. This page returns the student back to the preceding content page. You can edit this return jump, but most often, you would want to leave it as it is. If you do not mark the end of a branch with an **End of Branch** page, you will proceed out of the branch and on to the next question.

Summary

Moodle's assignments and lessons allow you to create course material that students interact with. This interaction is more engaging, and usually more effective, than courses consisting of static material that the students view. While you will probably begin creating your course by adding static material, the next step should usually be to ask, "How can I add interactivity to this course?" Lessons can even take the place of many static web pages, as they consist of web pages with a question at the end of each page.

7
Evaluating Students with Quizzes, Choices, and Feedback

Moodle gives you several options for evaluating your students. In this chapter, we will cover several of those options. In this chapter, we will cover the activity types listed in the following table:

Activity	Description
Choice ?	A choice is essentially a single, multiple-choice question that the instructor asks the class. The result can be displayed to the class, or kept between the individual student and the instructor. Choices are a good way to get feedback from the students about the class. You can plant these choices in your course ahead of time, and keep them hidden until you need the students' feedback. You can also add them as needed.
Quiz ☑	Questions that you create while making a quiz in one course can be reused in other courses. We'll cover creating question categories, creating questions, and choosing meaningful question names.
Feedback ◉	???

If you want to evaluate your students' knowledge, use a Quiz. If you want to evaluate their attitude towards the class, use Feedback. And if you want to share the results of question that you pose to the class, use a Choice.

Creating quizzes

Moodle offers a flexible quiz builder. Each question is a full-featured web page that can include any valid HTML code. This means that a question can include text, images, sound files, movie files, and anything else that you can put on a web page.

In most instructor-led courses, a quiz or test is a major event. Handing out the quizzes, stopping class to take them, and grading them can take a lot of the teacher's time. In Moodle, creating, taking, and grading quizzes is much faster. This means that you can use quizzes liberally throughout your courses. For example, you can:

- Use a short quiz after each reading assignment to ensure that the students completed the reading. You can shuffle the questions and answers to prevent sharing among the students, and make the quiz available only for the week or month in which the students are supposed to complete the reading.

- Use a quiz as a practice test. Allow several attempts, and/or use the **Adaptive** mode to allow students to attempt a question until they get it right. Then the quiz becomes both practice and learning material.

- Use a quiz as a pretest. Ask the students to complete a quiz even before they come to the course. The students can complete this pretest at a time and place that is convenient for them. Then, you can compare their scores on the pretest and their scores on the final test, and confirm that learning has occurred.

Question Banks

In this chapter, you will see how to create a quiz and add questions to the quiz. During that process, keep in mind that when you create a question, you are adding that question to Moodle's Question Bank.

The Question Bank is Moodle's collection of quiz questions. A Quiz is really just a place where you choose questions from the Question Bank, and display them all together. A Quiz can be deleted, but the questions still remain in the Question Bank.

The questions in the Question Bank can be categorized and shared. The real asset in your learning site is not the Quizzes, but the Question Bank that you and your fellow teachers build over time.

Configuring quiz settings

When you first create a quiz, you see the **Settings** page. The settings that you select on this page affect only that Quiz. Also, questions are added separately from the Quiz. So while these settings affect the Quiz that you are creating, they do not affect other Quizzes or the Questions that you will be adding to the Quiz.

The **Settings** page is divided into nine areas. Let's look at the settings under each area, from top to bottom.

General

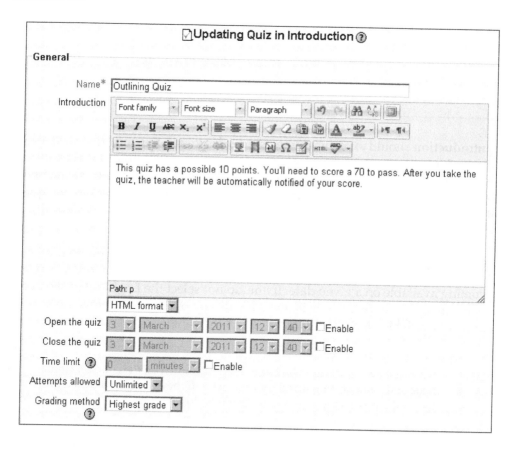

The **Name** of the quiz is displayed on the course's home page. The **Introduction** is displayed when a student selects the quiz, as shown in the following screenshot:

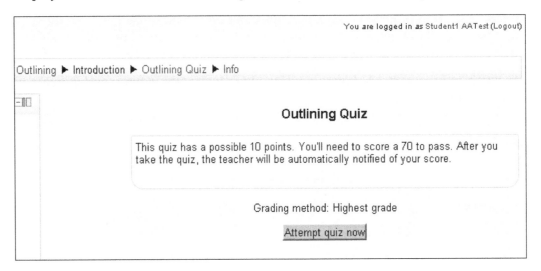

The **Introduction** should explain why the student is taking the quiz. It should also tell the student about any unusual features of the quiz, for example, if it uses an animation that requires the Flash plugin, or if it uses a pop-up window. Remember that once the student clicks on the **Attempt quiz now** button, they are into the quiz. So give the student everything they need to understand why and how to take the quiz before clicking on that button.

The **Open** and **Close** dates determine when the quiz is available. If you do not select the **Enable** checkbox for **Open the quiz**, the quiz will be permanently open, instead of becoming available on a given date. If you do not select the **Enable** checkbox for **Close the quiz**, then once the quiz is open, it will stay open permanently, instead of becoming unavailable on a given date.

 Note that even if the quiz is closed, it is still shown on the course's **Home Page** and students might still try to select it. If they do select a closed quiz, the students see a message saying that it is closed.

If you want to hide a quiz, further down on this page you will see the setting **Visible**. Change this setting to **Hide**, and the quiz will no longer be visible.

By default, a quiz does not have a **Time limit**. If you want to set a time limit, use this setting. When time runs out, the quiz is automatically submitted with the answers that have been provided up to that point. A time limit can help to prevent the use of reference materials while taking the quiz. For example, if you want students to answer the questions from memory, but all the answers are in the course textbook, setting a timer might discourage students from taking the time to look up the answer to each question.

Attempts allowed can be used to limit the number of times that a student can take the quiz. Further down the page, you can choose settings that require the student to wait between attempts. If, and only if, you enable multiple attempts, the time delay settings will take effect.

Layout

The settings under **Layout** control the order of the questions in the quiz, and how many questions appear on a page.

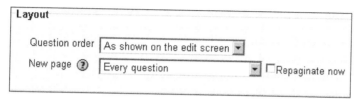

Question order determines whether the questions appear in the order that you place them when editing the questions, or in a random order. The random order will change each time the quiz is displayed. This discourages the sharing of quiz answers among students, and encourages them to focus on the wording when they retake a quiz.

New page determines where page breaks will fall. Will you have a page break after every question, every 2 questions, and so on? On the page where you edit the questions for the quiz, you can move these page breaks.

By default, all questions in a quiz are displayed on the same page. **New page** breaks the quiz up into smaller pages. Moodle inserts the page breaks for you. On the **Editing quiz** page, you can move these page breaks. If you want to break up your quiz into pages so that each hold the same number of questions, then this setting will work for you. If you want to break up your quiz into pages that hold different numbers of questions, then use this setting anyway, and edit the page breaks that Moodle creates for you.

Question behavior

The setting **Shuffle within questions** enables you to present the parts of a question in random order. This only works if three conditions are true. First, this option must be set to **Yes**. Second, the question must have several parts, for example as a multiple choice question or a matching question. This setting has no effect on something like a fill-in-the-blank question. Third, each question also has a "shuffle" setting of its own, and that must also be set to **Yes**.

The **Adaptive mode** setting allows multiple attempts **for each question**. This is different from **Attempts allowed**, which allows multiple attempts at the whole quiz. When you make a quiz adaptive, each question offers you the option to:

- Display a message if the student answered incorrectly, and redisplay the question.
- Display a message if the student answered incorrectly, and then display a different question.

Clicking on the **Show Advanced** button reveals two more settings.

Apply penalties will subtract a penalty from the quiz score, for a wrong answer. For each question that the student answers incorrectly, points are subtracted from the student's score. You can choose the penalty for each question when you create that question. This only works if three conditions are true. First, **Adaptive mode** must be set to **Yes**. Second, **Apply penalties** must also be set to **Yes**. Third, an amount for the penalty must be specified; this is done in the question itself.

Each attempt builds on the last only has an effect if multiple attempts are allowed. When this is enabled, each attempt that a student makes will display the results of the student's previous attempt. The student can then see how they answered and scored on the previous attempt.

The setting for **Each attempt builds on the last** is especially useful when you are using a quiz as a teaching tool, instead of an evaluation tool. **Attempts allowed** allows the student to keep trying the quiz. **Each attempt builds on the last** retains the answers from one attempt to another. Taken together, these two settings can be used to create a quiz that the student can keep trying until they gets it right. This transforms the quiz from a test into a learning tool.

Review options

Review options determine what information a student can see when they reviews a quiz, and when they can see that information.

Review options ⑦

Immediately after the attempt	Later, while the quiz is still open	After the quiz is closed
☑ Responses	☑ Responses	☐ Responses
☑ Answers	☑ Answers	☐ Answers
☑ Feedback	☑ Feedback	☐ Feedback
☑ General feedback	☑ General feedback	☐ General feedback
☑ Scores	☑ Scores	☐ Scores
☑ Overall feedback	☑ Overall feedback	☐ Overall feedback

The information the student can see is shown below:

Setting	Type of information displayed to the student
Responses	This is all of the answers that student had to choose from for a question.
Answers	These are the answers that the student chose.
Feedback	Each response for a question can have its own feedback. This setting refers to the feedback for each response that the student selected (that is, the feedback for each of the student's answers).
General feedback	Each question can have its own feedback. This feedback is displayed regardless of how the student answered the question. This setting displays that general feedback for each question.
Scores	The student's scores, or points earned, for each question.
Overall feedback	Overall feedback is given for the student's score on the quiz.

The settings for when the information is revealed are as follows:

Time Period	Meaning
Immediately after the attempt	Within two minutes of finishing the quiz.
Later, while the quiz is still open	Two minutes after the quiz is finished, for as long as the quiz is available to the student.
After the quiz is closed	After the date and time set in **Close the quiz** has passed. If you never close the quiz, this setting has no effect.

Display

The settings under **Display** affect information that is displayed while the student is taking the quiz.

If **Show the user's picture is set** to **Yes**, then while the student is taking the quiz, the student's profile picture and name will be displayed in the quiz window. This makes it easier for an exam proctor to confirm that the student is logged in as him or herself. The proctor can just look over the student's shoulder and see the student's picture and name on this screen.

The settings for **Decimal places in grades** and **Decimal places in question grades** affect the display of the grades that are shown to the student. The first setting affects the display of the overall grade for the quiz. The second setting affects the display of the grade for each, individual question.

No matter how many decimal places you display, Moodle's database calculates the grades with full accuracy.

When you create a course, you can add blocks to the left side bar and the right side bars. The setting for **Show blocks during quiz attempts** determines if these blocks are displayed while the student is taking the quiz. Normally, this is set to **No** so that the student is not distracted while taking the quiz.

Extra restrictions on attempts

If you enter anything into the **Require password** field, the student must enter that password to access the quiz.

With **Require network address**, you can restrict access to the quiz to particular IP address(es). For example:

- 146.203.59.235 is a single IP address. It would permit a single computer to access the quiz. If this computer is acting as a proxy, the other computers "behind" it can also access the quiz.
- 146.203 is a range of IP addresses. It would permit any IP address starting with those numbers. If those numbers belong to your company, then you effectively limit access to the quiz to your company's campus.
- 146.203.59.235/20 is a subnet. It would permit the computers on that subnet to access the quiz.

The **Enforced delay** settings prevent students from attempting the quiz without waiting between attempts. If you show the students the correct answers after they submit the quiz, you might want to set a delay between attempts. This prevents students from attempting the quiz, seeing the correct answers, and then immediately trying the quiz again while those answers are fresh in their memory.

If **Browser security** is set to **Full-screen popup...**, the quiz is launched in a new browser window. It uses JavaScript to disable copying, saving, and printing. However, this security is not foolproof and ins intended more as a deterrent.

Techniques for greater security

You should understand that the only way to make a test secure, is to give the test on paper, separate the students far enough apart so that they can't see each other's papers, place a proctor in the room to observe the students, and use different questions for each group that takes the test. There is no way to make a web-based test completely cheat proof. If you absolutely must give a web-based test that is resistant to cheating, consider these strategies:

- Create a very large number of questions, but have the quiz show only a small set of them. This makes the sharing of questions less useful.

- Shuffle the questions and the answers. This also makes the sharing of questions more difficult.

- Apply a time limit. This makes using reference material more difficult.

- Open the quiz for only a few hours. Have your students schedule the time to take the quiz. Make yourself available during this time to help with technical issues.

- Place one question on each page of the quiz. This discourages students from taking screenshots of the entire quiz.

Grades

If you allow several attempts, the grading method determines which grade is recorded in the course's gradebook: the **Highest**, **Average**, **First**, or **Last** grade.

Apply penalties only applies when a quiz is adaptive. For each question the student answers wrongly, points are subtracted from the student's score. You can choose the penalty for each question when you create that question. (See the setting for Adaptive, above)

Decimal digits apply to the student's grade.

Students may review

The **Students may review** setting controls if and when a student can review his/ her attempts at the quiz. If you allow the student to review the quiz **Immediately after** submitting his/her answers, but not **Later** or **After the quiz is closed**, then the student can review the quiz only once, immediately after submission. When the student navigates away from that review page, they will no longer be able to review the quiz.

In the matrix, **Responses** means the student's answers to the questions. **Scores** is the point value for each question. **Feedback** is individual feedback for each question. **Answers** is the correct answer(s) for each question. **General feedback** is feedback for the entire quiz.

Security

Show quiz in a "secure" window launches the quiz in a new browser window. JavaScript is used to disable copying, saving, and printing. This security is not foolproof. If you enter anything into **Require password**, the student must enter that password to access the quiz.

Overall feedback

Moodle enables you to create several different kinds of feedback for a quiz. You can create feedback for:

- The entire quiz, which changes with the student's score. This is called **Overall Feedback**, and uses a feature called **Grade Boundary**.

- A question, no matter what the student's score was on that question. All students receive the same feedback. This is called **General Feedback**. Each individual question can have its own **General Feedback**. The exact type of feedback that you can create for a question varies with the type of question.

- A response. This is feedback that the student receives when they selects that response (that answer) to a question.

The following screenshot shows **Overall Feedback** with **Grade Boundaries**. Students who score 90−100% on the quiz receive the first feedback, "You're a wizard..." Students who score 80−89.99% receive the second feedback, "Very good!...":

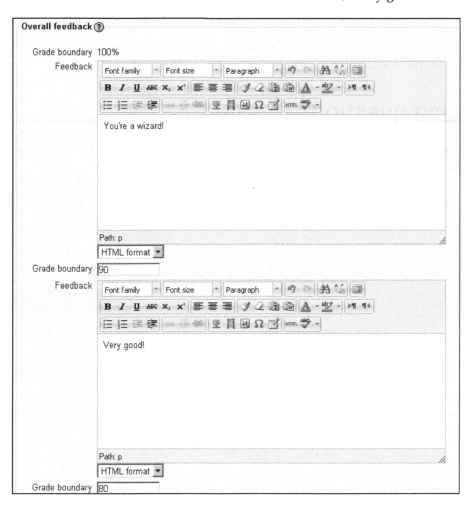

Common Module settings

Group mode works the same as it does for any other resource. However, because each student takes the quiz themselves, the only real use for the group setting in a quiz is to display the high score for a group in the **Quiz Results** block.

Visible shows or hides the quiz from students, but, as always, a teacher or course creator can still see the quiz.

Adding questions to a quiz

After you've selected the quiz from your course home page, you can add questions to the quiz. First, select **Settings | Quiz Administration | Edit quiz**. On the **Editing quiz** page, you can see the **Add a question...** button:

Before we look at detailed instructions for creating new questions, look at the button labeled **Question Bank contents**. Also, on the **Quiz administration** menu, you can see the option for **Question bank**. These enable you to work with the Question Bank.

The Question Bank

The Question Bank is the collection of quiz questions for your Moodle site. You have access to different questions in the Bank, depending upon where you are in your site.

In the following screenshot, the user is in the **Outlining** course. The user selected the Question Bank, and is now selecting the group of questions to work with:

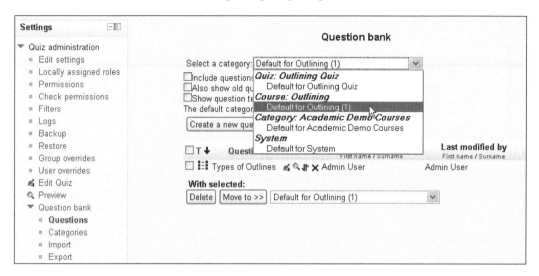

Notice that the user can select questions that are stored for just this quiz (**Quiz: Outlining Quiz**), questions that are stored for this course (**Course: Outlining**), the category in which the course resides (**Category: Academic Demo Courses**), or the entire site (**System**). If the user switched to another course, the questions for this quiz and course would be unavailable. But, questions for the new course would be available. Questions for the system are always available.

Sharing questions

If you want the questions that you create for this quiz to be available to other users of the site, then create the questions under **Question bank** and move them to the **Category** or to the **System** lists. Note that being able to access a question category depends on your security settings.

As shown in the section *Add questions to a quiz*, you can create questions directly to a quiz. As shown in the preceding section, you can also create questions in the Question Bank, and then later add these to the quiz. If you're in a hurry to create questions for a quiz, select **Edit Quiz** and start creating them. You can move them to the Question Bank later, if required.

You can display questions from one category at a time. To select that category, use the **Category** drop-down list.

If a question is deleted when it is still being used by a quiz, then it is not removed from the Question Bank. Instead, the question is hidden. The setting **Also show old questions** enables you to see questions that were deleted from the category. These deleted (or hidden, or old,) questions appear in the list with a blue box icon next to them.

 To keep your Question Bank clean and to prevent teachers from using deleted questions, you can move all of the deleted questions into a category called "Deleted questions". Create the category "Deleted questions" and then use **Also show old questions** to show the deleted questions. Select them and move them into "Deleted questions".

Moving questions between categories

To move a question into a category, you must have access to the target category. This means that the target category must be published, so that teachers in all courses can see it.

Select the question(s) to move, select the category, and then click on the **Move to** button.

Managing the proliferation of questions and categories

As the site administrator, you might want to monitor the creation of new question categories to ensure that they are logically named, don't have a lot of overlap, and are appropriate for the purpose of your site. As these question categories and the questions in them are shared among course creators, they can be a powerful tool for collaboration. Consider using the site-wide **Teachers forum** to notify your teachers and course creators of new questions and categories.

Creating and editing question categories

Every question belongs to a category. You manage question categories on the **Categories** tabbed page. There will always be a **Default** category, but before you create new questions, you might want to check to ensure that you have an appropriate category in which to put them.

To add a new category, do the following:

1. Select **Quiz administration | Question bank | Categories**.
2. Scroll to the **Add category** section, at the bottom of the page.

3. Select a **Parent** for the category. If you select **Top,** the category will be a top-level category. Or, you can select any other category to which you have access, and then the new category will be a child of the selected category.

4. In the **Name** field, enter a name for the new category.

5. In the **Category Info** field, enter a description of the new category.

6. Click on the **Add category** button.

To edit a category, do the following:

1. Select **Quiz administration | Question bank | Categories.**

2. Next to the **Category,** click on the ✍ icon. The **Edit categories** page is displayed.

3. You can edit the **Parent, Category name, Category Info,** and **Publish** settings.

4. When you have finished, click on the **Update** button. Your changes are saved and you are returned to the **Edit categories** page.

Creating a question

1. To create a quiz question, begin by selecting **Quiz administration | Edit Quiz.** Then, next to **Question Bank** contents, click on the **Show** link. The page will then display the questions that have been added to this quiz, and will also show the Question Bank.

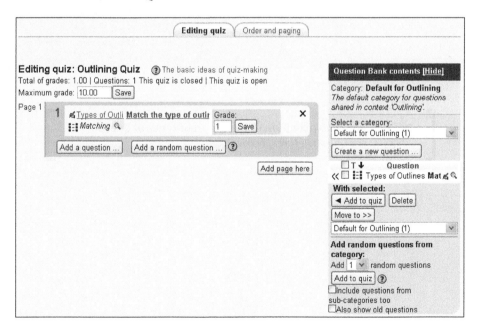

This is a two-step process. First, you will create a question, and then you will add this question to your quiz.

To create a question, do the following:

1. Click on the **Create a new question** button.
2. From the pop-up window, select the type of question that you want to create.

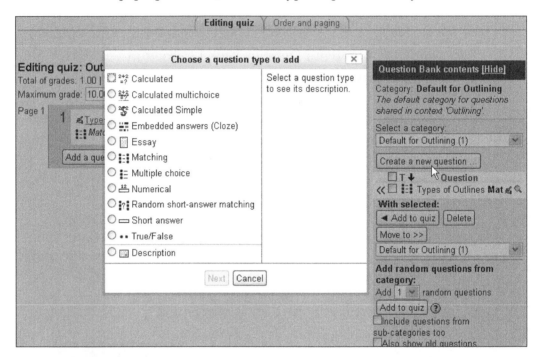

 For an explanation of the different types of questions, see *Question types*, below.

3. Click on the **Next** button. This brings you to the editing page for that question. The editing page will be different for each type of question, but some features are the same for all types of questions.

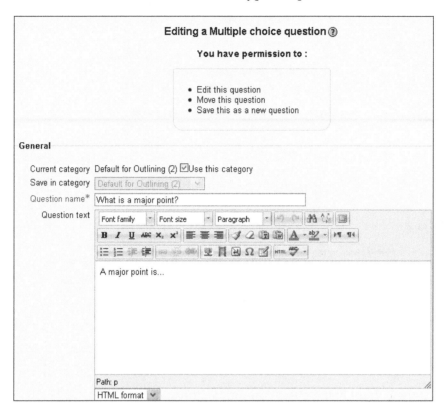

4. The **Name** of the question is what the teacher will see when building and reviewing the quiz. Students don't see this field. Make the name meaningful to the teacher. For example, "Leaf Question 1" would not be a very descriptive name, but "PrinciplesofBio-Chap8-Pg3" would tell you the source of that question. If you forget what a question says, you can always click on the 🔍 button next to the question to preview it.

5. The **Question text** is the actual question that the students will see.

6. **General feedback** is feedback that students will see for this question, no matter which answer they gave. For more about question feedback, see the section *Adding feedback to Questions and Quizzes*, earlier in this chapter.

7. Enter the choices (answers) for the question.

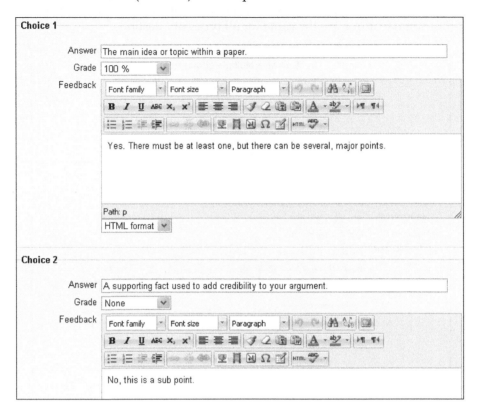

8. At the bottom of the page, you can tag the question.

9. After you save the question, it is added to the list of questions in that category.

10. To add the question to the quiz, select the checkbox next to the question, and then click on the **Add to quiz** button.

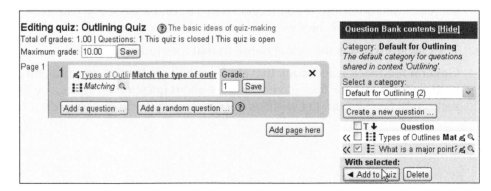

Question types

The following table explains the types of questions that you can create, and gives some tips for using them.

Type of question	Description and tips for using
Calculated	When you create a calculated question, you enter a formula that is displayed in the text of the question. The formula can contain one or more wildcards, which are replaced with numbers when the quiz is taken. Wildcards are enclosed in curly brackets.
	For example, if you type the question **What is 3 * {a}?**, Moodle will replace {a} with a random number. You can also enter wildcards into the answer field, so that the correct answer is **3 * {a}**. When the quiz is run, the question will display **What is 3 * {a}?** and the correct answer will be the calculated value of **3 * {a}**.
Description	This is not a question. It displays whatever web content you enter. When you add a description question, Moodle gives you the same editing screen as when you create a web page.
	Recall that under the **Quiz** tab, you can set page breaks in a quiz. If you want to break your quiz into sections, and fully explain each section before the student completes it, consider putting a **Description** on the first page of the section. For example, the Description could say "The following 3 questions are based on this chart," and show the chart just once.
Essay	When the student is given an essay question, they use Moodle's online rich-text editor to answer the question. However, if there is more than one essay question on a page, the rich-text editor appears only for the first essay question. This is a limitation of Moodle. To work around this, insert page breaks in your quiz so that each essay question appears on its own page. You enter page breaks on the **Quiz** tabbed page.
	Also, you might want to instruct your students to save their essay every few minutes.
Matching	After you create a matching question, you then create a list of subquestions, and enter the correct answer for each subquestion. The student must match the correct answer with each question. Each subquestion receives equal weight for scoring the question.

Type of question	Description and tips for using
Embedded Answers (Cloze)	An embedded answers question consists of a passage of text, with answers inserted into the text. Multiple-choice, fill-in-the-blank, and numeric answers can be inserted into the question. Moodle's help file gives the following example:

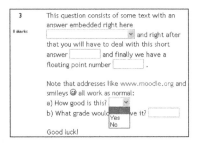

Notice that the question presents a drop-down list first, which is essentially a multiple-choice question. Then, it presents a short answer (fill-in-the-blank) question, followed by a numeric question. Finally, there's another multiple-choice question (the Yes/No drop-down) and another numeric question.

There is no graphical interface for creating embedded answers questions. You need to use a special format that is explained in the help files.

Multiple Choice	Multiple choice questions allow a student to select a single answer, or multiple answers. Each answer can count toward a specified percentage of the question's total point value.

When you allow a student to select only a single answer, you usually assign a positive score to the one correct answer and zero or negative points to all of the other, incorrect, answers. When you allow the student to select multiple answers, you usually assign partial positive points to each correct answer. That's because you want all of the correct answers to total 100%. You also usually assign negative points to each incorrect answer. If you don't bring down the question's score for each wrong answer, then the student can score 100% on the question just by selecting all of the answers. The negative points should be equal to or greater than the positive points, so that if a student just selects all of the answers, they won't get a positive score for the question. Don't worry about the student getting a negative score for the question, because Moodle doesn't allow that to happen-zero is the lowest possible score.

On the **Editing Quiz** page, if you have chosen to shuffle the answers, check all of the multiple choice questions that you use in the quiz. If any of them have answers like "All of the above" or "Both A. and C." then shuffling answers will ruin those questions. Instead, change them to multiple-answer questions, and give partial credit for each correct answer. For example, instead of "Both A. and C." you would say, "Select all that apply" and then give partial credit for A. and for C.

Type of question	Description and tips for using
Short Answer	The student types a word or phrase into the answer field. This is checked against the correct answer or answers. There may be several correct answers, with different grades.
	Your answers can use the asterisk a wildcard. You cam also set the answers to be case sensitive.
Numerical	Just as with a short-answer question, the student enters an answer into the answer field. However, the answer to a numerical question can have an acceptable error, which you set when creating the question. For example, you can designate that the correct answer is 5, plus or minus 1. Then, any number from 4 to 6 inclusive will be marked correct.
Random	When this type of question is added to a quiz, Moodle draws a question at random from the current category. The question is drawn at the time that the student takes the quiz. The student will never see the same question twice during a single attempt at the quiz, no matter how many random questions you put into the quiz. This means that the category you use for your random questions must have at least as many questions as the random ones that you add to the quiz.
Random Short-Answer Matching	Recall that a matching question consists of subquestions, and answers that must be matched to each subquestion. When you select **Random Short-Answer Matching**, Moodle draws random short-answer questions from the current category. It then uses those short-answer questions, and their answers, to create a matching question.
	To the student, this looks just like any other matching question. The difference is that the subquestions were drawn at random from short-answer questions in the current category.
True/False	The student selects from two options: True or False.

Adding feedback to a question

Moodle allows you to create several different kinds of feedback for a quiz. You can create feedback for:

- The entire quiz, which changes with the student's score. This is called Overall Feedback, and uses a feature called Grade Boundary.

- A question. The exact type of feedback that you can create for a question varies according to the type of question. In this section, we'll look at feedback for multiple choice questions. In the next section, *Assemble the Quiz*, we'll look at feedback for the entire quiz.

Types of feedback for a question

For a multiple choice question, you can create three kinds of feedback:

Type of feedback	Explanation and when to use it
General Feedback	If you create general feedback for a question, no matter what answer the student chooses, they will receive that feedback. Every student who answers the question gets the general feedback. If you think the student might get the correct answer by guessing, then you can use general feedback to explain the method of arriving at the correct answer. Also, consider using general feedback to explain the importance of the question.
Any correct response	A multiple choice question can have multiple answers that are 100% correct. For example, "From the list of people below, select one person who signed the Declaration of Independence." That list could include several people who signed, and each of them would be 100% correct. If the student selects any of those 100% correct answers, they will see the feedback for **Any correct response**. This is useful when you want to teach the student which answers are 100% correct, and why they are correct.
For any partially correct response	You can create a multiple choice question that requires the student to select several choices to get full credit. For example, "From the list of people below, select the two people who signed the Declaration of Independence." In that case, you could give each response a value of 50%. The student needs to choose both correct responses to receive the full point value for the question. If the student selects some - but not all - of the correct choices, they will see the feedback for **Any partially correct response**. This is useful when you want to teach the student the relationship between the correct responses.
For any incorrect response	Any response with a percentage value of zero or less is considered an incorrect response. If a student selects any incorrect response, they will see the feedback for **Any incorrect response**. This is useful when all incorrect responses have something in common, and you want to give the feedback about that commonality.

Remember that these types of feedback are not activated because the student chose a specific response. They are activated because the student chose any correct, partially correct, or incorrect response.

If you want to create feedback for individual responses, we will discuss that in the following section. *Feedback for individual responses*.

Feedback for individual responses

You can create feedback for any individual response to a question. A response is an answer that the student chooses or types. Each response can display its own feedback.

In the following example, notice how each response has its own feedback. In this example, if a student selects an incorrect response, they will see feedback for that specific response, and also the feedback for any incorrect response.

The following screenshot shows a multiple-choice question that uses several kinds of feedback. You're seeing this question from the course creator's point of view, not the student's. First, you can see General Feedback, "The truth is, most New Yorkers have never even thought about the "missing Fourth Avenue" issue.". After the question is scored, every student sees this feedback, no matter what the student's score.

Following that, you can see that **Choice 1** through **Choice 4** contain feedback for each response. This feedback is customized to the response. For example, if a student selects **Sixth Avenue** the feedback is "Nope, that name is taken. Sixth is also known as the "Avenue of the Americas."".

For this question, we don't need any feedback under **Any correct answer** or **Partially correct answer**. Those options are useful when you have multiple responses that are correct, or responses that are partially correct. In this case, only one response is correct and all other responses are incorrect.

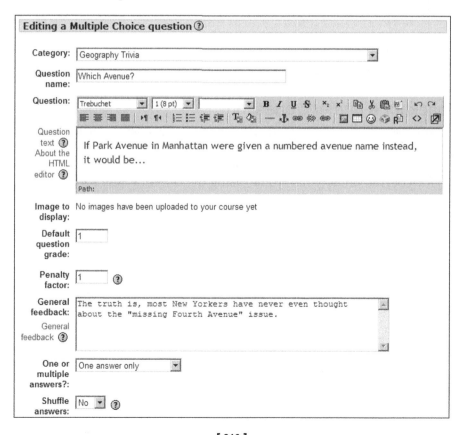

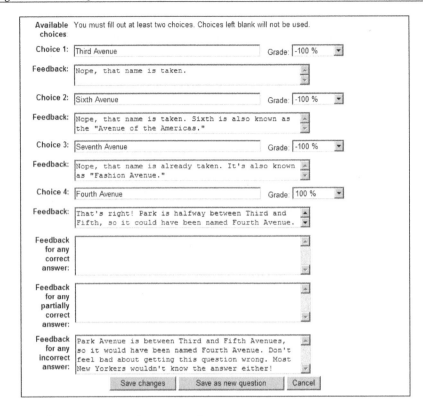

Feedback for a numeric question

The following screenshot shows feedback for a numeric answer question. In this screenshot, notice that the course creator is not using the HTML editor. Instead, the course creator is editing the questions in plain text. You can turn the HTML editor off or on for yourself under your Profile, using the **HTML Editor** setting.

Notice that the **General Feedback** explains how the question is solved. This feedback is displayed to everyone after answering the question, even those who answered correctly. You might think that if the student answered correctly, they don't need this explanation. However, if the student guessed or used a different method than that given in the **General Feedback**, explaining the solution can help the student learn from the question.

In a numeric answer question, the student types in a number for the answer. This means the student could enter literally any number. It would be impossible to create customized feedback for every possible answer, because the possibilities are infinite. However, you can create customized feedback for a reasonable number of answers. In this question, we've created responses for the most likely incorrect answers. After we've given this test to the first group of students, we'll need to review their responses for the most frequent incorrect answers. If there are any that we haven't covered, we'll need to add them to the feedback for this question.

In the following screenshot, notice that each response has customized feedback. **Answer 1** is correct. **Answer 2** would be the result of switching the two numbers while trying to solve the problem. Because this is a likely error, we've included feedback just for that answer, explaining the error the student made. **Answer 3** is the result of interpreting b3 as "b times 3" instead of "b cubed". This is also a likely error, so we've included feedback for that answer. **Answer 4** is a wildcard, and applies if the student submitted any answer other than the three above it.

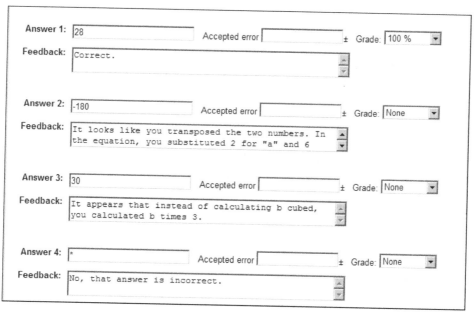

Assembling the quiz

After you have created the questions, you can begin adding the questions to a quiz. With the quiz selected, select **Settings | Quiz administration | Edit Quiz**.

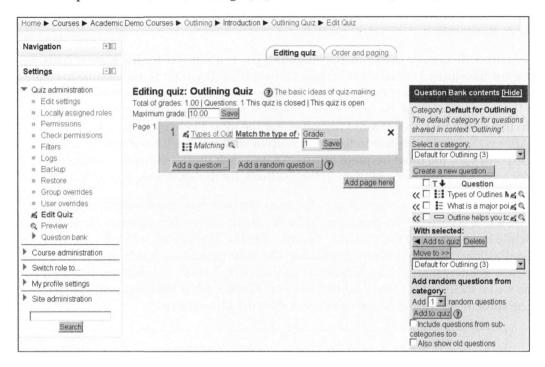

Most of the functions on the **Edit Quiz** page are self-explanatory. However, here are some tips for using them. Generally, you'll use the **Editing quiz** tabbed page to assemble the quiz, and the **Order and paging** tabbed page to place the questions in order and create page breaks.

The Editing quiz tabbed page

Under the **Editing quiz** tabbed page, you can:

- Add questions from the Question Bank.
- Create new questions.
- Assign each question a number of points.
- Assign the quiz a total number of points.

Let's look at some of the functions available on this tabbed page.

Maximum grade

The quiz's **Maximum grade** is the quiz's point contribution towards the course. In this example, the quiz is worth 10 points towards the student's total for the course.

The grade for each question will be scaled to the quiz's **Maximum grade**. For example, if this quiz had five questions worth 1 point each, but the **Maximum grade** is 10, then each question will contribute 2 points to the student's total grade for the course.

Grade for each question

Each question has a point value. The question's point value is scaled to the quiz's **Maximum grade**. For example, if a question has a grade of 2, and the quiz has a maximum value of 10, then that question is worth one-fifth of the quiz's grade.

In the preceding example, you can see that the maximum grade for the quiz is 10, and the grade for the question is 1. However, this is a matching question, with four choices. We would probably make this question worth 4 points, so that each correct match is worth 1 point.

Using the Question Bank contents

On the rightmost side of the page, you can see an area labeled **Question Bank contents**. You must click on the **unhide** link to display this area.

From the Question Bank, you can add questions that are stored under the:

- Quiz
- Course
- Category
- System

You can also create new questions from this page.

To add a question from the Question Bank:

1. Select the category that holds the question:

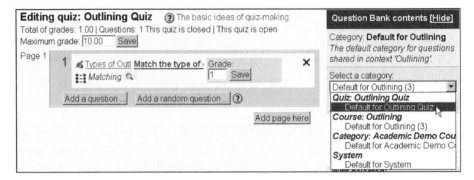

2. Select the question that you want to add, by selecting the checkbox next to the question.

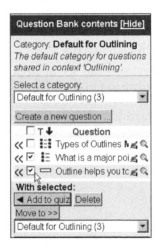

3. Click on the **Add to quiz** button, and the selected question(s) are added to the quiz.

4. Remember to assign a **Grade** to the questions that you add.

Adding random questions to a quiz

You can add a number of random questions to your quiz. In the following screenshot, notice that there are three questions in the selected category. Also notice that the user can add a maximum of three random questions from this category:

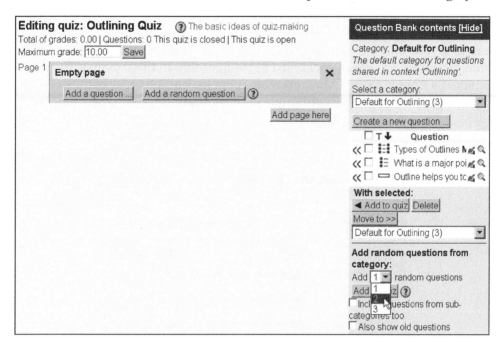

You can add random questions from several categories to the same quiz.

On the same attempt, the student will never see the same random question twice. However, the questions are reset between attempts, so a student could see the same question twice if they attempt the same quiz twice.

If a question is deleted when it is still being used by a quiz, then it is not removed from the question bank. Instead, the question is hidden. The setting **Also show old questions** enables you to inlcude questions that were deleted from the category. These deleted (or hidden, or old,) questions appear in the list with a blue box next to them.

The Order and paging tabbed page

You can change the order and page breaks on your quiz on the **Editing quiz** tabbed page. However, you have more options under the **Order and paging** tabbed page. Let's look at what you can do under that tab.

Changing the order of questions

You have several ways to rearrange questions. First, you can specify their order by entering a number into the field next to the question. In this example, the user has entered a 12 next to the **D.E.C.** question. Let's look at the order of the questions before the user clicks on the **Reorder questions** button:

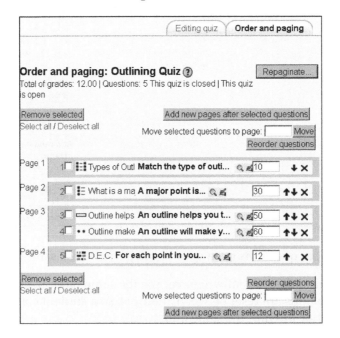

After clicking on **Reorder questions**, notice that the **D.E.C.** question has moved to second place. Note that Moodle has changed the ordering number for the question to **20 Page 4** is now empty, and can be deleted:

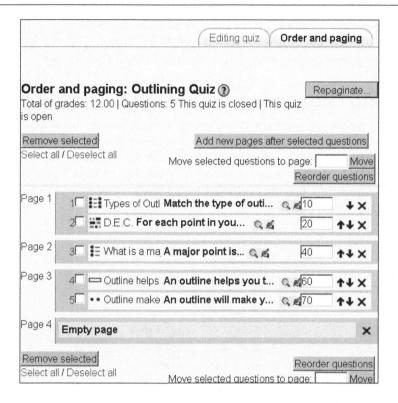

Another way to rearrange questions is to click on the up and down arrows next to each question.

Finally, you can select a question or questions using the check box to the left of each question, enter the page number for those questions into the box labeled **Move selected questions to page:**, and then click on the **Move** button.

Changing page breaks

If you put all of the questions in the quiz onto one page, if the student's browser refreshes or freezes before the quiz is submitted, they will lose the answers that they have already selected on that page. To avoid this, use page breaks to put a few questions on each page, so that your student can't lose more than a page of work.

 To remove a page, you should first move all the questions off that page, and then click on the **X** on the page.

To add a page, select the question that you want to precede the new page, and then click on the **Add new pages after selected questions** button. If you select several questions, then a new page is added after each of those questions.

Preventing Glossary auto linking in quiz questions

If you have a Glossary in your course, glossary words that are used in quiz questions will link to the associated glossary entries. If you don't want students to have this resource when they take the quiz, then go to the Glossary and change the setting **Automatically link glossary entries** to **No**. Alternatively, when typing a glossary word in a quiz question, use the online editor's HTML view to add the tag **<nolink> </nolink>** to the word, like this:

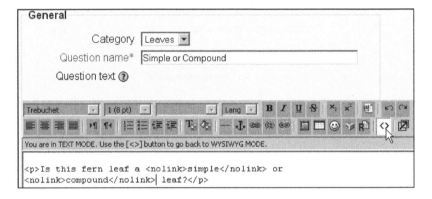

Preventing an open-book quiz

In most Moodle courses, quizzes are "open–book" affairs. This is because when the student is taking an online course, there is nothing to prevent the student from looking things up. If you want to prevent this, you can do so, with some manual intervention.

The easiest way to prevent a quiz from becoming "open book" is to put that quiz into a separate course topic, by itself. Then, hide all of the other course topics. This can be done with single click on each topic. Administer the quiz, and redisplay the topics afterwards.

Feedback

The Feedback module allows you to create surveys for your students. Do not confuse this with the Survey activity. In a Survey, you must choose from several pre-built surveys; you cannot build your own surveys. Also, do not confuse this with the Questionnaire module. The Questionnaire module is an add-on, whereas Feedback comes standard with Moodle 2.0.

Feedback isn't just for students

Obviously, you can use a Feedback activity to survey your students. But you can also use it for other purposes, for example to:

- Conduct a survey of the employees in your work place
- Collect data from people who have agreed to be research subjects
- Conduct public opinion surveys of the visitors to your site

The Feedback activity allows you to create different kinds of questions: multiple choices, drop-down selection, short answers, and more. You can share the results of a Feedback activity with the students, or keep it confidential.

Creating a Feedback activity

Creating a Feedback activity is similar to adding a Quiz. First, you add the activity, and then you add the questions. We'll cover both of these tasks in a separate section below.

To add a Feedback activity, do the following:

1. From the **Add an activity...** menu, select **Feedback**. Moodle displays the settings page for the activity.
2. In the **Name** field, enter a name for the Feedback activity. Your students will see this on the course home page.
3. Text and graphics that enter into the **Description** field, is displayed to students before they begin the activity. Use this information to explain the activity. Remember, this is a full-featured HTML editor, so you can put text, graphics, and media into the **Description**.
4. Under **Timing**, you can enter a time to open and close the activity. If you don't enter a time to open the activity, it is available immediately. If you don't enter a time to close the activity, it will remain open indefinitely.
5. The option to **Record User Names** affects only what the teacher sees. Students do not see each others' responses. If **Record User Names** is set to **Users' Names Will Be Logged and Shown With Answers**, then the teacher will be able to see a list of users who completed the Feedback, along with their answers.
6. If **Show analysis page after submit** is set to **Yes**, a summary of their results so is shown to the user after they submit their feedback.
7. If **Send E-Mail-notifications** is set to **Yes**, then course administrators are emailed whenever someone submits this feedback. This includes Teachers and Course Managers.

8. If **Multiple submissions** is set to **Yes**, then users can submit their feedback multiple times. When **Record User Names** is set to **Anonymous**, this setting is enabled and an unlimited number of anonymous users can submit feedback an unlimited number of times. When you track user names, this option allows each logged-in user to submit feedback an unlimited number of times.

Get this setting right the first time.

For some reason, Moodle doesn't allow you to change the **Multiple submissions** setting after someone has answered the Feedback activity. So you need to get this setting right before people start answering.

9. If you want Moodle to number the questions in your Feedback activity, select **Yes** for **Automated numbers**.

10. The page that you compose under **Page after submit** is displayed immediately after the user submits their answers. You can use this page to explain what happens after the activity. If you leave this blank, Moodle displays a simple message telling the user that their answers have been saved. At the bottom of this page, Moodle displays a **Continue** button.

11. The **URL for continue** field specifies the Web address of a page that you want the user to see after they view the **Page after submit**. If you leave this blank, the **Continue** button will take the user back to the course home page.

Careful with the URL for continue button!

You might be tempted to use the **URL for continue** button to send the user to another page in your site. However, bear in mind that, if you move this activity to another course, or another Moodle site, the URL might no longer apply.

12. Common module settings and **Restrict availability** work as they do for other activities. These are covered in a separate section of the book.

13. Click on the **Save and display** button to save the settings. Moodle then displays the **Questions** tab for this Feedback activity. It is then time to start adding questions.

To add Questions to a Feedback activity, follow the steps shown below:

1. Select the Feedback activity.

2. From the left-hand menu, select **Settings | Feedback administration | Questions**. If you have just created and saved the activity, this page will already be displayed.

3. Select the **Edit questions** tab.

4. From the drop-down list that is labeled **Add question to activity**, select the type of question that you want to add.

 Specific types of questions and their settings are covered in the next section. The rest of this procedure covers settings that are common to almost all question types.

5. If you mark a question as **Required**, the user must answer it in order to submit the feedback. The question will have a red asterisk next to it.

6. The **Question** field contains the text of the question. Unlike a quiz question, a feedback question can consist of only text.

7. The **Label** field contains a label that only Teachers will see, when viewing the results of the feedback. The most important reason for the **Label** field is that if export the results of the feedback to an Excel worksheet, then the Label is exported with the results. This allows you to match the feedback results with a short label in your database.

8. The **Position** field determines the order of the question, when you first add it to the feedback page. After the question has been added, you can override this number and move the question to any position on the page.

9. **Depend item** and **Depend value** can be used to make the appearance of a question dependent upon the answer to a previous question. For example, you might first ask someone, "Do you have a Twitter account?" If they answer **Yes**, you might display a question like, "How often do you tweet?" If they answer **No**, you would hide that subsequent question.

   From the **Depend item** drop-down list, select the question whose answer will determine if this question appears. Then, in the **Depend value** field, enter the answer that is needed to make this question appear.

10. For a discussion of the fields that apply to only one type of question, see the section on Question types.

11. Save the question.

Question types

The Feedback activity allows you to add several types of questions. Some of these are not actually questions, but you still add them from the same drop-down menu:

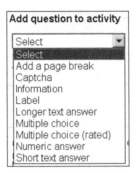

Adding a page break

Add a page break inserts a page break into the Feedback activity.

Avoiding bots with captcha

A captcha is a test to ensure that a human is filling out an online form. It displays a picture of some text, and the user must read and type in that text. If the user doesn't correctly type the text, the feedback form is rejected. This prevents software robots from automatically filling in your feedback and spamming your results.

Inserting information

You can use the **Information** question type to insert information about the feedback into the form. This information is added by Moodle, and submitted with the user's answers. At this time, the options are:

- **Responsestime**: The date and time the user submitted the feedback.
- **Course**: The short name of the course in which this Feedback activity appears.
- **Course category**: The short name of the category in which this Feedback activity appears.

Adding a Label

Adding a **Label** question to a Feedback is the same as adding a Label to a course home page. The Label can be anything that you can put on a web page. This is a good way to insert an explanation, instructions, or encouragement into the activity.

Creating a text box for a longer text answer

Use the **Longer text answer** question type question type to create a text box in which the user can enter a relatively long answer. You specify how many characters wide and how many lines high the text box is. If the user runs out of space, Moodle adds a scroll bar to the box, so that the user can keep on typing.

Displaying multiple choice questions

A multiple choice question displays a list of responses. There are three sub-types of multiple choice questions.

With a **multiple choice – multiple answers** question, Moodle displays a checkbox next to each response. The user can select as many responses as they want.

With a **multiple choice – single answer** question, Moodle displays a radio button next to each response. The user must select only one response from the list of options.

With a **multiple choice – single answer allowed (drop-down list)** question, Moodle displays a drop-down list of the responses. The user must select only one response from the drop-down list.

You create the responses for a multiple choice question by entering one response on each line, in the **Multiple choice values** field. For example, consider the following settings:

The above settings will create the following this question:

What portion of the emails that you receive do you actually answer?

○ I answer almost all or all of the emails I get.   ○ I answer most of the emails I get.   ○ I answer about half of the emails I get.   ○ I answer some of the emails I get.   ○ I answer very few of the emails I get.   ○ My inbox is a black hole; things go in, but nothing comes out.

 Notice the **Adjustment** setting for this question is set to **horizontal**. This causes the responses to be listed horizontally, across the page, instead of in a vertical list.

Notice the setting for **Hide "not selected" option**. If this is set to **No**, then Moodle adds a **Not selected** response to the list of responses that you create. If it is set to **Yes**, Moodle displays only the responses that you create.

Creating a multiple choice (rated) question

To the user, the **Multiple choice (rated)** type of question appears the same way as a multiple choice – single answer question. However, when you review the results, you will see a number that is associated with each answer. This allows you to calculate averages and perform other calculations with the data that you collect.

In the following example, the answers are rated 4 through 0:

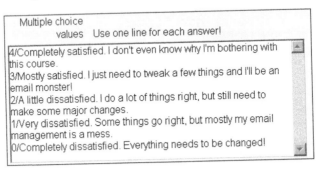

Multiple choice
values   Use one line for each answer!

4/Completely satisfied. I don't even know why I'm bothering with this course.
3/Mostly satisfied. I just need to tweak a few things and I'll be an email monster!
2/A little dissatisfied. I do a lot of things right, but still need to make some major changes.
1/Very dissatisfied. Some things go right, but mostly my email management is a mess.
0/Completely dissatisfied. Everything needs to be changed!

The user doesn't see these numbers when they select an answer. However, when the Teacher looks at the analysis for this question, the average is displayed:

(howsatisfiedworkflow) How satisfied are you with your current email workflow?	
- Completely satisfied. I don't even know why I'm bothering with this course. (4):	0
- Mostly satisfied. I just need to tweak a few things and I'll be an email monster! (3):	0
- A little dissatisfied. I do a lot of things right, but still need to make some major changes. (2):	1 (50.00 %)
- Very dissatisfied. Some things go right, but mostly my email management is a mess. (1):	1 (50.00 %)
- Completely dissatisfied. Everything needs to be changed! (0):	0
Average: 1.50	

In addition, when the results of the feedback are exported to Excel, the rating numbers are also exported. This allows you to perform advanced analysis on your results, using a spreadsheet.

Numeric answer

Use a **Numeric** question type to ask the user to enter a number. You can specify an exact value, or a range that you will accept.

Short text answer

A *Short text answer* question lets you limit the amount of text that the user can enter. You specify the size of the text entry box, and the amount of text that the box will accept.

Viewing feedback

Teachers and administrators can view the responses to a Feedback activity. You can view the responses one at a time, or can view a summary of all responses.

See individual responses

If **Record User Names** is set to **Users' Names Will Be Logged and Shown With Answers**, then the Teacher will be able to see a list of users who have completed the Feedback, and their answers. To see this list of responses, carry out the following steps:

1. Select the Feedback activity.

2. From the left-hand menu, select **Settings | Feedback administration | Show responses**.

3. For the user whose responses you want to see, click on the date.

The responses for that session will be displayed.

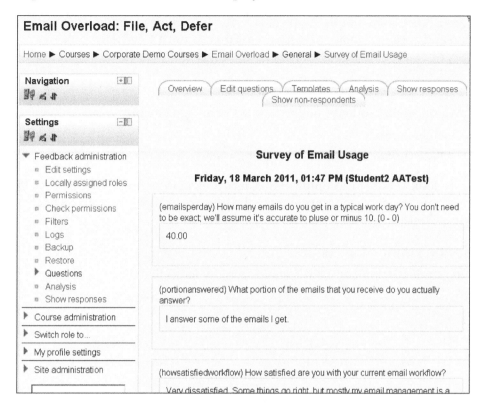

Note that if a user answers the Feedback several times, there will be a date for each time that the user answered.

For anonymous responses, instead of a name you will see a number.

Analyzing responses with the Analysis tab

On the **Analysis** tabbed page, you can see a summary of all the responses. On this page, you also have an **Export to Excel** button. Clicking on this button will download all of the Response data to a Microsoft Excel spreadsheet.

Choices

Moodle's Choice is the simplest type of activity. In a Choice activity, you create one question and specify a choice of responses. You can use a Choice to:

- Take a quick poll
- Ask students to choose sides in a debate
- Confirm the students' understanding of an agreement
- Gather consent
- Allow students to choose a subject for an essay or project

Before we look at how to accomplish this, let's look at the Choice activity from the student's point of view, and then explore the settings available to the Teacher when creating a Choice.

Student's point of view

From the student's point of view, a choice activity looks like this:

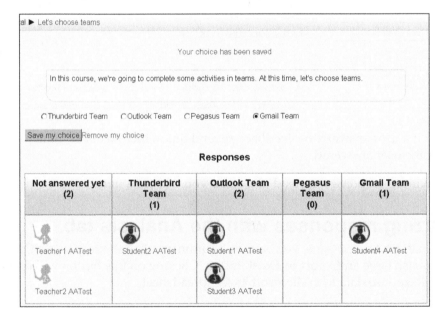

Notice a few things about this Choice activity:

- The student can see how many other students have chosen a response.
- There is a limit on the number of students who can choose each response.
- The student can remove their choice and submit again.

These are options that you can set for the activity. The teacher also could have hidden other students' responses, had no limit for the number who can choose each response, and prevented the student from changing their response.

Teacher's point of view

Before we discuss some of the uses for a choice activity; let's look at the settings available on the **Editing Choice** page. Then, we'll see how we can make creative use of these capabilities.

Limit

The **Limit** next to each choice allows you to limit how many students can select a given choice. In the preceding example, no more than four students can select each choice. So, once four students have selected a team, that choice becomes unavailable to subsequent students.

For Limits to take effect, **Limit the number of responses allowed** must be set to **Enable**.

Display Mode

In the preceding example, **Display Mode** is set to **Horizontal**. You can also arrange the choices vertically.

Publish results

You can choose whether to reveal the results of the Choice to the students, and if so, when.

In the example at the beginning of this section, **Publish results** was set to **Always show results to students**. This is why the student could see how many students had chosen each response. If it had been set to **Do not publish results to students**, then the activity would not have shown how many students had selected each response.

If you are going to limit the number of students who can choose a response, consider using **Always show results to students**. That way, the student can see how many others have chosen the response, and how many slots are left for each response.

Privacy of results

If you publish the results of the Choice, then you can then choose whether or not to publish the names of the students who have selected each response. In the example at the beginning of this section, **Privacy of results** was set to **Publish full result**, so a student completing the Choice could see who had already selected each response.

Allow students to change their minds

The setting **Allow choice to be updated** determines whether or not a student can change their answer after submitting it. If this is set to **Yes**, a student can retake the Choice activity until the activity is closed. However, they can only ever choose one option.

Summary

Feedback and **Choice** give teachers the opportunity to assess students, their attitudes, and their satisfaction with a course. Feedback is especially useful for assessing the class' attitude and experience at the beginning of the course. You can also use Feedback to create surveys for people who are not even taking a course, such as an employee survey or gathering research data.

The **Choice** activity is especially useful for having a structured, ongoing conversation between the students and teacher. You can create several of these, keep them hidden, and reveal them when you want to measure the students' attitude.

Moodle's **Quiz** activity is rich in feedback. The many different types of feedback allow you to turn a quiz into a learning activity. Consider using the quiz activity not just for testing, but also for teaching.

8
Adding Social Activities to Your Course

Social course activities encourage student-to-student interaction. Peer interaction is one of the most powerful learning tools that Moodle offers. It not only encourages learning, but also exploration. It also makes courses more interesting because students can share their knowledge, which increases student participation and satisfaction. This chapter teaches you how to add social resources to a course, and how to make the best use of them.

Chat

The Chat module creates a chat room where students can have real-time, online chats. Online chat has some unique advantages over an in-person classroom discussion. Students do not need to deal with a fear of public speaking, transcripts can be edited and used as course material, and conversation can proceed at a leisurely pace that gives participants time to think. The key to using these advantages is preparation. Prepare your students by ensuring that they understand chat room etiquette and know how to use the software. Prepare yourself by having material ready to copy and paste into the chat. And everyone should be prepared to focus on the goals and subject of that chat. More than any other online activity, chat requires that the teacher take a leadership role and guide the students to a successful learning experience.

When you add a chat room to a course, any student taking the course can enter that chat room at any time. The chat room can become a meeting place for the students taking the course, where they can come to collaborate on work and exchange information. If you give group assignments, or have students rate other students' assignments, consider adding a chat room to the course and encouraging students to use it. Also, consider saving transcripts of the chat sessions so that they can act as another reference tool for the students.

When you schedule a Chat, it appears on the course Calendar and is also displayed in the **Upcoming events** block, as shown in the following screenshot:

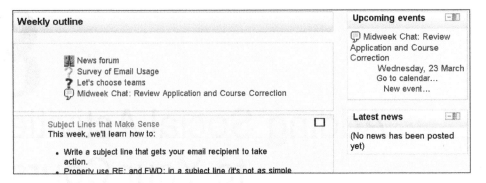

When the student selects the Chat, they see the **Description** that you entered when you created the Chat. You can use this **Description** to advise the student of the purpose of the Chat:

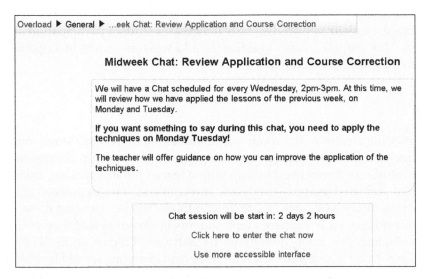

When you enter a Chat, it launches in a pop-up window, as shown below. Make sure that your students don't have pop ups blocked.

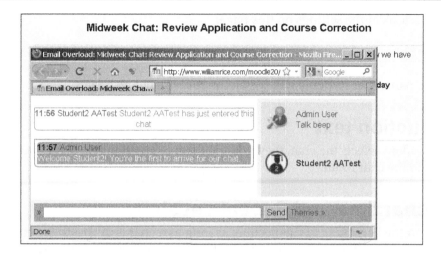

Let's have a look at the settings that you can specify when creating a Chat.

The Chat settings page

The **Editing Chat** page is where you create and select settings for a chat. When you first add a Chat, you will be taken to this page. In order to edit the settings of an existing Chat, select that Chat and then from the left-hand menu bar select **Settings | Chat administration | Settings**.

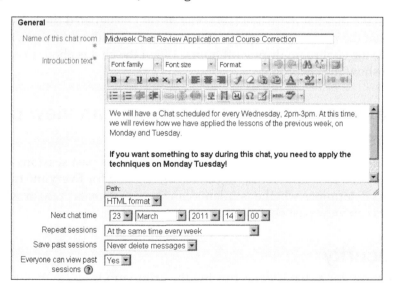

Let's take a look at the settings on this page:

Name

This is the name that students will see on the course's Home Page.

Introduction text

When a student selects the chat, they will see the introduction text before being passed into the chat room.

Next chat time and Repeat sessions

As stated in the beginning of this section, as long as a chat is visible to the student, they can enter that chat room at any time. Therefore, the settings for **Next chat time** and **Repeat sessions** don't open and close the chat. Instead, these settings put a time and date for the chat on the class calendar.

Chat times are listed in the **Calendar** and **Upcoming Events** blocks. Note that chat is not restricted to these times; they are only announced as a way for people in the course to "make a date" for the chat. Spontaneous chats have the best chance of happening if the course has a lot of students who frequent the course's Home Page. Also, consider adding the **Online Users** block, so that when students visit the site they will know who is online and can invite others into the chat room.

In order to make the chat room available only during designated times, you should make sure that the person running the chat is a Teacher with editing privileges, and also hide the chat room during off hours. When the chat is about to begin, the Teacher can show the chat room.

Save past sessions and Everyone can view past sessions

Through this setting, the past chats can be saved. The **Save past sessions** setting allows you to set a time limit for saving chats. The setting for **Everyone can view past sessions** determines whether students can view past chats (**Yes**) or whether only teachers can view past chats (**No**).

Chat security

The only security for a chat room is turning the group mode on, so that only students in a selected group can see each other in the chat room.

Remember that in the **Course Settings** page, you can set the **Enrolment duration** as **Unlimited**. This means that once a student is enroled in the course, she or he is always enroled until you manually unenrol the student. If you leave the course open to all students who were ever enrolled, consider segregating your chat by groups. Then, create a group that includes only the currently-enrolled students. This prevents previous students from giving away too much in the chat room.

Forum

Forums are one of Moodle's most powerful features. A well-run class forum can stimulate thoughtful discussion, motivate students to become involved, and result in unexpected insights.

You can add any number of forums to a course, and also to the site's Front Page. Anyone with access to the course will have access to the forums. You can use group mode to limit access to a forum to specific groups.

When a student enters a forum, the student sees the description entered during creation of the forum, as shown in the following screenshot:

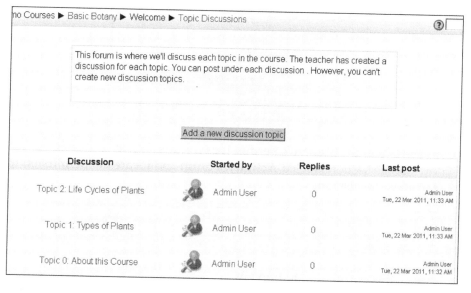

When writing a forum posting, the student uses the same online, WYSIWYG editor that you see when creating web pages in Moodle. Also, you can allow students to upload files into a forum. If you ask students to collaborate on assignments, or ask them to review each others' work, consider adding a forum specifically for discussing the assignment. Encourage the students to use the forum to preview each others' work and collaborate on the assignments.

Discussion equals topic

In the Moodle forum, discussions are the equivalent of topics or threads. Under **Settings | Forum administration | Permissions**, you can control who can create new discussions, and who can post new replies.

In the preceding screenshot, note that the introduction to the forum states that only the Teacher can create new discussions. Students can reply to the discussion, but cannot create new discussions. This was accomplished by using permissions. Here's how:

 Only an Administrator can perform this process. If you have only Teacher rights, get an Administrator to do this for you.

1. Select the Forum.
2. Select **Settings | Forum administration | Permissions**.
3. From the **Advanced role override** drop-down list, select **Student**.

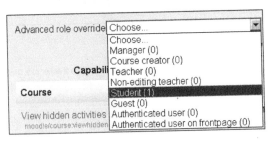

4. A page listing the Student's permissions for this activity is displayed. Scroll down to the section labeled **Activity: Forum** and locate the permission for **Start new discussions**.

5. Change this permission to **Prevent**.
6. At the bottom of the page, save the changes.

Using the News Forum to send mass emails

Moodle does not have a module specifically for sending email announcements. So when you want to send an email to everyone in a class, you can use the default **News Forum** that is automatically added to every class. By default, in the **News Forum**, the **Subscription mode** is set to **Forced subscription**, and only Teachers have the ability to post messages to the forum. When the teacher posts a message, everyone who is subscribed to the **Forum** receives the message via email. With everyone subscribed, the entire class will receive a copy of each posting by e-mail.

Multiple forums

Remember that a class can have as many **Forums** as you want. If your course uses groups, you can use groups in the forum. Also, you can hide old **Forums** and create new ones. This is useful if you run students through a course on a schedule. Just turning off the old **Forums** and creating new ones allows you to refresh a part of the course.

Forum settings

The **Settings** page is where you select the settings for a forum. Let's look at how each of the settings affects the user experience.

General settings

The following are some of the general settings.

Forum name

The Forum name is the name that students will see when the forum is listed on the course's Home Page.

Forum type

In Moodle, you can create several types of forums. Each type can be used in a different way. The types of forums are:

Type of Forum	Description
Single simple discussion	The entire forum appears on one page. The first posting, at the top of the page, is the topic for the forum. This topic is usually created by the Teacher. The students then post replies under this topic. A single-topic forum is most useful for short, highly-focused discussions.
Each person posts one discussion	Each student can create one and only one new topic. Everyone can reply to every topic.
Q and A	This is like a single-topic forum, in which the Teacher creates the topic for the forum. Students then reply to that topic. However, a student cannot see anyone else's reply until they have posted a reply. The topic is usually a question posed by the Teacher, and the students' replies are usually answers to that question.
Standard forum displayed in a blog-like format	In a standard forum, anyone can start a new topic. Teachers and students can create new topics and reply to existing postings. Displaying the discussion in a blog-like format makes both the title and the body of each discussion visible.
Standard forum for general use	In a standard forum, anyone can start a new topic. Teachers and students can create new topics and reply to existing postings. Only the titles of discussions are visible; you must click into a discussion to read the postings under it.

Forum introduction

When the student enters a forum, they will see the **Forum introduction** at the top of the forum's page. This text should tell the student what the forum is about. You can also use this introduction to tell the student if they can rate posts by other students, and even to link to a document with more extensive instructions for using the forum. This is possible because the **Introduction** is a full-featured web page that can hold anything that you can put on a standard web page.

Subscription mode

Selecting the **Force subscription** option subscribes all students to the forum automatically—even students who enrol in the course at a later time. Before using this setting, consider its long-term effect on the students who take your class.

If you re-use the same class for a later group of students, then the previous group will still be enroled. Do you want previous students to be notified of new postings in the current class's forum? If not, there are several solutions, such as:

- Don't force all students to be subscribed.
- Use groups to separate the current group of students in the class from previous groups.
- Create a fresh instance of the course for each new group.

If you select **Auto subscription**, everyone in the course is subscribed to the forum, but later they can unsubscribe. With **Force subscription**, the student cannot unsubscribe as long as they are enrolled in the course.

Read tracking for this forum?

When the **Read tracking for this forum**? setting is turned on, it highlights the messages that the student hasn't read.

If students are subscribing to the forum via email, then this feature is less useful because it won't reflect any posts read via email.

Maximum attachment size

Students can attach files to forum postings. This sets the maximum size of a file that the student can upload. The setting turns off the student's ability to upload files to the forum **Uploads are not allowed**.

Maximum number of attachments

The **Maximum number of attachments** setting specifies the maximum number of files that can be attached to one post. Note that this is not the maximum for the whole forum.

Post threshold for blocking Settings

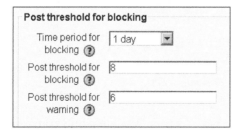

The **Post threshold for blocking** setting helps you to prevent the forum from being taken over by a few prolific posters. Users can be blocked from posting more than a given number of postings in a given amount of time. As they approach the limit, they can be given a warning.

In the preceding example, after a student makes a sixth post for the day, the system will warn them that they are approaching the limit for the number of posts per day. After eight posts, the student cannot post any more posts that day.

Ratings

In a forum, a "rating" is really a "grade". When you enable ratings, you are really allowing the Teacher to give each forum posting a grade. In the following screenshot, you can see the first posting in the forum, which was made by the Teacher. Below that, you can see the reply left by Student1. The student's reply was rated by the Teacher:

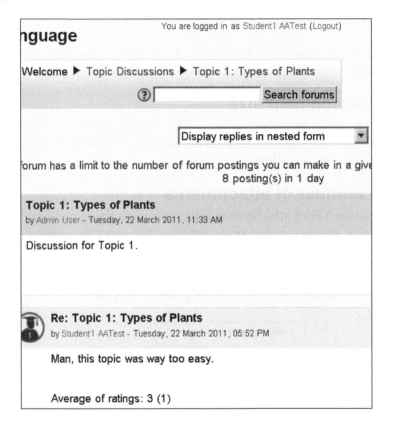

By default, only Teachers, non-editing Teachers, and course managers can rate forum postings. If you want the students to be able to rate postings in a forum, follow the steps given in the section. *Enable students to rate forum postings*, below. You do that on the **Permissions** page. Make sure you save your work before leaving the **Settings** page.

Only an Administrator can perform this process. If you have only Teacher rights, get an Administrator to do this for you.

Enable students to rate forum postings

1. Select the Forum.

2. Select **Settings | Forum administration | Permissions**.

3. From the **Advanced role override** drop-down list button, select **Student**.

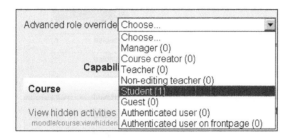

4. A page listing the Student's permissions for this activity is displayed. Scroll down to the section labeled **Activity: Forum** and locate the permission for **Rate posts**.

5. Select the radio button for **Allow**.

6. Click on the **Save changes** button.

Glossary

The **Glossary** activity is one of the most underrated features of Moodle. On the surface, a glossary is a list of words and definitions that students can access. However, a course creator can allow students to add to a **Glossary**. This transforms the glossary from a static listing of vocabulary words to a collaborative tool for learning.

When this setting is turned on, whenever a word from a **Glossary** appears in the course, it is highlighted in gray. Clicking on the word brings up a pop-up window containing the word's **Glossary** entry.

You can use a glossary to build a class directory, a collection of past exam questions, famous quotations, or even an annotated collection of pictures.

Enable glossaries for your site

Under **Site Administration | Plugins | Manage Filters**, the site administrator can turn on **Glossary Auto-Linking**.

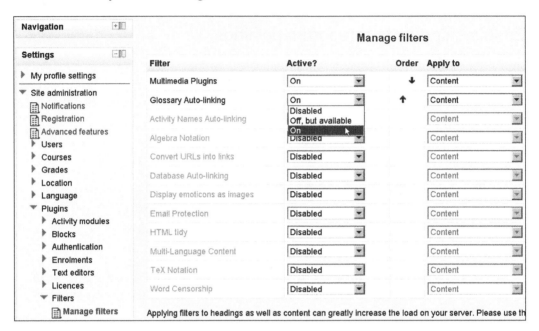

Help! My glossary won't work!

If you create a glossary and just can't get it to work, check with your Site Administrator that the glossary plugin is enabled.

Adding glossary entries

Selecting a **Glossary** from the course menu displays the glossary's introductory page. On this page, you can edit and browse the glossary. The teacher can always edit a glossary in their course. You can also permit students to submit new glossary entries (more on that later).

The following screenshot shows the **Browse** tabbed page, where you can add a new entry:

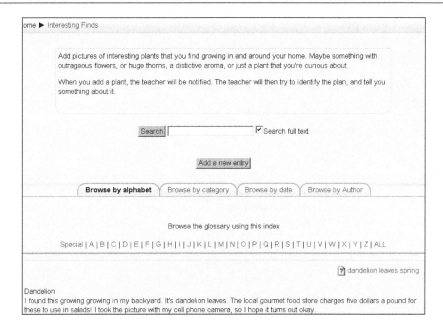

Create new **Glossary** entries by clicking on the **Add a new entry** button. This button appears below every tab when you're browsing the glossary, so it's always available. The following screenshot displays the top half of the new entry page:

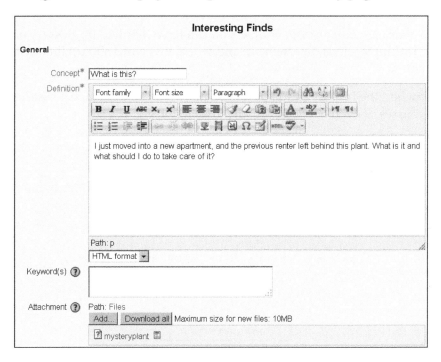

On this page, **Concept** is the term that you are adding to the **Glossary**. **Keyword(s)** are synonyms, the equivalent of a "see also" in an index or dictionary. These terms will link to the same definition as the concept.

Notice that you can add a picture or media file to the **Definition**, using the icons in the tool bar: ▓ ▓.

You can also upload these kinds of files as an **Attachment**, which is what the user in this example chose to do.

The following screenshot displays the bottom half of the **Add a new entry** window:

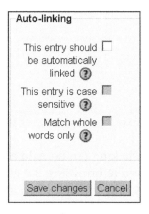

When this word appears in your course, you can have it link to its glossary entry. The **Auto-linking** options determine if, and when, this word should link to its glossary entry.

For the Teacher, the **Import** and **Export** links allow you to exchange glossaries between courses or even between Moodle installations:

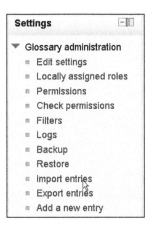

You might want to begin a course with a small glossary, and let students add to it as they discover new concepts. If you do this, export the starting glossary so that you have it available for the next course. The next time that you teach the course, you can choose to export everything in the completed course except student information and the glossary. In the new copy, just create a new, blank **Glossary** and import the starting **Glossary**.

Also, note that the editing window allows you to include hyperlinks in the definition (the 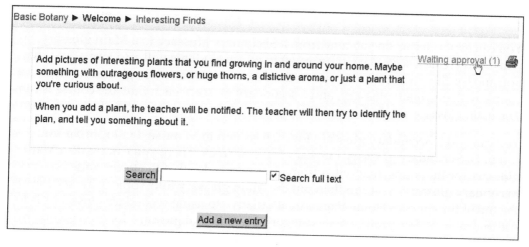 icon). This can be used to link to freely-available information on the Web, such as information from Wikipedia, at `http://www.wikipedia.org/`.

When you create a **Glossary**, in the **Settings** window you choose whether terms that students add are approved automatically, or whether they need the Teacher's approval. If **Approved by default** is turned off, new terms would await the Teacher's approval before being added. In the following screenshot, notice the link in the upper-right corner for **Waiting approval**:

Global versus local glossary

By default, a glossary applies only to the course in which it resides. However, you can choose to make a glossary global, in which case the words from that glossary will be highlighted and clickable wherever they are in your site. The work done in one course then becomes available to all of the courses on your site. If your site's subject matter is highly focused, consider using a global glossary. If your site's subject matter is very broad, as would be the case for a university-wide learning site, you should use local glossaries to avoid confusion. For example, imagine you have a course on chemistry and another on statistics. Both use the word "granular," but chemistry uses it to indicate a powdered substance while statistics uses it to indicate a fine level of detail.

[Only an Administrator can make a glossary into a global glossary. If you
have only Teacher rights, get an Administrator to do this for you.]

Main and secondary glossaries

If you want students to be able to add entries to a **Glossary**, you must make it a
Secondary glossary. Prior to Moodle 1.7, only teachers could add terms to a **Main
glossary**. A **Secondary glossary** had only the terms that the students and the Teacher
add to it. Since Moodle 1.7 and the introduction of Roles, you can override these
settings and allow students to add entries to the main glossary through the Override
roles capability.

[Only an Administrator can override roles.]

You can export terms one-at-time from a **Secondary glossary** to a **Main glossary**. So
you could create a secondary glossary(s) to which students will add terms, and then,
you and/or the students could export the best terms to the main glossary. Imagine a
course with one main glossary, and a secondary glossary each time the course is run.
The main glossary would become a repository of the best terms added by each class.

You can add a **Secondary glossary** for each section in a course. For example, you
can put a **Secondary glossary** into each topic or week. Then, you can create a **Main
glossary** for the course that will automatically include all of the terms added to each
Secondary glossary. You can then put the **Main glossary** into Topic 0, the section at
the top of the course's Home Page. An alternative to using secondary glossaries is to
use one main glossary, and create categories within that glossary for each section in
the course. This keeps all glossary entries in one place.

If you want the course to have only one glossary, and you want students to be able to
add to it, make it a **Secondary glossary**. Even though the term "Secondary" implies
that there is also a primary or main glossary, this does not have to be the case. You
can have just a **Secondary glossary** (or more than one) in a course, without a
Main glossary.

Ratings

You can give students the ability to rate glossary entries, just like they can rate forum postings. The question is, what do you want students to rate? The glossary entry's clarity? Its helpfulness? Your writing skill in creating the entry? You'll need to consider what you want students to rate, and create a custom scale that supports this rating. You determine who can rate glossary entries, and what scale to use, on the **Settings** page, as shown in the following screenshot:

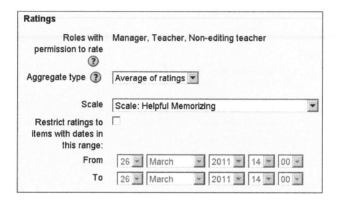

In the preceding screenshot, the course creator is applying a custom scale called **Helpful Memorizing** to the glossary. This custom scale was created before the Teacher came to this page.

After creating a custom scale, the Teacher went to the glossary's **Settings** page, as shown in the preceding screenshot, and selected it under Scale.

Notice that only the course Manager, Teachers, and Non-editing Teachers can rate the entries in this glossary. The next step is for the Teacher to modify the permissions, to allow students to rate entries.

This three-part process is covered in the following subsections.

Allowing students to rate glossary entries:

Allowing students to rate glossary entries consists of a three-part process:

1. Create the rating scale
2. Select the scale for the glossary
3. Give students permission to use ratings

Create the rating scale

1. Select **Settings | Grade administration | Scales**.

2. Click on the **Add a new scale** button.

3. On the new **Scale** page, give the scale a **Name**. Only the teacher will see this name.

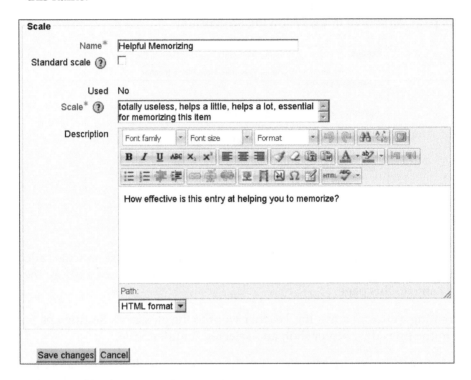

4. In the **Scale** field, enter the values that the user will select when giving their rating.

5. In the **Description** field, enter a short description that will help you to remember the purpose of this scale.

6. **Save** your changes.

Select the scale for the glossary

1. Go to the glossary's **Settings** page.

2. For the **Scale** field, select the scale that you just created.

3. Modify any other settings that you want to on this page.

4. **Save** your changes.

Students will now be able to rate each glossary entry on how helpful it is to memorize the material. From the student's point of view, the result looks like this:

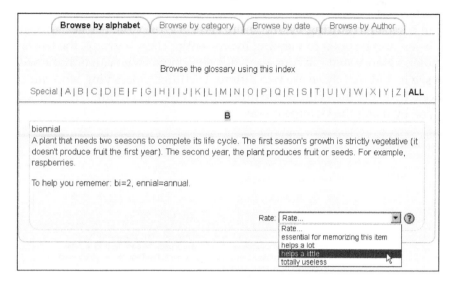

Wiki

The Moodle Wiki module allows students to collaborate on a group writing project, build a knowledge base, and discuss class topics. Because a wiki is easy to use, interactive, and organized by date, it encourages collaboration among the participants. This makes it a powerful tool for capturing group knowledge. The key difference between a forum and a wiki is that when users enter a forum, they see a thread devoted to a topic. Each entry is short. The users read through the thread one entry at a time. The result is that the discussion becomes prominent. In a wiki, users see the end result of the writing. To see the history of the writing, they must select a **History** tab. The result is that the end result of the writing becomes prominent.

Old wiki content is never deleted and can be restored. Wikis can also be searched, just like other course material. In the following section, we'll look at the settings on the **Editing Wiki** page and how these settings affect the user experience.

Using the wiki type and group mode to determine who can edit a wiki

A wiki can be open to **editing** by: the entire class, a group, the teacher, or a single student. It can also be open to **viewing** by: the entire class, a group, the teacher, or single student. Notice that the course creator determines who can **edit** the wiki, and who can **see** it, and that these are two different settings. Specifying who can edit the wiki is done by using the **Wiki mode** drop-down box. Specifying who can see the wiki is done by using the **Groups** mode.

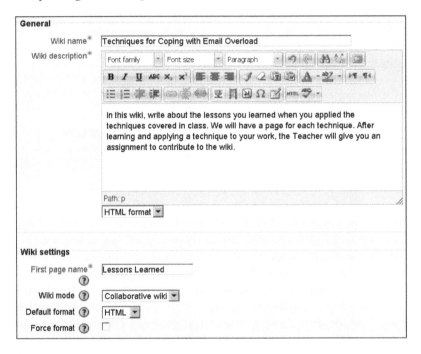

Making a wiki editable by only a single student appears to turn the wiki into a personal journal. However, the difference between a single-student wiki and a journal is that a journal can be seen only by the student and the Teacher. You can keep a single-student wiki private, or, you can open it for viewing by the student's group or the entire class.

Default format

The **Default format** setting determines whether wiki authors use standard wiki markup or HTML code when editing. If you're using the HTML editor for other student activities, setting this to **HTML only** can simplify this activity for your students. They will get the familiar HTML editor, and don't need to learn the wiki markup language. However, if your students are accustomed to wikis, you may want to select **Creole**. This enables them to use a common wiki markup, which is faster for experienced typists.

First page name

The name on the first page of the wiki will be taken from this field.

If there is one wiki for the entire class, when the first student enters the wiki, that student will see the starting page(s). If that first student edits any page, the next student who enters will see the edited version, and so on. If there is one wiki for each group in the class, then each group will get a "fresh" wiki, containing only the starting page(s) that you created. Similarly, if each student gets their own wiki, then each student will see those starting pages when they enter their wiki.

Workshop

A workshop provides a place for the students in a class to see an example project, upload their individual projects, and see and assess each other's projects. When a teacher requires each student to assess the work of several other students, the workshop becomes a powerful collaborative grading tool.

Workshop strategies

Workshops can be ungraded, peer graded, instructor graded, or a combination of peer and instructor graded. Workshops allow you to create very specific assessment criteria for the graders to use. Also, workshops let you set due dates for submitting work, and for grading work. You can use these and other features to build a strategy for making the best use of workshops in your courses.

Peer assessment of assignments

One strategy for workshops is to have students assess each other's work, before submitting that same work as a graded assignment. For example, you could create a workshop where students assess each other's subject matter, outlines, and hypothesis for their term papers. Or they could assess each other's photos for specific technical and artistic criteria before submitting them to the instructor for grading.

Timing of submissions and assessments

Workshops allow you to set different due dates for submitting work, and for assessing other student's work. If you set both due dates the same, so many students might submit their work just before the submission deadline that they cannot all be assessed before the assessment deadline. Consider setting the submission deadline well before the assessment deadline. Then, before opening up the assessment ability to the students, examine the work submitted and ensure that it's close to what you expected or were trying to elicit from the students. You might even want to use the time between submission and assessment to refine your assessment criteria, in response to the work submitted.

The four questions

The fields in the workshop window give you many choices. No matter what you enter into each field, your many decisions can be summed up as:

- What will you have each student do? Create a file offline and upload it to the workshop? Write a journal entry? Participate in an online chat? Perform some offline activity and report on it via email or Wiki? Although the workshop window allows the student to upload a file, you can also require any other activity from the student.

- Who will assess the assignments? Will the Teacher assess all assignments? Will students be required to assess other students' assignments? Will each student self-assess their work?

- How will the assignments be assessed? You can determine the number of criteria upon which each assignment is assessed, the grading scale, and the type of grading.

- When will students be allowed to submit their assignments and assessment? The assignment becomes available as soon as you show it. However, you can require students to assess an example before being allowed to submit their own work, and you can also set a deadline for submitting assignments.

All of the fields that we cover in the following subsections are variations on these questions. The online help does a good job of explaining how to use each field. Instead of repeating how to use each field here, we will focus on how your choices affect the student and Teacher experience.

The Edit Settings page

The workshop activity is the most complex tool currently available in Moodle. Workshops are designed so that a student's work can be submitted and offered for peer review within a structured framework. Workshops provide a process for both instructor feedback and peer feedback on open-ended assignments, such as essays and research papers. They provide a place for the students in the class as well as the teachers to make the best use of Moodle. There are easy-to-use interfaces for uploading assignments, performing self-assessments, and peer reviews of other students' papers. The key to the workshop is the scoring guide, which is a set of specific criteria for making judgments about the quality of a given work. These are several fields under workshop. They will be explained in the following sections.

Name and introduction

The settings under **General** partially answer the question: what will you have each student do?

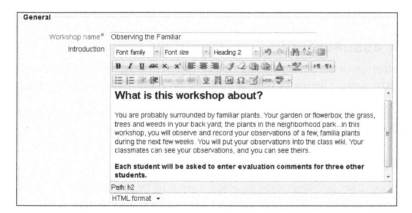

Your students will see and click on the **Name**. The **Introduction** should give instructions for completing the workshop. If you want to provide printer-friendly instructions, you can upload a `.pdf` file to the course files area, and put a link to this document in the workshop description.

Workshop Features

The settings under **Workshop Features** answer the question: who will assess the assignments?

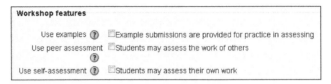

Use examples

If the workshop uses examples, then users can assess example(s) of the work provided by the teacher. The user's assessment of the example is then compared to the assessment provided by the teacher. This enables users to practice assessing work, before they assess each other's work.

Users receive a grade for how well their assessment agrees with the assessment provided by the teacher. However, the grade is not counted in the gradebook.

Use peer assessment

If the workshop uses peer assessment, each user will be given submissions from other users to assess. The users will be graded on their assessments of their peers.

The number of peers that each user assesses, and how their assessments are graded, is set elsewhere on this page.

Use self assessment

If the workshop uses self assessment, each user will be given their own work to assess. The user will be graded on their assessments of their own work.

Grading settings

The **Grading settings** fields determine the maximum points that a student can earn for a workshop.

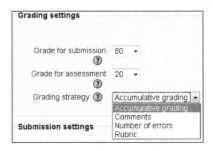

Grade for submission is the maximum number of points that a student can be given by the grader.

Grade for assessments is the grade that the student receives for grading other submissions. This grade is based on how close the assessment by the student is to the average of all assessments for that same submission. For example, Student A submits work. Students B, C, and D assess the work and give scores of 10, 9, and 5. The average assessment is 8, so students B and C would receive higher marks for their assessments than student D. In essence, the Grade for assessments is the "grade for grading".

If you did not enable **Use peer assessment** under **Workshop features**, then this grade is irrelevant.

Grading strategy

A workshop assignment is quite flexible in the type of grading scheme used. This setting determines the overall scheme. The various options for this setting are described below.

Accumulative

In the **Accumulative** grading strategy, the grade for each element is added upto arrive at the accumulated grade. This style of grading allows you to present the reviewer with a numeric scale. You can also present the reviewer with Yes or No questions, such as "Does this workshop meet the requirement?". Or you can present the reviewer with a grading scale, such as "Poor, Fair, Good, or Excellent". If you use a Yes or No or a grading scale, you will assign a point value to each response. Consider informing the reviewer of the value of each response. For example, instead of just writing:

- Poor
- Fair
- Good
- Excellent

Consider writing:

- Poor (1 point)
- Fair (2 points)
- Good (3 points)
- Excellent (4 points)

Comments

When the **Comments** grading strategy is selected, students can comment upon each assessment element but do not select a grade. The teacher can grade the students' comments. In that case, the workshop is transformed from one where students grade each other to where the teacher grades each student's comments.

This may be especially useful when you want to have a structured discussion about material that you present to the students. As the course creator, you can present the students with material uploaded to the workshop, or use the workshop's description to direct the students to the material that they must assess. After the students view the material, they enter the workshop and leave comments according to the elements presented. Because the workshop presents the students with evaluation elements, and because it requires that they complete each element, your discussion is more structured than if you use a Wiki or forum.

Number of errors

When you choose this option, students evaluate a workshop using a series of Yes or No questions. Usually, you create questions to evaluate whether the submission met a requirement, such as "Does the student present a variety of opinions?"

When writing one of these questions, make sure that it can be answered using only Yes or No. A sign that you need to revise your question is the presence of the word "or". For example, don't write "Did the student describe the plant well enough to distinguish it from others, or, is there still doubt as to which plant the student is describing?" Such a question cannot be answered Yes or No.

The answer to an evaluation question is sometimes very clear, and sometimes subjective. For example, the question "Did the student describe the plant well enough to distinguish it from others?" is subjective. One reviewer might think the student did an adequate job of describing the plant, while another might think otherwise. These questions can be a good way to perform subjective peer evaluations of each student's work.

If the work requires a more objective evaluation, such as "Did the student include all five identifying features covered in this lesson?" you may not need a workshop. That kind of objective evaluation can be easily performed by the Teacher, by using an assignment.

Rubric

For a rubric grading scale, write several statements that apply to the project. Each statement has a grade assigned to it. The reviewers choose the one statement that best describes the project. This single choice completes the review.

You can create several of these elements, and the reviewers must select a statement for each of them.

Submission settings

The submission settings are where you enter instructions for the users, and determine how many files they can upload, and how large these files can be upload. This is where you partially answer the question: what will you have each student do?

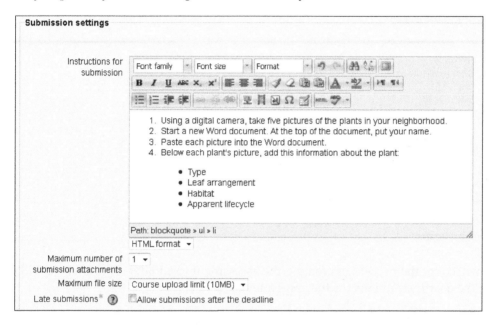

The user will see the **Instructions for submission** when they navigate to the workshop.

The **Maximum number of submission attachments** and **Maximum file size** determine how many files the user can upload, and what size these files can be.

Late submissions allows users to submit their work after the deadline. The deadline is set further down the page.

Assessment settings

The settings in this section are used to give the users instructions on how to perform their assessments, and, to determine when to present the user with examples to assess.

The actual criteria used in the assessment are not created on this page. Instead, the criteria are created under **Settings | Workshop administration | Edit assessment form**, as shown in the example below:

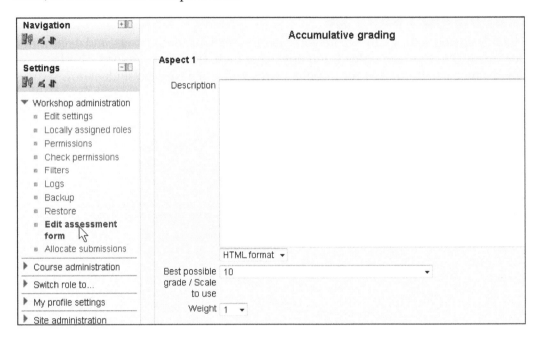

We will cover the process of creating the assessment form later. For now, we will just give the user instructions for the assessment:

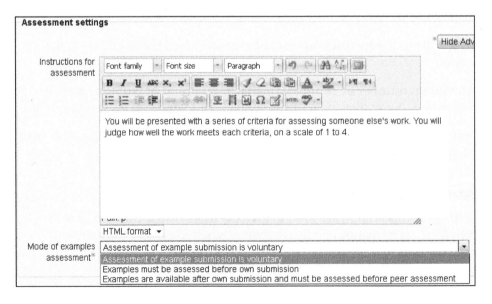

If the **Mode of assessment** is grayed out and unavailable, that is because the setting for **Use example** is not selected (further up the page).

Access control

The settings under this section answer the question: when will students be allowed to submit their assignments and assessment?

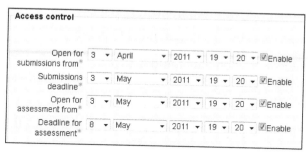

Notice that the submissions and assessments can open on the same day. However, assessments cannot open before submissions (there would nothing to assess).

The Edit assessment form page

On the **Edit assessment form** page, you enter the assessment criteria. The exact contents of this page will change depending upon the type of assessment that you selected on the **Workshop settings** page.

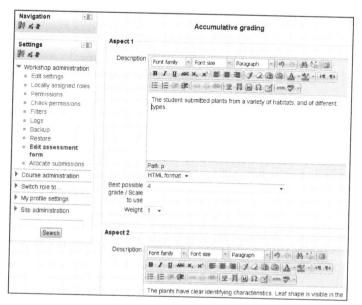

Making the maximum grade a multiple of the number of assessment elements allows the students to more easily interpret their grades. For example, suppose a workshop will be assessed on five elements. For each element, the assessor will choose from four statements:

- The workshop does not meet this requirement in any way (0 points).
- The workshop partially meets this requirement (1 point).
- The workshop meets this requirement (2 points).
- The workshop exceeds this requirement (3 points).

Using the above statements, element would be worth a maximum of three points. With five elements, the workshop would have a maximum grade of 15. This would make it easy for the student to interpret his or her grade.

From the student's point of view, the assessment form looks like this:

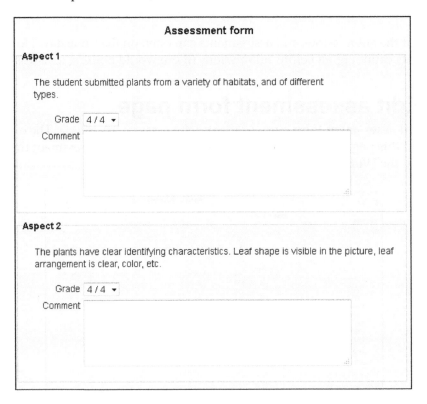

Notice that for each assessment criteria, the student can enter comments. This is a default setting for the workshop.

Add an example to the workshop

After you save the workshop settings and assessment form, you can add an example to your workshop. Selecting the workshop will give you a screen like this:

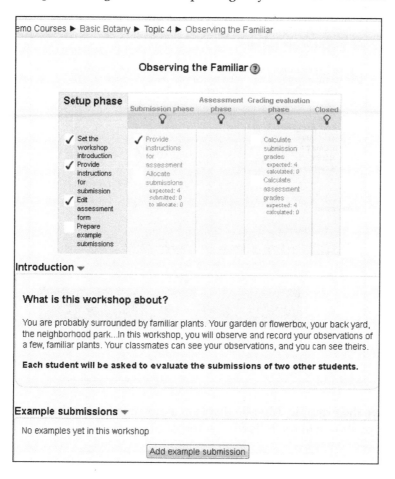

To add an example submission, begin by clicking on the **Add example submission** button. This brings you to a page that displays the same assessment instructions that your users will see, and where you can upload the example to be assessed:

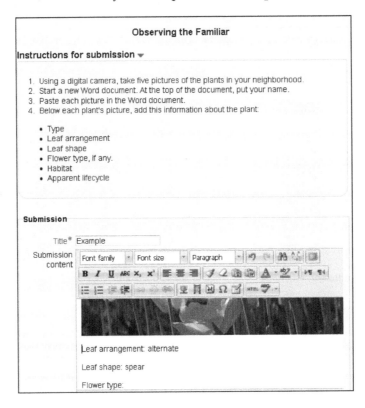

After you save the example, Moodle displays a message saying that you must assess the example, as shown in the following screenshot:

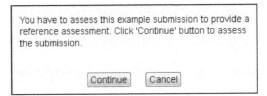

After you assess the example, Moodle returns you to the workshop's home page. You will see the progress that you have made, as shown in the following screenshot:

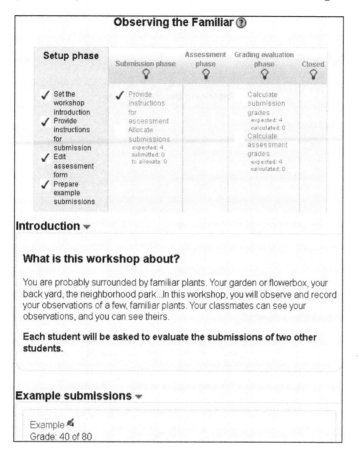

Notice that the next step would be for the Teacher to allocate the student submissions for assessment. However, no one has submitted anything yet. At this point, the Teacher has to wait for students to submit their work.

Students submit their work

Once a student selects the workshop, they will see a page similar to the example shown below:

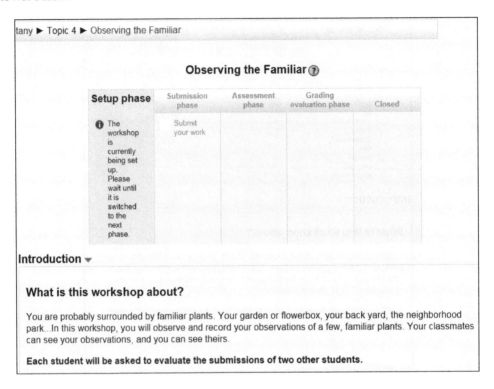

Even though the teacher has finished setting up the workshop and is ready for the students to submit their work, the students still see a message: **The workshop is currently being set up. Please wait until it is switched to the next phase**.

The Teacher must manually switch the workshop from one phase to the next. Even if you're done with the set-up and are ready to accept submissions, Moodle doesn't know that.

To switch to the next phase, the Teacher must click on the light bulb above that phase. In our example, the Teacher clicks the light bulb above the Submission phase, and sees the following message:

You are about to switch the workshop into the **Submission phase**. Students may submit their work during this phase (within the submission access control dates, if set). Teachers may allocate submissions for peer review.

Continue   Cancel

Now when the student selects this workshop, they see a prompt to submit work, as shown in the following screenshot:

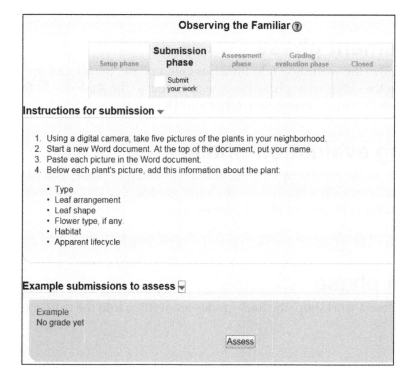

Notice that the student can also assess the example at this point. On the **Settings** page for this workshop, for **Mode of examples assessment**, we selected **voluntary**. Therefore, the example is not required. If we had made assessing the example mandatory, the student would receive a message that they cannot submit work until the example has been assessed.

Allocating submissions

As soon as students begin submitting their work, you can start allocating those submissions to other students for assessment. Do this under **Workshop administration | Allocate submissions**. You can allocate submissions manually or randomly.

If you perform a random allocation, then all of the submissions that have been received up to that point in time will be allocated to other students for assessment. However, submissions sent in after the random allocation will not be automatically allocated. You will need to perform another random allocation for subsequent submissions, until the workshop is complete.

Assessment phase

When you move the workshop into the assessment phase, the allocations that you made during the submission phase become available to the students. In this phase, the students will actually assess each other's work.

Grading evaluation phase

When you move the workshop into the grading evaluation phase, you can tell Moodle to automatically calculate the student's grades. You can also override these grades and enter your own grades, if necessary.

At this stage, students can no longer modify the submissions they have sent in.

Closed phase

When you close a workshop, the final grades are written into the course's Gradebook.

Summary

Moodle offers several options for student-to-student and student-to-teacher interaction. When deciding which social activities to use, consider the level of structure and amount of student-to-student and student-to-teacher interaction you want. For example, chats and Wikis offer a relatively unstructured environment, with lots of opportunity for student-to-student interaction. They are good ways of relinquishing some control of the class to the students. A forum offers more structure because entries are classified by topic. It can be moderated by the Teacher, making it even more structured. A workshop offers the most structure, by virtue of the set assessment criteria that students must use when evaluating each other's work. Note that as the activities become more structured, the opportunity for students to get to know one another is decreased.

You may want to introduce a chat and/or forum at the beginning of a course, to build "esprit de corps" among the students, then move into a collaborative Wiki, such as a group writing project. Finally, after the students have learned more about each other and are comfortable working together, you might use a workshop for their final project.

9
Blocks

Every block adds functionality to your site or your course. This chapter describes many of Moodle's blocks, helps you decide which ones will meet your goals, and tells you how to implement them.

A block displays information in a small area in one of the side columns. For example, a block can display a **Calendar**, the latest news, or the students enrolled in a course. Think of a block as a small applet, or widget.

When configuring your Moodle site, you can choose to display, hide, and position blocks on the site's Front Page. When configuring a course, you can also show, hide, and position blocks on the course's Home Page. The procedure is the same whether working on the site's Front Page or a course's Home Page. The site's Front Page is essentially a course. You can also give students permission to add blocks to their personal, My Moodle page.

Many blocks are available to you in a standard Moodle installation. You can also install additional blocks, which available from http://moodle.org/.

Configuring where a block appears

In early versions of Moodle, when you added a block to a course, that block appeared only on the course's Home Page. It did not appear on any resource or activity pages in the course. With version 2, you can now configure a block to appear on the course's Home Page, and on all the resource and activity pages for the course. You can also configure a block to appear on all of the courses in a specific category.

Configuring where a block appears is done by using the settings for **Page context** and **Restrict to these page types**. For example, in the following screenshot, the user is configuring the **Blog menu block** in the **Email Overload** course:

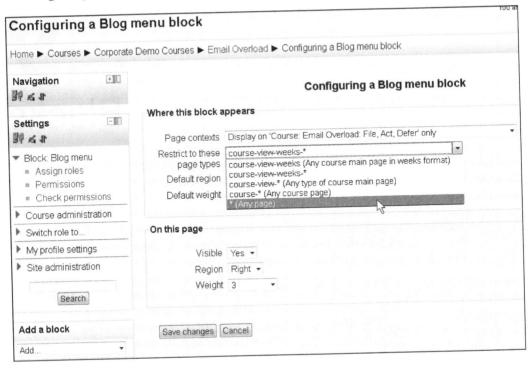

- These settings work in combination to determine where a block appears. In some places, some of these settings have no effect. The following is a list of the combinations that you might find most useful.

- When a block is added to a course's home page, and you want it to appear on only the course's home page, set **Page contexts** to **Display on course name only** and set **Restrict to these page types** to **course-***.

- When a block is added to a course's home page, and you want it to appear on every page in that course (all of the activities and resources), set **Page contexts** to **Display on course name and any pages within it** and set **Restrict to these page types** to *****.

- When a block is added to a category home page, and you want it to appear on the home page of every course in that category, set **Page contexts** to **Display on course name only** and set **Restrict to these page types** to **course-***.

When a block is added to a category home page, and you want it to appear on the every page of every course in that category, set **Page contexts** to **Display on course name only** and set **Restrict to these page types** to *.

Types of blocks

Moodle gives you many standard blocks that you can add to your courses. Some of the most useful are discussed in the following sections.

Activities block

The **Activities** block lists all of the types of activities available in the course:

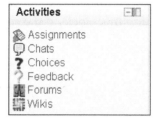

If a specific type of activity is not used in the course, the link for that type is not presented. The activity type is only shown if your course contains at least one instance of that type. When a user clicks on the type of activity, all activities of that type for the course are listed. In the example below, the user clicked on **Assignments** in the **Activities** block and a list of the assignments in the course is presented:

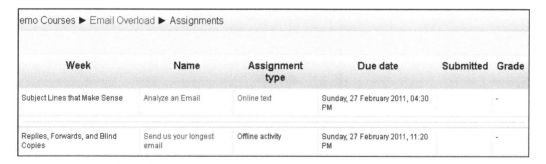

Week	Name	Assignment type	Due date	Submitted	Grade
Subject Lines that Make Sense	Analyze an Email	Online text	Sunday, 27 February 2011, 04:30 PM		-
Replies, Forwards, and Blind Copies	Send us your longest email	Offline activity	Sunday, 27 February 2011, 11:20 PM		-

 If this block is on the site's Front Page, clicking on a type of activity gives a list of the activities on the Front Page (and not for the entire site!).

Blog menu block

By default, every Moodle user has a personal blog on the site. Selecting this block puts the blog menu into the course's sidebar:

Notice that this block provides shortcuts to blog entries about the course. If blogging will be a part of the course, include this block on the course's Home Page.

Blog tags block

This block displays a list of all of the blog tags used on the site. The tags are listed in alphabetical order. The more blog entries that use a tag, the larger the tag appears in the block:

Calendar block

Workshops, assignments, quizzes, and events appear on the **Calendar**:

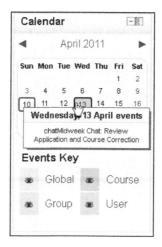

In the preceding screenshot, you can see that the user is pointing to an event that begins on the 13th. A pop-up window shows the name of the event. This event was added to a course, so it is a course-wide event.

When the course creator or administrator clicks on one of the four links at the bottom of the **Calendar** block, it disables the display of that type of event. For example, if this **Calendar** is displayed on a course's Home Page, you might want to disable the display of global events and user events by clicking on those links. This would result in the **Calendar** displaying only events for the course and the groups in the course.

Comments block

The Comments block allow]s anyone with access to it, to leave and read comments. The comments are all saved, so you can accumulate quite a long list of comments.

In the following screenshot, the user Student1 is logged in. Notice that Student1 can delete his comment, but not the comment left by the course administrator:

Of course, the course and site administrator can delete anyone's comments.

As all comments are saved, and the list can get long, you probably want to limit the comment block to a single course. That is, you don't want to add a comment site wide, or to all the courses in a category. If you do, the block could become crowded with comments (unless this is the effect that you want).

Consider adding a **Comments** block to an activity or a resource, and using the first comment to encourage students to leave their feedback, like this:

Course completion block

The **Course completion** block works with the course completion tracking function. Please see *Chapter 10, Features for Teachers,* for a detailed discussion of course completion tracking.

Courses block

The Courses block displays the courses that the student is enrolled in, plus a link to **All courses** at the bottom of the block. Notice that the **Navigation** block displays only the courses that the student is enrolled in. It does not give the student a link to the list of all course categories:

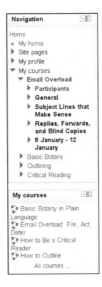

Course/site description

The **Course/Site Description** block displays the course summary, taken from the course's **Settings** page. This is the same course summary that is displayed when someone clicks on the Information ❶ icon in the course listing on the front page of the site.

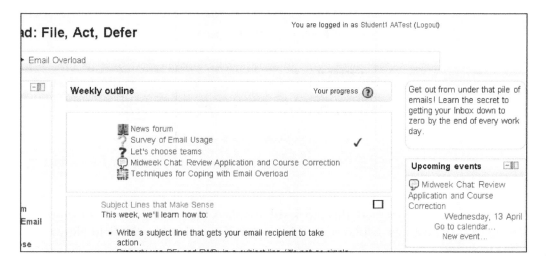

HTML block

The **HTML** block creates a block in the sidebar that can hold any HTML (any web content) that you can put on a web page. Most experienced web users are accustomed to the content in sidebars being an addition to the main content of a page. For example, we put menus and interesting links in the sidebars in most blogging software. I suggest you adhere to that standard and use the HTML block to hold content that is an interesting addition to, but not part of, the course. For example, you could put an annotated link to another site of interest.

Think of an HTML block as a miniature web page that you can put into the sidebar of your course.

When you edit an HTML block, Moodle provides the same full-featured web page editor that you get when adding a web page to a course.

Latest news block

When you create a new course, by default it has a News forum. The **Latest news** block displays the most recent postings from this forum.

Even if the forum is renamed, this block still displays the postings for this forum. The number of postings displayed in this block is determined by the field **News items to show**.

Recall that the Front Page of your site is another course. If the **Latest news** block is displayed on the site's Front Page, it displays the latest postings from the sitewide news forum, or **Site News** on the **Course Settings** page.

If you have set the News forum to email students with new postings, you can be reasonably sure that the students are getting the news, so you might not need to display this block. However, if the news items are of interest to visitors not enrolled in the course, or if the course allows guest access, you probably want to display this block.

Login block

If a visitor is not logged in, Moodle displays small **Login** links in the upper-right corner and bottom center of the page. However, the links are not very noticeable. The **Login** block is much more prominent. The main advantage to the **Login** block over the small **Login** links is the block's greater visibility.

If you want the **Login** block to be displayed on every page of your site, set **Page contexts** to **Display throughout the entire site** and **Restrict to these page types** to *.

After the user logs in, this block disappears.

Main menu block

The **Main menu** block is available only on the site's Front Page. Anything that can be added to a course can be added to this block, as you can see from the pull-down menus labeled **Add a resource** and **Add an activity**.

In my example site, I use the **Main menu** to convey information about the site and how to use the site. I want visitors to be able to easily get instructions for enroling and using courses. Perhaps I should change the name of this block to **How to Use this Site**. I can do that by looking in the `moodle.php` file under the language folder, for this line:

```
$string['mainmenu'] = 'Main menu';
```

Change `Main menu` to whatever you want to be displayed for the name of the menu.

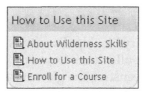

Messages block

The **Messages** block provides a shortcut to Moodle's Messages center. It displays the latest messages received. This is a shortcut to the same page you would reach by selecting **Settings | My profile | Messages**.

Online Users block

The **Online Users** block displays a list of the users who are in the current course at the present time. If it is on the site's Front Page, is shows people who are online on the site. Every few minutes, the block is updated:

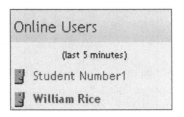

Quiz results block

The **Quiz results** block is available only if there is a quiz in the course. It displays the highest and/or lowest grades achieved on a quiz within a course. You can anonymize the students' names in the block, if you prefer.

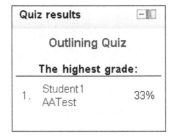

Random Glossary Entry block

Moodle's **Random Glossary Entry** block pulls entries from a selected glossary, and displays them in a block. It can pull entries from any glossary that is available to that course. In the following screenshot, the glossary that the block is using is a class directory, where each student is an entry in the glossary:

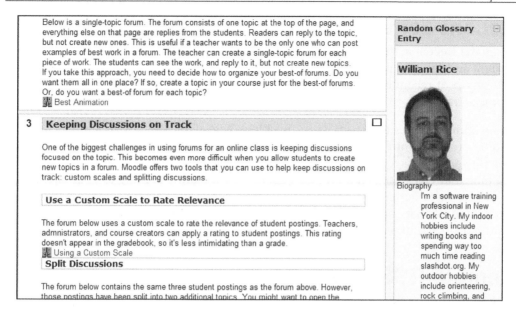

Even though the name of the block is "Random" Glossary Entry, you can control the order in which entries are pulled from the glossary, and how often the block displays a new entry. For example, in the following screenshot, the Random Glossary Entry block is set to display each entry in order, and to change the entry displayed each day:

Here are some ideas for using the Random Glossary Entry block for something other than a glossary:

- Highlights of work that past students in this class have submitted. If the class is working on a long-term project, create a glossary that contains the best work submitted by previous classes who completed that project. Display the glossary while the current class is working on that project.

- Inspirational or informative quotes related to the field of study.

- If you're teaching in a corporate setting, consider putting rules and procedures into their own glossaries. You could create a separate glossary for each type of rule or procedure, for example, a Human Resources Policies glossary, a Purchase Order glossary, and so on. Then, display random entries from these glossaries in the appropriate courses.

- Past exam questions and their answers. Students can use this as another resource to prepare for your exams.

- Funny anecdotes related to the field of study.

- Common mistakes and their corrections. For example, how to spot software bugs, or common foreign language grammar errors.

Recent activity block

When the **Recent activity** block is added to a course's Home Page, it lists all of the student and teacher activity in that course since the user's last login. The link for **Full report of recent activity** displays a page that enables you to run reports on course activity.

When added to the site's Front Page, this block lists all of the student and teacher activity on the Front Page, but not in the individual courses, since the user's last login. If someone is logged in as a guest user, this block displays activity since the last time that Guest logged in. If guest users are constantly coming to your site, this block may be of limited use to them. One strategy is to omit this block from the site's Front Page, so that anonymous users don't see it, and add it only to courses that require users to authenticate.

Remote RSS Feeds block

When the **Remote RSS Feeds** block is added to a course Home Page, the course creator chooses or creates RSS feeds to display in that block.

This example below shows an RSS feed from an adventure racing site. This feed is the result of the configuration shown in the following screenshot.

A feed can be added by the Site Administrator, and then selected by the course creator for use in an RSS block. Alternatively, when the Course Creator adds the RSS block, they can add a feed at that time. The new feed then becomes available to all other Course Creators, for use in all other courses. This is similar to the way quiz questions work. All quiz questions, no matter who created them, are available to all Course Creators for use in their courses.

Search forums block

The **Search forums** block provides a search function for forums. It does not search other types of activities or resources. When this block is added to the site's Front Page, it searches only the forums on the Front Page.

When it's added to a course's Home Page, it searches only the forums for that course. This block is different from the **Search courses** field that automatically appears on the site's Front Page. The **Search courses** field searches course names and descriptions, not forums.

Topics block

The **Topics** block displays links to the numbered topics or weeks in a course. Clicking on a link advances the page to that topic. This block does not display the names of the topics. If you want to display links to the topics that show their names, you'll need to create those links yourself. The following screenshot shows an example of this:

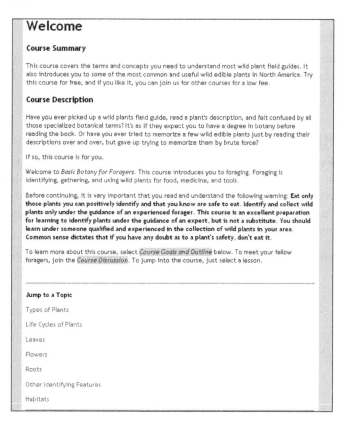

Here's one way to create those links:

1. While viewing the Home Page of the course, in the address bar of your browser you will see the web address of the course. In my example, it was `http://moodle.williamrice.com/course/view.php?id=4`. Select and copy this address.

2. In Topic 0, add a label. Do this by clicking on the **Add a resource** drop-down menu and selecting **Insert a label**.

3. You should see a word processor-like window, where you enter the text of the label. In my example, I added a horizontal rule and then typed **Jump to a Topic**. You can add any text that you want to use to introduce these links.

4. Type the name of the first topic, such as **Types of Plants**.

5. Select the name of the topic by dragging across it.

6. Click on the **Link** button to create the link. You should see a pop-up window where you can enter the URL of the link.

7. In the **Insert Link** pop-up window, paste the link that you copied before. This is the link to the course's Home Page. Immediately after the link, type the hash sign (#) and the number of the topic or week.

8. Repeat steps 4 through 7 for each topic.

9. When you have finished with the **Edit label** window, click on the **Save changes** button to return to your course's Home Page. You will now see the links in Topic 0.

Upcoming Events block

The **Upcoming Events** block is an extension of the **Calendar** block. It gets event information from your calendar. By default, the **Upcoming Events** block displays 10 events; the maximum is 20. It looks ahead a default of 21 days; the maximum is 200. If there are more upcoming events than the maximum chosen for this block, the events furthest away will not be shown.

This block is helpful for reminding students of the tasks that they need to complete in the course.

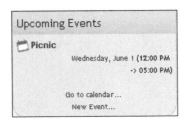

Summary

When deciding which blocks to display, consider the comfort level of your students. If they're experienced web surfers, they may be comfortable with a full complement of blocks displaying information about the course. Experienced web surfers are adept at ignoring information they don't need (when was the last time you paid attention to a banner ad on the Web?). If your students are new computer users, they may assume that the presence of a block means that it requires their attention or interaction. Remember that you can turn blocks on and off as needed.

10
Features for Teachers

Moodle offers several features that are of special interest to teachers. These focus on determining how well your students are progressing through a course. Reports and logs show you who has done what on your site or in your course. Grades not only tell you how well your students are scoring, but can also be curved and weighted very easily.

Logs and reports

Moodle keeps detailed logs of all activities that users perform on your site. You can use these logs to determine who has been active on your site, what they did, and when they did it.

Some reports are available at the course level. Teachers can access these reports. Other reports are available at the site level. You must be a Site Administrator to access these reports. Both sets of reports are covered in this chapter.

Moodle has a modest report viewing system built into it. However, for sophisticated log analysis, you need to look outside of Moodle.

To view the logs and reports for a course, you must be logged in as a Teacher or a Manager. Then, select **My courses | name of course | Reports**.

You can use the **Reports** page to display three different kinds of information. From top to bottom, they are:

- Raw logs
- Activity reports
- Participation reports

Let's look at each one separately.

View course logs

Notice that Moodle's display of the log files can be filtered by course, participant, day, activity, and action. You can select a single value for any of these filters:

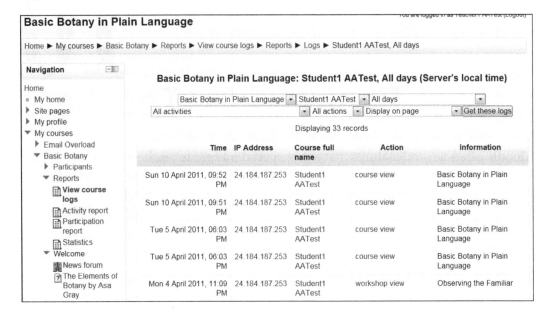

You cannot select multiple values for any of these filters. That is, you cannot look at the logs for two courses at the same time, or four participants at the same time, or for a few days at the same time. If you want a more sophisticated view of the logs, you must use a tool other than Moodle's built-in log viewer.

Fortunately, you can download the logs as text files and import them into another tool, such as a spreadsheet. To download the logs, use the last drop-down list on the page, as shown in the following screenshot:

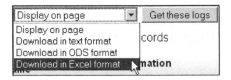

For example, you could use Excel's data menu to format, chart, and analyze the data. A complete discussion of Excel's data functions is beyond this book, but there are many sources of help for these functions.

The following figure is an example of a table created in Excel from imported data. I've sorted the data by participant (**Full name**), so that at a glance, I can see which users are most active:

	A	B	C	D	E	
1	Course	Time	IP Address	Full name	Action	Information
2	FreePics	2007 February 24 19:34	82.27.68.16	LisaMarie Alexandria	course view	Free Wild Pictures
3	FreePics	2007 January 16 19:43	82.27.73.24l	LisaMarie Alexandria	course view	Free Wild Pictures
4	FreePics	2007 January 16 19:23	82.27.73.24l	LisaMarie Alexandria	resource view	Common Burdock in the Spring
5	FreePics	2007 January 16 19:23	82.27.73.24l	LisaMarie Alexandria	course view	Free Wild Pictures
6	FreePics	2007 January 16 19:23	82.27.73.24l	LisaMarie Alexandria	course enrol	Deer Habits
7	Debris Huts	2007 February 18 16:43	86.136.132.	Bradford Sorens	course view	Debris Huts
8	Debris Huts	2007 February 18 16:43	86.136.132.	Bradford Sorens	course enrol	Debris Huts
9	Bow Drill	2007 February 18 16:43	86.136.132.	Bradford Sorens	course view	Bow Drill Firestarting
10	Bow Drill	2007 February 18 16:43	86.136.132.	Bradford Sorens	course enrol	Debris Huts
11	Tracking Basic	2007 February 18 16:42	86.136.132.	Bradford Sorens	user view all	
12	Tracking Basic	2007 February 18 16:41	86.136.132.	Bradford Sorens	course view	Tracking Basics
13	Tracking Basic	2007 February 18 16:41	86.136.132.	Bradford Sorens	course enrol	Debris Huts
14	Water's Edge	2007 February 18 16:40	86.136.132.	Bradford Sorens	course enrol	Debris Huts
15	Water's Edge	2007 February 18 16:40	86.136.132.	Bradford Sorens	course view	By the Water's Edge
16	FreePics	2007 February 18 16:31	86.136.132.	Bradford Sorens	course view	Free Wild Pictures
17	FreePics	2007 February 18 16:31	86.136.132.	Bradford Sorens	resource view	Wild Plant Pictures
18	FreePics	2007 February 18 16:31	86.136.132.	Bradford Sorens	course view	Free Wild Pictures
19	FreePics	2007 February 18 16:31	86.136.132.	Bradford Sorens	course enrol	Debris Huts

Notice that the preceding table contains information from several courses. You can see this from Column A. There are two ways to get information from several courses in the same place. First, you could run the report as an Administrator, from the administrative interface. This enables you to run a report for all courses on the site. Second, as a Teacher, you could download the data from each course separately, and combine it into one Excel worksheet.

Viewing Activity reports

An Activity report offers a user-friendly view of the activity in a single course. Whereas the logs show complete information, an activity report shows only the course items, what was done in each item, and the time of the latest activity for that item. When you first select Activity reports from the menu, you are presented with a list of all of the activities in the course, as shown in the following screenshot:

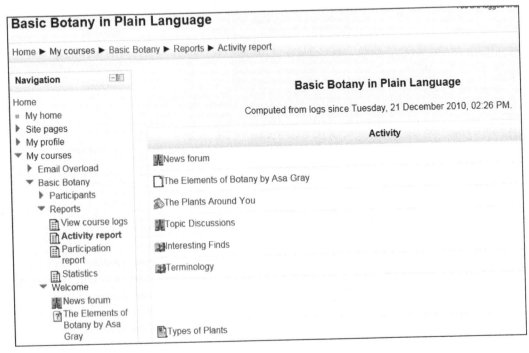

From this list, select the activity for which you want to generate a report. You are taken to that activity. In this example, the teacher selected **The Plants Around You**:

Notice that the Activity report only acts as a link to the activities in a course. Once you select an activity, you will use that activity's method for viewing a report.

Participation report

The Participation report is especially useful for discovering which students need to complete an activity, and sending them a reminder to complete it. In the following example, the teacher is looking at the report for the activity called **Interesting Finds**. This is a glossary activity. The teacher is displaying only records for the students in the class, but wants to see only records of students' posts to the glossary:

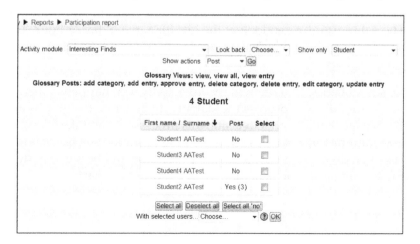

In this demonstration course, the teacher wants all of the students to contribute (post) to the glossary. So, the teacher will send a message to Student1, Student3, and Student4. To do this, they select the students and then from the **With selected users...** drop-down list, selects **Send a message**, as shown in the following screenshot:

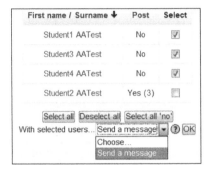

This takes the teacher to a page where they can create and send a message. The message will be sent to the students' email addresses, and will also be stored in their Moodle messages.

Statistics

Statistics is a feature that is available only to Site Administrators. If you run a website, you might be familiar with using site statistics to track the usage of your site. These statistics are recorded by the web server and displayed using a statistics analyzer. In Moodle, if the Administrator enables site statistics, Moodle will record statistics about each course and the site, just as your web server records statistics about your website. Moodle will also produce graphs to display the statistics, similar to a statistics analyzer.

The statistics page shows how many hits the different pages in your Moodle site have had. The Administrator can look at the hits for a given day or hour. The statistics page does not show which users visited these pages. For that, you will need to use the site logs.

If you enable site statistics, Moodle will record activity as it happens. Then, at a time that you specify, Moodle will process the statistics to generate the graphs and charts on the Statistics page. For a very active site, this processing can take a long time. Therefore, the Administrator should specify a time when the site is not busy serving students. Also, you do not want the statistics processing and backup routines to run at the same time, so you should schedule them a few hours apart.

How to enable site statistics:

1. Select **Site administration | Server | Statistics**.

2. Select the **Enable statistics** checkbox.

3. Select the appropriate settings to specify when, and for how long, to run the statistics.

4. Click on the **Save changes** button.

Using scales for feedback, rating, and grading

In Moodle, you can use scales to rate or grade forums, assignments, quizzes, lessons, and workshops. These scales can be used by anyone who is grading or evaluating a student's work. For example, if a workshop is being graded by other students, then the students can use the scale selected by the teacher to grade that workshop. Being able to apply a scale to so many types of activities is a powerful way to make your courses more interactive and engaging.

Moodle comes with two pre-existing scales. One is called "Separate and Connected Ways of Knowing". This scale allows students to describe an item as connected to other knowledge in the course, or separate from the other knowledge. It isn't useful as a way to grade students, but instead is used to stimulate discussion about the item.

The other built-in scale that Moodle offers is numeric. You can assign a maximum number of points, from **1** to **100**, to an item. Whoever is rating or grading the item selects a numeric grade from a drop-down list.

Moodle also allows you to create custom scales. For example, in the following screenshot, you can see that the student is looking at an activity named **Terminology**. This is a glossary that contains terms that the student must memorize for the course.

In the lower-right corner of the page, the student is rating this glossary entry. The teacher created a custom scale for this course. The scale allows students to rate how helpful something is for memorizing the glossary entry. The teacher then applied this custom scale to the glossary.

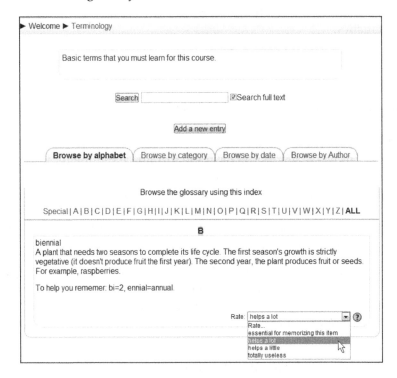

Note that once the teacher created the custom scale, they could have applied it to any activity in the course. For example, the course could have a forum where students exchange tips on memorizing terminology. Then, the students could rate each post to that forum on how helpful it is for memorization.

How to create a custom scale

A Site Administrator can create a custom scale at the site level. Then, that scale can be applied by all of the teachers to their activities. A teacher can create a custom scale at the course level. Then, that scale can be applied to the activities in just that course.

1. Select **Settings | Grade administration | Scales**. If you're creating a scale for the entire site, select **Site administration | Grades | Scales**.

   The Scale page is displayed. The scale for **Separate and Connected Ways of Knowing** is listed, as are any other custom scales for this course (or for this site).

2. Click on the **Add a new scale** button. The **Edit page** is displayed, as shown below.

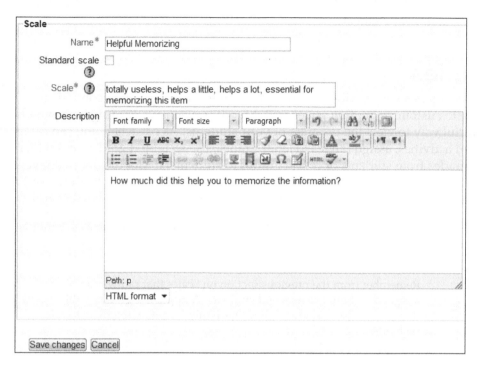

3. When a teacher applies this scale to an activity, they will see the **Name** that you enter here. Students who use the scale will never see the **Name**.

4. The **Scale** field holds the entries that the user will see when using this scale. Compare the text in the **Scale** field of the preceding screenshot, to the text that appears in the drop-down list of the screenshot before that.

5. When a teacher sees this scale in the list, they will see the **Description** that you enter here. Students who use the scale will never see the **Description**.

6. Save your changes.

The scale is now ready to be applied.

How to apply a scale to an activity

Once a custom scale has been created, you need to apply it to an activity.

1. When logged in as a Teacher, Administrator, or Course Manager, select the activity.

2. Look on that activity's **Edit settings** page.

3. Find the section labeled **Ratings**.

4. From the **Scale** drop-down list, select the scale that you want to apply.

5. Save your changes.

Grades

Moodle offers a very flexible reporting tool for grades. When you combine the ability to customize grading scales with Moodle's extensive grading tools, you have a powerful way to view the progress of your students. As a teacher, you can categorize graded activities, assign ranges to letter grades, use weighted grades, and either hide grades from students or reveal grades to students. If Moodle doesn't have the reporting capabilities that you want, you can download grades in text-only or Excel format and use a spreadsheet to chart and analyze them.

Anything that can have a scale applied to it can be graded: forums, assignments, quizzes, lessons, workshops, and more.

 Remember from the previous section on Scales that ratings can be assigned by both teachers and students. A rating is a grade, so this means that you can have students grade each other by allowing them to rate each other.

Viewing grades

To access grades, select the course whose grades you want to see, and then select **Grade administration | Grader Report**. This displays a summary of the grades for that course, as shown in the following screenshot:

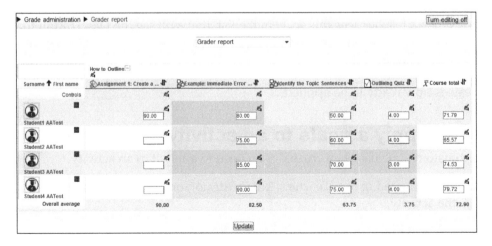

Notice that Student2, Student3, and Student4 have not completed the first assignment in this course. Also notice that the Teacher can override the grades being displayed by entering new ones, and then clicking on the **Update** button.

In our example course, the Teacher wants to investigate the lack of grades for **Assignment1**. So they will click on the name of the assignment, which takes the Teacher out of the **Grader report** and into the Assignment itself. Notice that now the navigation bar at the top of the page shows that we are viewing the assignment:

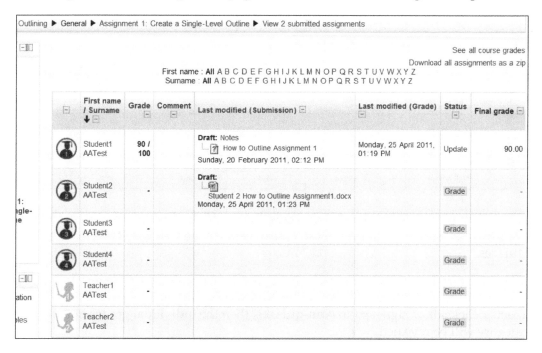

Now that the Teacher is viewing the submissions for the assignment, they can see that Student2 submitted a paper but it has not been graded. Clicking on the submission will download or open it. Clicking on the **Grade** link will allow the Teacher to enter a grade and optional comments for the submission.

The **Grader report** is the Teacher's starting point for examining the grades for a course. It also allows the Teacher to enter updated grades. From there, you can click into individual activities and investigate or modify grades.

Categorizing grades

Each of the graded activities can be put into a category. Note that you put activities into categories, not students. If you want to categorize students, you need to put them into groups.

Viewing grade categories

Categorizing the graded activities in a course enables you to quickly see how your students are doing with various kinds of activities. If you do not assign an activity to a category, by default it belongs to the category **Uncategorized**. The following screenshot shows a course that uses the categories of **Quizzes** and **Non-quizzes**. These were created by the Teacher because they were concerned that some students have test anxiety, so the Teacher wanted to compare the students' performance on tests to other activities:

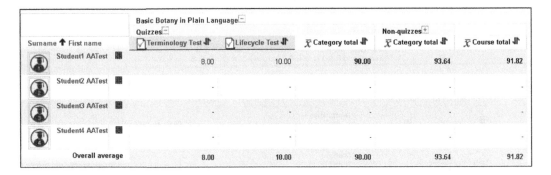

Notice that in the category labeled **Quizzes**, the grades for two quizzes are showing: **Terminology Test** and **Lifecycle Test**. It also displays the **Category total** for **Quizzes**.

In the category labeled **Non-quizzes**, the report displays only the **Category total**. Grades for the individual activities under **Non-quizzes** are not displayed. If the Teacher clicks the + sign next to **Non-quizzes**, then the individual grades in that category will be revealed.

In this example, the Teacher can see that Student1's scores on the quizzes are consistent with the student's score on the non-quiz activities. Categorizing the activities made it easy to see the comparison.

Creating grade categories

Categories are created, and items are moved into categories, in the same window.

How to create a grade category

To create a grade category, follow the steps shown below:

1. Select **Settings | Grade administration | Categories and items**.
2. From there, you can select **Simple view** or **Full view**.

3. At the bottom of the page, click on the **Add category** button. The **Edit category** page is displayed.

4. Complete the required fields the page, and save your changes.

How to assign an item to a grade category

To assign an item to a grade category, follow the steps shown below:

1. Select **Settings | Grade administration | Categories and items | Simple view**.

2. Select the item(s) that you want to assign to the category.

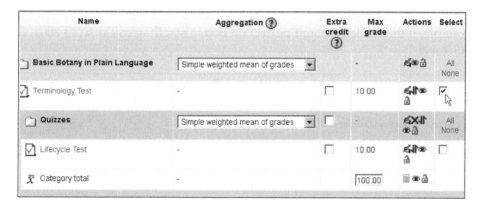

3. At the bottom of the page, from the drop-down list, select the category into which you want to move the item(s).

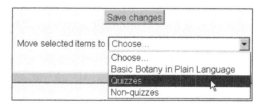

4. Click on the **Save changes** button.

The most important point here is to determine what kind of question you want to answer when you examine student grades, and create categories that enable you to answer that question. For example, "How do my students do on quizzes versus more interactive activities, such as workshops and forums?" To answer that question, create a category just for quizzes, and you can answer that question just by viewing the grades. Or, "How do my students do on offline activities versus online activities?" To answer that question, create Online and Offline grading categories.

Remember, these categories are not "written in stone". If your needs change, you can always create and assign new grading categories later, as needed.

Using extra credit

You can designate any activity as being for 'extra credit'. When an item is designated as extra credit, its points are not added to the total possible points for the category. In this example, the **Terminology test** has been designated as extra credit. If it were not designated as extra credit, the total points needed for a 100% in this category would be 20. But in this case, the total points needed to achieve a 100% is 10. That means in this example, if the student scored perfect on both tests, they could score 200% for this category!

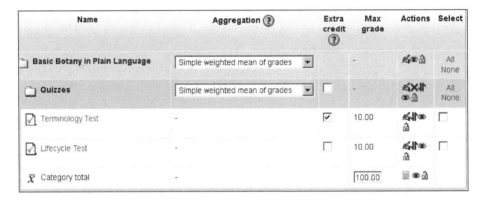

You can also create a category just for extra credit activities. The extra credit setting is on the **Edit category** page. Alternatively, you can use the extra credit setting on selected activities. Both approaches will work.

Weighing a category

You can, and probably should, assign a weight to a grade category. By default, a weight of 100 is applied to every category. This means that each category contributes equally to the course total. In the following screenshot, you can see that both categories are assigned a weight of 100. The course has a weight of 100:

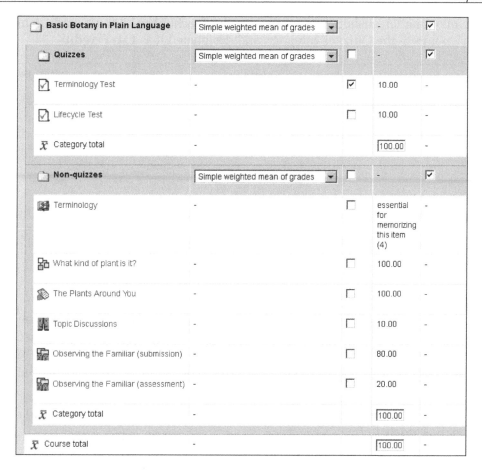

No matter what numbers you enter for category totals, you can enter any number for the course total. The category totals will contribute proportionately to the course total.

Compensating for a difficult category by adding points

You might want to add extra points to everyone's grade, to compensate for an especially difficult assignment. The easiest way to add extra points to everyone's grade in the class is to add an extra grade item to a category and then give everyone the points for that item.

In the following screenshot, you can see that the Teacher has added a grade item worth 2 points to the **Quizzes** category, and designated it as **Extra credit**:

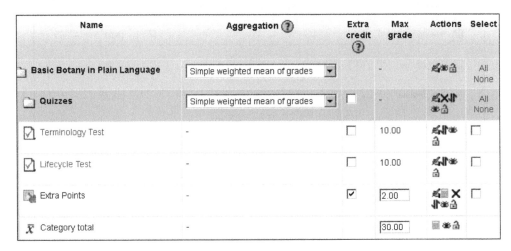

The Teacher then added this grade item by clicking on the **Add grade item** button at the bottom of the page. When you add a grade item instead of an activity, you must enter the grade for each student manually. This is because there is no activity in Moodle for the student to perform, so Moodle cannot calculate a grade for the student.

In order to add grades to the grade item go to **Course administration | Grades | Grader report**. On this page, manually enter the grades for the grade item, and then click on the **Update** button:

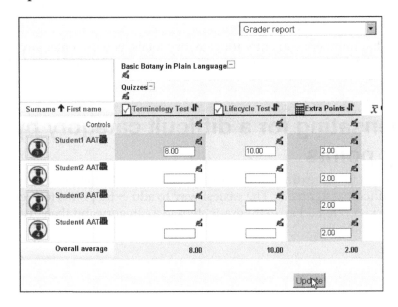

Another way to add extra points is to simply override the automatic grading of the assignments. In this example, the Teacher could have simply entered manual grades for either Test. However, that would have made it more difficult and tedious to determine how many points were manually added to the grades. By creating an extra credit grading item, we can see exactly how much was added to the grades.

The Teacher forum

You cancreate a **Forum** that only Teachers can access. This is especially useful when several teachers collaborate on a course. To create a teacher-only forum, add a normal forum and then change the security so that Students and Guests cannot access it. When a Student tries to access the forum, they will receive a message stating **You do not have the permission to view discussions in this forum**. Teachers will be able to access the forum.

How to make a forum (or any activity or resource) available to Teachers only

To make a forum (or any other activity or resource) available to Teachers only, carry out the steps shown below:

1. Log in to the course as a Teacher or a Course Manager.
2. Select the forum.
3. From the **Settings** for the forum, select **Permissions**, as shown in the following screenshot:

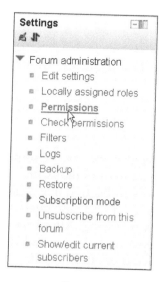

4. From the **Advanced role override** drop-down list, select **Student**:

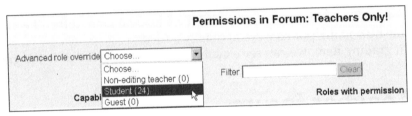

5. Under **Activity: Forum**, change all of the Student permissions to **Prohibit**:

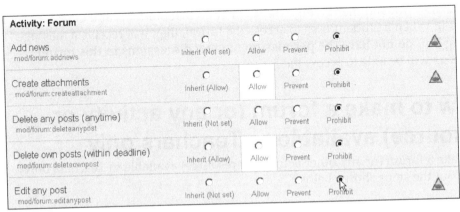

6. Save your changes.

7. In the lower-right corner, for **Change another role**, select **Guest**.

8. Again, under **Activity: Forum**, change all of the Guest permissions to **Prohibit**.

9. Save your changes.

The result is a forum that Students and Guests can see the name of, but cannot access.

Summary

Managing a successful course requires two-way communication between the teacher and students, whether in a classroom or online. Constantly monitoring a course's logs and grades gives you an early indication that a class may need a mid-course correction. You can use questions, surveys, and chats to discover specific problems and challenges that the students are facing. After bringing the course back on track, custom grading scales, extra credit, and curves can help you to equalize the grades. When teaching online, make a habit of often checking the logs and grades.

Index

HTML online
  reference link 154

I

IMS Enterprise File
  about 92
  reference link 93
installer script
  about 50
  config.php 50, 51
  configuration settings 50, 51
  copyright 55
  database settings, specifying 54, 55
  database tables 51
  database tables, created by install.php 57,
    58
  directories, specifying 52
  install.php 51, 52
  server, checking 56
  web address, specifying 52
interactive course material
  assignment 165
  lesson 165
Internet Explorer
  URL 67

J

jumps settings, lesson setting
  next or previous page 190
  random question within content page 191
  specific pages 190
  this page 190
  unseen question within cluster 190, 191

L

language
  about 97, 98
  additional languages, installing 100, 101
  files 98, 99
  language settings, configuring 101
language settings
  configuring 101, 102
  Excel encoding 102
  sitewide locale 102
Latest news block 286

layout settings, quiz settings
  configuring 201
LDAP 93
lesson activity
  about 165, 174-177
  content pages 194, 195
  editing 193, 194
  first question page, adding 184, 185
  question pages, creating 188
  settings, configuring 177, 178
lesson settings
  configuring 177, 178
  flow control 180, 182
  general settings 178
  grade options 179
  pop-up window 183, 184
links
  adding, to course 146-149
Login block 286

M

Main menu block 287
manual accounts method, authentication
    methods 70
matching question 215
math filters
  about 112
  Algebra Notation filter 112
  TeX Notation filter 112
media
  adding, to course 157, 158
  video, embedding on Moodle page 159, 160
  video or audio, adding to Moodle page 158
Messages block 287
Mnet Remote Enrolments 96
Moodle
  about 7
  activities 11, 26
  activity reports, viewing 298, 299
  Chat module 241
  Choice activity 238
  course, organizing 160
  course activities 165
  course categories 121
  course logs, viewing 296, 297
  course material 26

T

teachers point of view, Choice activity 239
test accounts, for Moodle site
  creating 64, 66
  fields 64, 65
TeX Notation filter 112
Topics block 291, 292
Topics format 131
true/false question 217

U

Upcoming Events block 292
user accounts
  creating manually 70
  suspending 70, 71
username
  changing, in Moodle 76

W

web pages
  adding, to course 149
  composing, in HTML editor 154
  image file, inserting 153
  images, adding 151
  linked picture, inserting 151, 152
  Moodle's HTML editor 150
  text, pasting into Moodle page 150, 151
  uploading, to Moodle 154

Weekly format 131
Wiki module
  about 259
  default format setting 261
  editing, group mode using 260
  editing, wiki type using 260
  first page name 261
Workshop Features
  examples, using 264
  peer assessment, using 264
  self assessment, using 264, 265
Workshop module
  about 261
  assessment phase 276
  closed phase 276
  edit assessment form page 269, 270
  edit settings page 263
  evaluation phase, grading 276
  example, adding 271-273
  strategies 261
  submissions, allocating 276
  work, submitting 274, 275
Workshop strategies
  about 261
  assignments, assessing 261
  due dates, setting for submissions and
    assessments 262
WYSIWYG tools 154

Thank you for buying
Moodle 2.0 E-Learning Course Development

About Packt Publishing

Packt, pronounced 'packed', published its first book "*Mastering phpMyAdmin for Effective MySQL Management*" in April 2004 and subsequently continued to specialize in publishing highly focused books on specific technologies and solutions.

Our books and publications share the experiences of your fellow IT professionals in adapting and customizing today's systems, applications, and frameworks. Our solution based books give you the knowledge and power to customize the software and technologies you're using to get the job done. Packt books are more specific and less general than the IT books you have seen in the past. Our unique business model allows us to bring you more focused information, giving you more of what you need to know, and less of what you don't.

Packt is a modern, yet unique publishing company, which focuses on producing quality, cutting-edge books for communities of developers, administrators, and newbies alike. For more information, please visit our website: www.packtpub.com.

About Packt Open Source

In 2010, Packt launched two new brands, Packt Open Source and Packt Enterprise, in order to continue its focus on specialization. This book is part of the Packt Open Source brand, home to books published on software built around Open Source licences, and offering information to anybody from advanced developers to budding web designers. The Open Source brand also runs Packt's Open Source Royalty Scheme, by which Packt gives a royalty to each Open Source project about whose software a book is sold.

Writing for Packt

We welcome all inquiries from people who are interested in authoring. Book proposals should be sent to author@packtpub.com. If your book idea is still at an early stage and you would like to discuss it first before writing a formal book proposal, contact us; one of our commissioning editors will get in touch with you.

We're not just looking for published authors; if you have strong technical skills but no writing experience, our experienced editors can help you develop a writing career, or simply get some additional reward for your expertise.

Moodle 1.9 Teaching Techniques

ISBN: 978-1-849510-06-6   Paperback: 216 pages

Creative ways to build powerful and effective online courses

1. Motivate students from all backgrounds, generations, and learning styles

2. When and how to apply the different learning solutions with workarounds, providing alternative solutions

3. Easy-to-follow, step-by-step instructions with screenshots and examples for Moodle's powerful features

Moodle 1.9 for Teaching 7-14 Year Olds: Beginner's Guide

ISBN: 978-1-847197-14-6   Paperback: 236 pages

Effective e-learning for younger students using Moodle as your Classroom Assistant

1. Focus on the unique needs of young learners to create a fun, interesting, interactive, and informative learning environment your students will want to go on day after day

2. Engage and motivate your students with games, quizzes, movies, and podcasts the whole class can participate in

3. Go paperless! Put your lessons online and grade them anywhere, anytime

4. Ideal for teachers new to Moodle: easy to follow and abundantly illustrated with screenshots of the solutions you'll build

Moodle 1.9 Math

ISBN: 978-1-847196-44-6   Paperback: 276 pages

Integrate interactive math presentations, build
feature-rich quizzes, set online quizzes and tests,
incorporate Flash games, and monitor student
progress using the Moodle e-learning platform

1. Get to grips with converting your mathematics
   teaching over to Moodle

2. Engage and motivate your students with
   exciting, interactive, and engaging online
   math courses with Moodle, which include
   mathematical notation, graphs, images, video,
   audio, and more

3. # Integrate multimedia elements in math
   courses to make learning math interactive
   and fun

Moodle 2.0 Administration

ISBN: 978-1-849516-04-4   Paperback: 427 pages

An administrator's guide to configuring, securing,
customizing, and extending Moodle

1. A complete guide for planning, installing,
   optimizing, customizing, and configuring
   Moodle

2. Learn how to network and extend Moodle for
   your needs and integrate with other systems

4. A complete reference of all Moodle system
   settings

CPSIA information can be obtained at www.ICGtesting.com
Printed in the USA
LVOW03s1321030114

367941LV00004B/30/P